Entertainment Directory

SYDNEY
TRAVEL GUIDE
2020

*SHOPS, RESTAURANTS, **ARTS**, ENTERTAINMENT & NIGHTLIFE*

The Most Positively
Reviewed And Recommended
Places In The City

EGP
Editorial

SYDNEY

TRAVEL GUIDE

2020

SHOPS, RESTAURANTS, ARTS, ENTERTAINMENT & NIGHTLIFE

SYDNEY TRAVEL GUIDE 2020
Shops, Restaurants, Arts, Entertainment & Nightlife

© Barry M. Bradley, 2020
© E.G.P. Editorial, 2020

Printed in USA.

ISBN-13: 9781081459000

INDEX

SYDNEY TRAVEL GUIDE 2020

Shops, Restaurants, Arts, Entertainment & Nightlife

*This directory is dedicated to Sydney Business Owners and Managers
who provide the experience that the locals and tourists enjoy.
Thanks you very much for all that you do and thank for being the "People Choice".*

*Thanks to everyone that posts their reviews online and
the amazing reviews sites that make our life easier.*

*The places listed in this book are the most positively reviewed
and recommended by locals and travelers from around the world.*

*Thank you for your time and enjoy the directory that is
designed with locals and tourist in mind!*

TOP 500 SHOPS

The Most Recommended by Locals & Trevelers

(From #1 to #500)

#1
The Queen Victoria Building
Category: Shopping Center
Average Price: Expensive
Area: Sydney
Address: 455 George St Sydney
New South Wales
Phone: +61 2 9265 6800

#2
Westfield Sydney
Category: Local Flavor,
Shopping Center
Average Price: Modest
Area: Sydney
Address: 188 Pitt Street Sydney
New South Wales
Phone: +61 2 8236 9200

#3
Kinokuniya Bookstore
Category: Bookstore
Average Price: Modest
Area: Sydney
Address: 500 Geroge St Sydney
New South Wales
Phone: +61 2 9283 8203

#4
The Strand Arcade
Category: Shopping Center
Average Price: Expensive
Area: Sydney
Address: 414 George St Sydney
New South Wales
Phone: +61 2 9232 4199

#5
David Jones
Category: Department Store
Average Price: Exclusive
Area: Sydney
Address: 65-77 Market St Sydney
New South Wales
Phone: +61 2 9266 5544

#6
World Square Shopping Centre
Category: Shopping Center
Average Price: Modest
Area: Sydney
Address: 644 George St Sydney
New South Wales
Phone: +61 2 8669 6900

#7
Priceline Pharmacy World Square
Category: Drugstore
Average Price: Modest
Area: Sydney
Address: 644 George St Sydney
New South Wales
Phone: +61 2 9268 0042

#8
Myer
Category: Cosmetics, Beauty Supply,
Department Store
Average Price: Expensive
Area: Sydney
Address: 436 George St Sydney
New South Wales
Phone: +61 2 9238 9111

#9
My Sweet Memory
Category: Office Equipment, Café
Average Price: Inexpensive
Area: Sydney
Address: 95 Bathurst St Sydney
New South Wales
Phone: +61 2 8971 7465

#10
Lululemon
Category: Sports Wear
Average Price: Inexpensive
Area: Sydney
Address: 330C George St Sydney
New South Wales
Phone: +61 2 9233 8292

#11
Kim Sun Young Beauty Salon
Category: Hair Salon, Cosmetics,
Beauty Supply, Eyelash Service
Average Price: Inexpensive
Area: Sydney
Address: 369 Pitt St Sydney
New South Wales
Phone: +61 2 9267 7066

#12
Utopia
Category: Music, DVDs
Average Price: Modest
Area: Sydney
Address: 511 Kent St Sydney
New South Wales
Phone: +61 2 9571 6662

#13
Gaffa
Category: Art Gallery
Average Price: Modest
Area: Sydney
Address: 281 Clarence St Sydney
New South Wales
Phone: +61 2 9283 4273

#14
Harbourside
Category: Shopping Center,
Local Flavor
Average Price: Modest
Area: Sydney
Address: 2-10 Darling Dr Sydney
New South Wales
Phone: +61 2 8204 1888

#15
Australian Diamond Brokers
Category: Jewelry, Bridal
Average Price: Expensive
Area: Sydney
Address: 70 Castlereagh St Sydney
New South Wales
Phone: +61 2 9232 2328

#16
Galaxy Bookshop
Category: Bookstore
Average Price: Modest
Area: Sydney
Address: 131 York St Sydney
New South Wales
Phone: +61 2 9267 7222

#17
The Tea Cosy
Category: Coffee, Tea, Gift Shop
Average Price: Modest
Area: Sydney
Address: 33 George St Sydney
New South Wales
Phone: +61 2 9247 3233

#18
AMP Retail Plaza
Category: Shopping Center
Average Price: Inexpensive
Area: Sydney
Address: 50 Bridge St Sydney
New South Wales
Phone: +61 2 9257 1823

#19
Zara
Category: Women's Clothing,
Men's Clothing
Average Price: Modest
Area: Sydney
Address: 77 Pitt St Sydney
New South Wales
Phone: +61 2 9216 7000

#20
Lush Fresh Hand Made Cosmetics
Category: Cosmetics, Beauty Supply
Average Price: Modest
Area: Sydney
Address: 455 George St Sydney
New South Wales
Phone: +61 2 9283 5746

#21
Games Paradise
Category: Toy Store
Average Price: Expensive
Area: Sydney
Address: 357 Pitt St Sydney
New South Wales
Phone: +61 2 9267 2069

#22
Oscar Wylee Eyewear
Category: Eyewear, Opticians
Average Price: Inexpensive
Area: Sydney
Address: 320 Sussex St Sydney
New South Wales
Phone: +61 2 8355 4646

#23
Saigon Fabrics
Category: Fashion
Average Price: Expensive
Area: Sydney
Address: 78 Erskine St Sydney
New South Wales
Phone: +61 2 9299 0778

#24
Varoujan Jewellers
Category: Jewelry
Average Price: Expensive
Area: Sydney
Address: Shop 3048, Level 3 Sydney
New South Wales
Phone: +61 2 9232 2329

#25
Westfield
Category: Shopping Center
Average Price: Exclusive
Area: Sydney
Address: 100 Market St Sydney
New South Wales
Phone: +61 2 9358 7858

#26
Red Eye Records
Category: Music, DVDs, Vinyl Records
Average Price: Modest
Area: Sydney
Address: 143 York St Sydney
New South Wales
Phone: +61 2 9267 7440

#27
Lawson's Record Centre
Category: Music, DVDs
Area: Sydney
Address: 380 Pitt St Sydney
New South Wales
Phone: +61 2 9267 3434

#28
Alex & Alex Shoes
Category: Shoe Store
Average Price: Expensive
Area: Sydney
Address: 68 Erskine St Sydney
New South Wales
Phone: +61 2 9299 0097

#29
Red Eye Records
Category: Vinyl Records
Area: Sydney
Address: King Street 66 Sydney
New South Wales
Phone: +61 2 9233 8177

#30
Atelier De Velo
Category: Coffee, Tea, Bikes
Area: Sydney
Address: 156 Clarence St Sydney
New South Wales
Phone: +61 2 9045 1204

#31
Ted's Cameras
Category: Photography Store, Services
Area: Sydney
Address: 317 Pitt St Sydney
New South Wales
Phone: +61 2 9264 1687

#32
Skin Deep Clothing Company Pty
Category: Men's Clothing
Area: Sydney
Address: 251 Elizabeth St Sydney
New South Wales
Phone: +61 2 9264 1239

#33
Clarence Street Cyclery
Category: Bikes
Area: Sydney
Address: 104 Clarence St Sydney
New South Wales
Phone: +61 2 9299 4962

#34
Eckersley's Art & Craft
Category: Hobby Shop
Average Price: Modest
Area: Sydney
Address: 93 York St Sydney
New South Wales
Phone: +61 2 9299 4151

#35
Peter Alexander
Category: Women's Clothing,
Men's Clothing, Lingerie
Average Price: Modest
Area: Sydney
Address: Pitt Street Sydney
New South Wales
Phone: +61 2 9223 7451

#36
The National Opal Collection
Category: Accessories, Jewelry
Average Price: Expensive
Area: Sydney
Address: 60 Pitt St Sydney
New South Wales
Phone: +61 2 9247 6344

#37
Abbey's Bookshop
Category: Bookstore
Average Price: Modest
Area: Sydney
Address: 131 York St Sydney
New South Wales
Phone: +61 2 9264 3111

#38
Red Eye Records
Category: Music, DVDs
Average Price: Modest
Area: Sydney
Address: 370 Pitt St Sydney
New South Wales
Phone: +61 2 9262 9755

#39
Tiffany & Co.
Category: Jewelry
Average Price: Exclusive
Area: Sydney
Address: 28 Castlereagh St Sydney
New South Wales
Phone: 1800 731 131

#40
Madame Tussauds Sydney
Category: Art Gallery
Average Price: Modest
Area: Sydney
Address: Aquarium Pier Sydney
New South Wales
Phone: 1800 205 851

#41
Rox Gems & Jewellery
Category: Jewelry
Area: Sydney
Address: The Strand Arcade Sydney
New South Wales
Phone: +61 2 9232 7828

#42
Antique Print Room
Category: Antiques, Art Gallery
Area: Sydney
Address: Shop 7, Queen Victoria
Building, 455 George St Sydney New
South Wales
Phone: +61 2 9267 4355

#43
Telstra Store World Square
Category: Electronics, Mobile Phones
Area: Sydney
Address: 644 George St Sydney
New South Wales
Phone: +61 2 8576 5574

#44
R.M. Williams
Category: Shoe Store, Men's Clothing
Average Price: Expensive
Area: Sydney
Address: 389 George St Sydney
New South Wales
Phone: +61 2 9262 2228

#45
Camera Service Centre
Category: Appliances & Repair,
Photography Store, Services
Area: Sydney
Address: 1st Floor, 203 Castlereagh St
Sydney New South Wales
Phone: +61 2 9264 7091

#46
Typo
Category: Cards, Stationery
Average Price: Inexpensive
Area: Sydney
Address: 2-10 Darling Dr Sydney
New South Wales
Phone: +61 2 9281 4400

#47
Strand Hatters
Category: Shopping
Average Price: Exclusive
Area: Sydney
Address: 412 George St Sydney
New South Wales
Phone: +61 2 9231 6884

#48
Wittner Shoes
Category: Shoe Store, Outlet Store
Average Price: Modest
Area: Sydney
Address: 580 George St Sydney
New South Wales
Phone: +61 2 9267 5318

#49
Adyar Bookstore
Category: Books, Mags, Music, Video
Average Price: Modest
Area: Sydney
Address: 99 Bathurst Street Sydney
New South Wales
Phone: +61 2 9267 8509

#50
Jack London
Category: Men's Clothing
Average Price: Expensive
Area: Sydney
Address: Shp 1061/ 680 George St
Sydney
New South Wales
Phone: +61 2 9261 2012

#51
Missha
Category: Cosmetics, Beauty Supply
Area: Sydney
Address: 455 George St Sydney
New South Wales
Phone: +61 2 9267 8007

#52
Strand Souvenirs & Opals
Category: Jewelry
Area: Sydney
Address: 220 George St Sydney
New South Wales
Phone: +61 2 9251 5140

#53
Joe Button
Category: Women's Clothing,
Men's Clothing
Average Price: Modest
Area: Sydney
Address: Level 5, 428 George Street
Sydney New South Wales
Phone: +61 2 8005 6327

#54
The Laser Lounge
Category: Hair Removal,
Cosmetics, Beauty Supply
Area: Sydney
Address: 12B Westpac Place Sydney
New South Wales
Phone: +61 2 8922 8190

#55
Ralph Nicola
Category: Antiques
Area: Sydney
Address: 428 George St Sydney
New South Wales
Phone: +61 2 9223 8744

#56
Jason Ree
Category: Jewelry
Area: Sydney
Address: 428 George St Sydney
New South Wales
Phone: +61 2 9235 2133

#57
Speaker's Corner
Category: Local Flavor,
Botanical Garden, Art Gallery
Area: Sydney
Address: The Domain Sydney
New South Wales
Phone: +61 2 9713 5780

#58
Mondial Neuman
Category: Jewelry
Area: Sydney
Address: Shop G17, 455 George St
NSW New South Wales
Phone: +61 2 9283 6584

#59
Morris And Sons
Category: Framing, Knitting Supplies,
Fabric Store
Average Price: Modest
Area: Sydney
Address: 50 York St Sydney
New South Wales
Phone: +61 2 9299 8588

#60
The Bespoke Corner
Category: Customized Merchandise
Average Price: Modest
Area: Sydney
Address: 35 Shelley St Sydney
New South Wales
Phone: +61 4 1461 4769

#61
Office National
Category: Computers
Average Price: Inexpensive
Area: Sydney
Address: 203B Castlereagh St Sydney
New South Wales
Phone: +61 2 9267 6065

#62
Oxford
Category: Men's Clothing
Average Price: Expensive
Area: Sydney
Address: Skygarden, Pitt St Sydney
New South Wales
Phone: +61 2 9223 3840

#63
Harrolds
Category: Department Store
Average Price: Exclusive
Area: Sydney
Address: 77 Castlereagh St Sydney
New South Wales
Phone: +61 2 9232 8399

#64
S.A. Hair Nail & Beauty Supplies
Category: Shopping
Area: Sydney
Address: 8th Floor, Dymocks Building
428 George St Sydney
New South Wales
Phone: +61 2 9221 4188

#65
Monsterthreads
Category: Fashion
Area: Sydney
Address: 500 George Street Sydney
New South Wales
Phone: +61 2 9550 3009

#66
Gregory Jewellers
Category: Jewelry
Area: Sydney
Address: 67 Castlereagh St Sydney
New South Wales
Phone: +61 2 9233 3510

#67
Wynyard Yousave Chemist
Category: Drugstore, Health & Medical
Area: Sydney
Address: Shop 1/ 60 Carrington St
Sydney New South Wales
Phone: +61 2 9299 2858

#68
Hype D C
Category: Shoe Store
Average Price: Expensive
Area: Sydney
Address: Shop 25&26G, Sydney Central
Plaza. Cnr Pitt St And Market St Sydney
New South Wales
Phone: +61 2 9221 5688

#69
So Good Jewellery
Category: Jewelry
Average Price: Expensive
Area: Sydney
Address: Shop 21 501 George St
Sydney New South Wales
Phone: +61 2 9267 8465

#70
Lincraft
Category: Fabric Store
Average Price: Expensive
Area: Sydney
Address: 68 York St Sydney
New South Wales
Phone: +61 2 9279 4288

#71
Gateway Retail
Category: Shopping Center
Area: Sydney
Address: 1 Macquarie Place Sydney
New South Wales
Phone: +61 2 9256 6900

#72
Bloch
Category: Shopping
Average Price: Expensive
Area: Sydney
Address: 117 York Street Sydney
New South Wales
Phone: +61 2 9261 2856

#73
Comic Kingdom
Category: Comic Books
Average Price: Modest
Area: Sydney
Address: 71 Liverpool St Sydney
New South Wales
Phone: +61 2 9267 3629

#74
Made On Earth
Category: Home Decor
Average Price: Modest
Area: Sydney
Address: 50 Pitt St Sydney
New South Wales
Phone: +61 2 9252 2322

#75
Flowers On Martin Place Pty
Category: Florist
Average Price: Modest
Area: Sydney
Address: 1 Martin Pl Sydney
New South Wales
Phone: +61 2 9232 1451

#76
Apple Store
Category: Computers, Mobile Phones
Average Price: Expensive
Area: Sydney
Address: 367 George St Sydney
New South Wales
Phone: +61 2 8083 9400

#77
Digi Direct
Category: Electronics
Area: Sydney
Address: 75 King St Sydney
New South Wales
Phone: +61 2 9262 2330

#78
Voi Designer Fashion House
Category: Women's Clothing,
Outlet Store, Leather Goods
Area: Sydney
Address: 72 Castlereagh St Sydney
New South Wales
Phone: +61 2 9224 1100

#79
Page 2
Category: Flowers, Gifts
Area: Sydney
Address: 455 George St Sydney
New South Wales
Phone: +61 2 9261 2650

#80
Joe Bananas
Category: Men's Clothing
Average Price: Expensive
Area: Sydney
Address: G45 Queen Victoria Building
NSW New South Wales
Phone: +61 2 9264 2733

#81
Cara&Co Concept Store
Category: Shopping
Average Price: Modest
Area: Sydney
Address: 188 Pitt Street Sydney, NSW
Sydney New South Wales
Phone: +61 2 9226 9999

#82
Town Hall Square
Category: Shopping Center,
Local Flavor
Average Price: Modest
Area: Sydney
Address: 464-480 Kent St Sydney
New South Wales
Phone: +61 2 9265 1596

#83
Telstra Store Pitt Street
Category: Electronics, Mobile Phones
Average Price: Expensive
Area: Sydney
Address: 245 Pitt St Sydney
New South Wales
Phone: +61 2 8576 3380

#84
Kelly's Discount Books
Category: Bookstore, Music, DVDs
Average Price: Inexpensive
Area: Sydney
Address: 583 George St Sydney
New South Wales
Phone: +61 2 9267 5910

#85
Ecoo Jewellery
Category: Jewelry
Average Price: Expensive
Area: Sydney
Address: 1 Macquarie Pl Sydney
New South Wales
Phone: +61 2 9251 4849

#86
Trophy Land
Category: Shopping
Average Price: Modest
Area: Sydney
Address: 309 Kent St Sydney
New South Wales
Phone: +61 2 9279 0009

#87
Perfect Vision Optical
Category: Eyewear, Opticians
Average Price: Modest
Area: Sydney
Address: 412 George St Sydney
New South Wales
Phone: +61 2 9221 1010

#88
Card King Wynyard
Category: Cards, Stationery
Area: Sydney
Address: 301 George Street Sydney
New South Wales
Phone: +61 2 9299 8031

#89
Next Byte
Category: Electronics, Computers
Average Price: Modest
Area: Sydney
Address: 66 Clarence St Sydney
New South Wales
Phone: +61 2 9367 8585

#90
Chifley Plaza
Category: Shopping Center
Area: Sydney
Address: 2 Chifley Sq Sydney
New South Wales
Phone: +61 2 9221 6111

#91
Sydney Luggage Centre
Category: Luggage
Area: Sydney
Address: Cnr Kent & Bathurst Sts
Sydney New South Wales
Phone: +61 2 9267 1139

#92
Giordano Australia Pty
Category: Women's Clothing
Area: Sydney
Address: 525 George St Sydney
New South Wales
Phone: +61 2 9267 7422

#93
Florentine Australia
Category: Office Equipment,
Cards, Stationery, Costumes
Average Price: Expensive
Area: Sydney
Address: Shop 22, Queen Victorian
Building, 455 George St Sydney
New South Wales
Phone: +61 2 9264 6055

#94
Trek & Travel
Category: Outdoor Gear
Average Price: Expensive
Area: Sydney
Address: 447 Kent St Sydney
New South Wales
Phone: +61 2 9261 3435

#95
SES Fashion
Category: Women's Clothing
Area: Sydney
Address: 325 George St Sydney
New South Wales
Phone: +61 2 9262 5322

#96
Design Tshirts Store Graniph
Category: Men's Clothing
Average Price: Expensive
Area: Sydney
Address: Shop RG09, The Galeries
Victoria, 500 George Street Sydney
New South Wales
Phone: +61 2 9261 5250

#97
Urban News
Category: Newspapers & Magazines
Area: Sydney
Address: 1 Harbour St Sydney
New South Wales
Phone: +61 2 9266 0889

#98
Hondarake
Category: Bookstore
Average Price: Modest
Area: Sydney
Address: 465 Kent St Sydney
New South Wales
Phone: +61 2 9261 5225

#99
Metalicus
Category: Women's Clothing
Area: Sydney
Address: 455 George St
New South Wales
New South Wales
Phone: +61 2 9261 0555

#100
Montblanc
Category: Jewelry, Watches,
Cards, Stationery
Average Price: Expensive
Area: Sydney
Address: 117 King St Sydney
New South Wales
Phone: +61 2 9231 5671

#101
Watches of Switzerland
Category: Watches
Area: Sydney
Address: 199 George St Sydney
New South Wales
Phone: +61 2 9251 0088

#102
Art Equity Pty Ltd
Category: Art Gallery
Area: Sydney
Address: 66 King St Sydney
New South Wales
Phone: +61 2 9262 6660

#103
Little Joe
Category: Women's Clothing
Average Price: Expensive
Area: Sydney
Address: Corner Pitt Street Mall And
Market Street Sydney New South Wales
Phone: +61 2 8246 9197

#104
The Family Jewels
Category: Jewelry
Area: Sydney
Address: St James Arcade80
Castlereagh Street Sydney
New South Wales
Phone: +61 2 9233 5152

#105
Pen-Ultimate
Category: Office Equipment
Area: Sydney
Address: QVB, George Street Sydney
New South Wales
Phone: +61 2 9264 4991

#106
Quarter Twenty One
Category: Café, Personal Shopping
Area: Sydney
Address: Pitt Street Sydney
New South Wales
Phone: +61 2 8072 7755

#107
Harvey Norman
Category: Department Store, Electronics
Area: Sydney
Address: 19-29 Martin Pl Sydney
New South Wales
Phone: +61 2 8236 6600

#108
Cue
Category: Women's Clothing
Average Price: Expensive
Area: Sydney
Address: Shop 18-20 Ground Floor. Qvb
Building 455 George Street. Sydney
New South Wales
Phone: +61 2 9264 9822

#109
Rebel Sport
Category: Sporting Goods
Average Price: Modest
Area: Sydney
Address: Mid City Cntr, 197 Pitt St
Sydney New South Wales
Phone: +61 2 9221 8633

#110
Doctor Who Popup Shop
Category: Pop-Up Shop
Average Price: Modest
Area: Sydney
Address: 644 George St Sydney
New South Wales
Phone: +61 2 8669 6900

#111
Vintage Clothing Shop
Category: Used, Vintage
Area: Sydney
Address: 80 Castlereagh St Sydney
New South Wales
Phone: +61 2 9238 0090

#112
Dinosaur Designs
Category: Jewelry, Home Decor
Area: Sydney
Address: Strand Arcade, 412-414
George St Sydney New South Wales
Phone: +61 2 9223 2953

#113
Paul And Joe
Category: Women's Clothing
Area: Sydney
Address: Westfield Centre Point Sydney
New South Wales
Phone: +61 2 8246 9082

#114
Kikki-K
Category: Office Equipment,
Home Decor
Area: Sydney
Address: 455 George St Sydney
New South Wales
Phone: +61 2 8264 0123

#115
Fleur Wood
Category: Women's Clothing
Area: Sydney
Address: Westfield Shopping Centre Pitt
St Sydney New South Wales
Phone: +61 2 8246 9128

#116
Lenas Gourmet Kiosk
Category: Café, Flowers, Gifts,
Newspapers & Magazines
Area: Sydney
Address: 30 The Promenade Sydney
New South Wales
Phone: +61 2 9279 2848

#117
Dymocks
Category: Bookstore
Area: Sydney
Address: 686 George St Sydney South
New South Wales
Phone: +61 2 9286 3565

#118
Steve Madden
Category: Shopping
Area: Sydney
Address: 188 Pitt Street Sydney
New South Wales
Phone: +61 2 9233 8685

#119
Yd.
Category: Men's Clothing
Area: Sydney
Address: 450 George St, Shop 18G
Sydney New South Wales
Phone: +61 2 9239 0955

#120
Roman Daniels Menswear
Category: Men's Clothing
Area: Sydney
Address: Hunter Street 20 Sydney
New South Wales
Phone: +61 2 9233 2260

#121
Love & Hatred
Category: Jewelry
Average Price: Expensive
Address: Shop 59/61, Strand Arcade,
412-414 George Street Sydney
New South Wales
Phone: +61 2 9233 3441

#122
Allans Music + Billy Hyde
Category: Musical Instruments
Area: Sydney
Address: 228 Pitt St Sydney
New South Wales
Phone: +61 2 9283 7711

#123
J Farren-Price Jewellers
Category: Watches
Area: Sydney
Address: Shop 2, St James Arcade 80
Castlereagh St Sydney
New South Wales
Phone: +61 2 9231 3299

#124
Declic
Category: Men's Clothing
Area: Sydney
Address: 61 - 101 Phillip Street Sydney
New South Wales
Phone: +61 2 9221 0223

#125
Australian Opal Cutters Factory
Category: Jewelry
Area: Sydney
Address: 295- 301 Pitt St Sydney
New South Wales
Phone: +61 2 9261 2442

#126
Florsheim Shoe Shops, The
Category: Shoe Store
Area: Sydney
Address: 500 George St Sydney
New South Wales
Phone: +61 2 9264 3358

#127
Theeyecarecompany
Category: Eyewear, Opticians,
Optometrists
Average Price: Expensive
Area: Sydney
Address: 261 George St Sydney
New South Wales
Phone: +61 2 9241 2121

#128
Bristol & Brooks
Category: Flowers, Gifts
Average Price: Expensive
Area: Sydney
Address: SHOP 8 Chifley Plaza 2
Chifley Sq Sydney New South Wales
Phone: +61 2 9232 8699

#129
Camper Shoes
Category: Shoe Store
Area: Sydney
Address: 455 George Street Ground
Floor, Queen Victoria Building Sydney
New South Wales
Phone: +61 2 9261 3910

#130
JB Hi-Fi
Category: Electronics
Average Price: Expensive
Area: Sydney
Address: 412 - 414 George Street
Sydney New South Wales
Phone: +61 2 9222 9877

#131
Marcs
Category: Women's Clothing,
Men's Clothing
Average Price: Modest
Area: Sydney
Address: 455 George St Sydney
New South Wales
Phone: +61 2 9221 5575

#132
Telstra Store George St Sydney
Category: Mobile Phones
Area: Sydney
Address: 400 George St Sydney
New South Wales
Phone: +61 2 8257 4439

#133
Paddy Pallin
Category: Outdoor Gear
Average Price: Expensive
Area: Sydney
Address: 507 Kent St Sydney
New South Wales
Phone: +61 2 9264 2685

#134
Portico Books
Category: Bookstore
Area: Sydney
Address: 1 Jamison St Sydney
New South Wales
Phone: +61 2 9290 3556

#135
Gifts At The Quay
Category: Flowers, Gifts
Average Price: Modest
Area: Sydney
Address: 199 George St Sydney
New South Wales
Phone: +61 2 9247 8881

#136
Mid City Centre
Category: Shopping Center
Area: Sydney
Address: Pitt Street Mall Sydney
New South Wales
Phone: +61 2 9210 4209

#137
T-Bar
Category: Women's Clothing,
Men's Clothing
Average Price: Expensive
Area: Sydney
Address: 644 George St Sydney
New South Wales
Phone: +61 2 9261 1366

#138
Jim & Jane
Category: Shopping
Area: Sydney
Address: 412-414 George Street
Sydney New South Wales
Phone: +61 2 8065 0908

#139
**The Metropolitan
Museum of Art Store**
Category: Jewelry, Art Gallery,
Home Decor
Area: Sydney
Address: 455 George St Sydney
New South Wales
Phone: +61 2 9283 3799

#140
Imagination
Category: Shopping
Average Price: Modest
Area: Sydney
Address: 245 Pitt Street Sydney
New South Wales
Phone: +61 2 8065 0892

#141
Christopher Hanna Cosmedical
Category: Men's Hair Salon,
Cosmetics, Beauty Supply
Average Price: Exclusive
Area: Sydney
Address: 128 Castlereagh St Sydney
New South Wales
Phone: +61 2 9283 0151

#142
Just White
Category: Toy Store
Area: Sydney
Address: 455 George St Sydney
New South Wales
Phone: +61 2 9261 2503

#143
Optus 'Yes' Shop
Category: Electronics
Area: Sydney
Address: 397 George St Sydney
New South Wales
Phone: +61 2 8064 0200

#144
Kookai
Category: Women's Clothing
Average Price: Modest
Area: Sydney
Address: 440 George St Sydney
New South Wales
Phone: +61 2 9235 0293

#145
Performing Arts Bookshop
Category: Bookstore
Average Price: Modest
Area: Sydney
Address: 262 Pitt St Sydney
New South Wales
Phone: +61 2 9267 2257

#146
The Paperplace
Category: Shopping
Area: Sydney
Address: 111 Elizabeth St Sydney
New South Wales
Phone: +61 2 9233 2979

#147
King of The Pack-Wynyard
Category: Tobacco Shop
Average Price: Modest
Area: Sydney
Address: Shop G30, 301 George Street
Sydney New South Wales
Phone: +61 2 9299 6547

#148
Page 1
Category: Cards, Stationery
Area: Sydney
Address: 455 George St Sydney
New South Wales
Phone: +61 2 9264 8634

#149
Catalog Clothing
Category: Women's Clothing
Area: Sydney
Address: 189/569 George Street
Sydney New South Wales
Phone: +61 2 9283 1366

#150
Swarovski
Category: Jewelry
Area: Sydney
Address: 455 George St Sydney
New South Wales
Phone: +61 2 9261 4699

#151
Everything Home
Category: Home & Garden,
Discount Store, Cards, Stationery
Average Price: Modest
Area: Sydney
Address: Shop W2, 301 George Street
Sydney New South Wales
Phone: +61 2 9299 8866

#152
Colette
Category: Shopping
Average Price: Modest
Area: Sydney
Address: 455 George St Sydney
New South Wales
Phone: +61 2 9261 0921

#153
Karlangu Aboriginal Art
Category: Art Gallery
Area: Sydney
Address: 129 Pitt St Sydney
New South Wales
Phone: +61 2 9252 5430

#154
JB Hi Fi
Category: Electronics
Average Price: Modest
Area: Sydney
Address: 680 George St Sydney
New South Wales
Phone: +44 29 262 9400

#155
AMP Capital Shopping Centres
Category: Shopping Center
Average Price: Inexpensive
Area: Sydney
Address: 50 Bridge St St Sydney
New South Wales
Phone: +61 2 9257 5000

#156
Ron Bennett
Category: Men's Clothing,
Accessories, Formal Wear
Area: Sydney
Address: 253 Pitt St Sydney
New South Wales
Phone: +61 2 9264 7485

#157
Ted Baker
Category: Men's Clothing,
Women's Clothing
Area: Sydney
Address: Corner Pitt Street And
Market Street Sydney New South Wales
Phone: +61 8 4513 04278

#158
Molton Brown
Category: Cosmetics, Beauty Supply
Average Price: Expensive
Area: Sydney
Address: Shop 39 Ground Floor, Queen
Victoria Building, George St Sydney
New South Wales
Phone: +61 2 9267 5110

#159
Quay Pharmacy
Category: Drugstore
Area: Sydney
Address: 3 Alfred St Circular Quay
New South Wales
Phone: +61 2 9241 3566

#160
Kagui Shoes-Metcentre
Category: Shoe Store
Area: Sydney
Address: Shop T5, 60 Margaret Street
Sydney New South Wales
Phone: +61 2 9241 7777

#161
Imagination World
Category: Women's Clothing
Area: Sydney
Address: Shop G4 245 Pitt St Sydney
New South Wales
Phone: +61 2 8065 0892

#162
Burberry
Category: Fashion
Average Price: Exclusive
Area: Sydney
Address: 343 George St Sydney
New South Wales
Phone: +61 2 8296 8588

#163
CBD Pharmacies
Category: Drugstore
Area: Sydney
Address: 92 Pitt St Sydney
New South Wales
Phone: +61 2 9221 0180

#164
Down Town Souvenirs
Category: Gift Shop
Area: Sydney
Address: 476 George St Sydney
New South Wales
Phone: +61 2 9264 3838

#165
City Recital Hall
Category: Music, DVDs
Area: Sydney
Address: Angel Place 2-12 Sydney
New South Wales
Phone: +61 2 9231 9000

#166
Samsung Experience Store
Category: Electronics
Area: Sydney
Address: 450 George St Sydney
New South Wales
Phone: +61 2 8076 7777

#167
Beauty Grace
Category: Cosmetics, Beauty Supply
Average Price: Expensive
Area: Sydney
Address: 61 Market St Sydney
New South Wales
Phone: +61 2 9266 3200

#168
John Chen Gallery
Category: Art Gallery
Area: Sydney
Address: George St Sydney
New South Wales
Phone: +61 2 9267 0700

#169
City Bike Depot
Category: Sporting Goods
Area: Sydney
Address: 305 Kent St Sydney
New South Wales
Phone: +61 2 9279 2202

#170
Leona Edmiston Australia Pty
Category: Women's Clothing
Average Price: Expensive
Area: Sydney
Address: 2 Chifley Square Sydney
New South Wales
Phone: +61 2 9230 0322

#171
Cotton On
Category: Women's Clothing,
Men's Clothing
Area: Sydney
Address: 680 George St Sydney
New South Wales
Phone: +61 2 9283 3787

#172
Forcast
Category: Women's Clothing
Area: Sydney
Address: Shop 3, 630-634 George
Street Haymarket New South Wales
Phone: +61 2 9283 0097

#173
Fashion Passion
Category: Women's Clothing
Area: Sydney
Address: 301 George St Sydney
New South Wales
Phone: +61 2 9299 8866

#174
Jb Hi-Fi
Category: Electronics
Average Price: Modest
Area: Sydney
Address: Galleries Sydney
New South Wales
Phone: +61 2 9888 4730

#175
Opal Fields
Category: Jewelry
Area: Sydney
Address: 190 George St The Rocks
New South Wales
Phone: +61 2 9247 6800

#176
Strand Coins
Category: Antiques
Area: Sydney
Address: 412 George St Sydney
New South Wales
Phone: +61 2 9231 6694

#177
Peter Sheppard Shoes
Category: Shoe Store
Area: Sydney
Address: 188 Pitt Street Sydney
New South Wales
Phone: +61 2 9232 6904

#178
Soyo Shoes
Category: Shoe Store
Area: Sydney
Address: 570 George Street Sydney
New South Wales
Phone: +61 2 9283 0886

#179
Honey Birdette
Category: Lingerie
Average Price: Expensive
Area: Sydney
Address: 188 Pitt St Sydney
New South Wales
Phone: +61 2 8246 9165

#180
Mountain Designs
Category: Sporting Goods
Average Price: Modest
Area: Sydney
Address: 499 Kent St Sydney
New South Wales
Phone: +61 2 9267 3822

#181
Mojo Music
Category: Bar, Vinyl Records
Average Price: Modest
Area: Sydney
Address: 73 York St Sydney
New South Wales
Phone: +61 2 9262 4999

#182
Dirt Cheap Cameras
Category: Photography Store, Services
Area: Sydney
Address: Shop 1, 32 York Street Sydney
New South Wales
Phone: +61 2 9299 9985

#183
Naked Truth
Category: Lingerie
Average Price: Expensive
Area: Sydney
Address: 537 George St Sydney
New South Wales
Phone: +61 2 9267 5898

#184
Incu
Category: Men's Clothing,
Women's Clothing
Average Price: Expensive
Area: Sydney
Address: The Galeries Victoria, Shop
Rg 19-20 500 George St Sydney New
South Wales
Phone: +61 2 9283 7622

#185
Mecca Cosmetica
Category: Cosmetics, Beauty Supply
Average Price: Expensive
Area: Sydney
Address: 500 George St Sydney
New South Wales
Phone: +61 2 9261 4911

#186
The Galeries
Category: Shopping Center
Average Price: Modest
Area: Sydney
Address: 500 George St Sydney
New South Wales
Phone: +61 2 9265 6888

#187
Payless Shoes
Category: Shoe Store
Area: Sydney
Address: 317 George St Sydney
New South Wales
Phone: +61 2 9299 7572

#188
Paws A While
Category: Toy Store, Home Decor
Area: Sydney
Address: Shop 43, Queen Victoria
Building, 455 George St Sydney New
South Wales
Phone: +61 2 9261 2952

#189
Edward Meller
Category: Shoe Store
Area: Sydney
Address: 80 Castlereagh Street Sydney
New South Wales
Phone: +61 2 9232 1807

#190
RDX
Category: Men's Clothing
Area: Sydney
Address: Hop 27/28G Sydney Central
Plaza Sydney New South Wales
Phone: +61 2 9233 5775

#191
Factorie
Category: Women's Clothing,
Men's Clothing
Area: Sydney
Address: 395 George Street Sydney
New South Wales
Phone: +61 2 9262 2835

#192
Fred Perry
Category: Women's Clothing,
Men's Clothing
Area: Sydney
Address: 412 George St S
New South Wales
Phone: +61 2 9223 1488

#193
Gap
Category: Women's Clothing,
Men's Clothing, Children's Clothing
Average Price: Modest
Address: 188 Pitt Street Sydney
New South Wales
Phone: +61 2 9232 1157

#194
Frat House
Category: Women's Clothing,
Men's Clothing
Area: Sydney
Address: Shop B1.55, 420 George
Street, Level 1 Sydney New South Wales
Phone: +61 2 9232 4149

#195
Sydney Souvenir Warehouse
Category: Toy Store, Sports Wear
Area: Sydney
Address: 80 Liverpool St Sydney
New South Wales
Phone: +61 2 9264 6535

#196
Paxtons
Category: Photography Store, Services,
Average Price: Expensive
Area: Sydney
Address: 285 George St Sydney
New South Wales
Phone: +61 2 9299 2999

#197
Flowers For Everyone
Category: Florist
Area: Sydney
Address: 2 Market St Sydney
New South Wales
Phone: +61 2 9264 4033

#198
Perfect Mowing Sydney
Category: Gardeners, Nursery,
Gardening, Furniture Store
Average Price: Inexpensive
Area: Sydney
Address: Sussex St 274 Sydney
New South Wales
Phone: +61 2 8417 2227

#199
Vodafone World Square
Category: Local Flavor, Mobile Phones
Average Price: Inexpensive
Area: Sydney
Address: 680 George St Sydney
New South Wales
Phone: +61 2 9283 1393

#200
Lowes
Category: Men's Clothing
Area: Sydney
Address: 468 George St Sydney
New South Wales
Phone: +61 2 9267 2744

#201
Page One
Category: Women's Clothing
Area: Sydney
Address: 273 George Street, Sydney
New South Wales
Phone: +61 2 9252 6895

#202
Via Condotti
Category: Shoe Store
Area: Sydney
Address: 455 George St Sydney
New South Wales
Phone: +61 2 9269 0188

#203
Dick Smith Electronics
Category: Electronics
Area: Sydney
Address: 7A Barrack St Sydney
New South Wales
Phone: +61 2 9299 5835

#204
Sambag
Category: Fashion
Area: Sydney
Address: 188 Pitt St Sydney
New South Wales
Phone: +61 2 9233 4938

#205
Dick Smith Electronics
Category: Electronics
Average Price: Modest
Area: Sydney
Address: 421 George St Sydney
New South Wales
Phone: +61 2 9262 5799

#206
Horace Rice Sporting Sales
Category: Sporting Goods
Area: Sydney
Address: 8 Spring St Sydney
New South Wales
Phone: +61 2 9233 3665

#207
Foto Riesel Camera House
Category: Photography Store, Services
Area: Sydney
Address: 360 Kent St Sydney
New South Wales
Phone: +61 2 9299 6745

#208
Dioptics
Category: Eyewear, Opticians
Area: Sydney
Address: Ste 101, 147 King St Sydney
New South Wales
Phone: +61 2 9221 0049

#209
Rochefort Tailor And Shirtmaker
Category: Men's Clothing, Sewing,
Alterations
Area: Sydney
Address: 185 Elizabeth St Sydney
New South Wales
Phone: +61 2 9264 4408

#210
GS Diamonds
Category: Jewelry
Area: Sydney
Address: 23 QVB 435 George St
Sydney New South Wales
Phone: 1300 952 556

#211
Witchery
Category: Women's Clothing,
Accessories
Area: Sydney
Address: Met Centre, 273 George St
Sydney New South Wales
Phone: +61 2 9252 8450

#212
Campo Marzio Design
Category: Accessories
Area: Sydney
Address: Shop 63 Lower Ground 1,
QVB, 455 George St Sydney
New South Wales
Phone: +61 2 9261 3816

#213
Witchery
Category: Children's Clothing,
Women's Clothing, Accessories
Area: Sydney
Address: 413 George St Sydney
New South Wales
Phone: +61 2 9279 1877

#214
Vendome Sydney
Category: Watches, Jewelry, Luggage
Area: Sydney
Address: 12 Castlereagh St Sydney
New South Wales
Phone: +61 2 8069 2316

#215
Dymocks
Category: Bookstore
Average Price: Modest
Area: Sydney
Address: 424 George St Sydney
New South Wales
Phone: +61 2 9235 0155

#216
Duo Jewellery
Category: Jewelry
Area: Sydney
Address: 412-414 George St Sydney
New South Wales
Phone: +61 2 9221 7627

#217
Kim Sun Young Beauty Salon
Category: Cosmetics, Beauty Supply,
Hair Extensions, Eyelash Service
Average Price: Modest
Area: Sydney
Address: 580 George Street Sydney
New South Wales
Phone: +61 2 9264 0707

#218
Ron Bennett Big Men's Clothing
Category: Men's Clothing, Formal Wear
Area: Sydney
Address: 143 York St Sydney
New South Wales
Phone: +61 2 9264 6365

#219
Hetty Belle Lingerie
Category: Lingerie, Sleepwear
Area: Sydney
Address: Sydney
New South Wales
Phone: +61 2 9388 3766

#220
L'Occitane
Category: Cosmetics, Beauty Supply
Area: Sydney
Address: George Street 455 Sydney
New South Wales
Phone: +61 2 9283 5211

#221
Adina Jozsef
Category: Jewelry
Area: Sydney
Address: 250 Pitt St Sydney
New South Wales
Phone: +61 2 9267 0122

#222
Organic Babe & Kids Wear
Category: Children's Clothing
Area: Sydney
Address: George St Sydney
New South Wales
Phone: 1300 729 808

#223
Witchery
Category: Women's Clothing,
Men's Clothing, Children's Clothing
Area: Sydney
Address: 211 Pitt St Sydney
New South Wales
Phone: +61 2 9232 7732

#224
**Masterpiece Jewellery
Opals & Gems**
Category: Jewelry, Accessories
Area: Sydney
Address: 2 East Circular Quay Sydney
New South Wales
Phone: +61 2 9252 5218

#225
Business Furniture Direct Pty
Category: Furniture Store
Area: Sydney
Address: Unit 25, No 287, Victoria Road
Sydney New South Wales 2116
Phone: +61 2 9680 0851

#226
Giulians
Category: Jewelry
Area: Sydney
Address: 199 George St Sydney
New South Wales
Phone: +61 2 9525 2051

#227
HIT Equipment International
Category: Wholesale Store
Area: Sydney
Address: 88 Philip St Sydney
New South Wales
Phone: 1300 856 970

#228
Paxtons Camera Video Digital
Category: Books, Mags, Music, Video
Average Price: Exclusive
Area: Sydney
Address: Basement Level, 285 George
St Sydney New South Wales
Phone: +61 2 9299 2999

#229
Witchery
Category: Women's Clothing,
Accessories
Area: Sydney
Address: Chifley Plaza, 2 Chifley Sq
Sydney New South Wales
Phone: +61 2 9223 0412

#230
Georges Cameras
Category: Photography Store, Services
Average Price: Expensive
Area: Sydney
Address: 387 George St Sydney
New South Wales
Phone: +61 2 9299 2323

#231
The Latin Store
Category: Home Decor
Average Price: Exclusive
Address: 455 George St Sydney
New South Wales
Phone: +61 2 9283 0410

#232
Canturi
Category: Jewelry
Average Price: Exclusive
Area: Sydney
Address: 80 Castlereagh St Sydney
New South Wales
Phone: +61 2 9246 2888

#233
E-Cigarettes
Category: Vape Shop, Tobacco Shop
Area: Sydney
Address: 161 George St Sydney
New South Wales
Phone: +61 4 1255 54412

#234
Twinkle Diamonds
Category: Jewelry
Area: Sydney
Address: 250 Pitt St Sydney
New South Wales
Phone: +61 2 9261 5005

#235
WINAICO Australia Pty
Category: Electronics
Area: Sydney
Address: 393 George St Sydney
New South Wales
Phone: +61 2 8091 2771

#236
Witchery David Jones
Category: Women's Clothing,
Accessories
Area: Sydney
Address: 86-108 Castlereagh St Sydney
New South Wales
Phone: +61 2 9266 6265

#237
Diamonds By Design
Category: Jewelry
Area: Sydney
Address: 428 George St Sydney
New South Wales
Phone: +61 2 9232 1611

#238
**City Stationery Office
Choice Pitt Street**
Category: Office Equipment
Average Price: Modest
Area: Sydney
Address: 82 Pitt Street Sydney
New South Wales
Phone: +61 2 9221 8052

#239
Beauty Salon Upstairs
Category: Cosmetics, Beauty Supply
Area: Sydney
Address: 375 George St Sydney
New South Wales
Phone: +61 2 9299 3533

#240
Joseph's Shoes
Category: Men's Clothing
Average Price: Exclusive
Area: Sydney
Address: 249 Pitt St Sydney
New South Wales
Phone: +61 2 9264 6079

#241
Woosh Sydney
Category: Men's Clothing
Average Price: Modest
Area: Sydney
Address: 644 George St World Square
New South Wales 2002
Phone: +61 2 9286 3927

#242
Coach Leatherware
Category: Leather Goods
Area: Sydney
Address: Ground Floor, 455 George St
Sydney New South Wales
Phone: +61 2 8666 0600

#243
Star Jewels
Category: Jewelry, Watches
Area: Sydney
Address: 109 Pitt St Sydney
New South Wales
Phone: 1800 201 141

#244
Daiso
Category: Shopping
Area: Sydney
Address: 5 Hunter St Sydney
New South Wales
Phone: +61 2 9231 1298

#245
Anania Jewellers
Category: Jewelry
Area: Sydney
Address: 235 Clarence St Sydney
New South Wales
Phone: +61 2 9299 4251

#246
More Than A Handful
Category: Lingerie
Area: Sydney
Address: Level 1, 70 Druitt St Sydney
New South Wales
Phone: +61 2 9264 4264

#247
Mick Simmons Sport
Category: Sports Wear
Area: Sydney
Address: 478 George St, Next To Hilton,
Opposite Qvb Sydney
New South Wales
Phone: +61 2 9264 2744

#248
Karen Millen
Category: Women's Clothing
Area: Sydney
Address: Myer Sydney City 436 George
St Sydney New South Wales
Phone: +61 2 9037 4141

#249
Witcheryman David Jones
Category: Men's Clothing
Area: Sydney
Address: 65-77 Market St Sydney
New South Wales
Phone: +61 2 9266 5869

#250
Office Furniture Now
Category: Office Equipment
Area: Sydney
Address: 101 Bathurst St Sydney
New South Wales
Phone: 1300 670 746

#251
Oxford Shop
Category: Department Store
Area: Sydney
Address: 680 George St Sydney
New South Wales
Phone: +61 2 9318 2211

#252
Pearsons Florist
Category: Florist
Area: Sydney
Address: 273 George St Sydney
New South Wales
Phone: +61 2 9251 1666

#253
Affinity Diamonds
Category: Jewelry
Area: Sydney
Address: 155 King St Sydney
New South Wales
Phone: +61 2 9221 0717

#254
Acupuncture & Beauty Centre
Category: Cosmetics, Beauty Supply,
Traditional Chinese Medicine
Area: Sydney
Address: Unit 95/515 Kent St Sydney
New South Wales
Phone: +61 4 0332 8807

#255
Cartier Boutique
Category: Jewelry
Average Price: Exclusive
Area: Sydney
Address: 43 Castlereagh St Sydney
New South Wales
Phone: 1800 130 000

#256
Flowers For Everyone
Category: Florist
Area: Sydney
Address: Allianz Centre 2 Market St
Sydney New South Wales
Phone: +61 2 9264 4033

#257
Daniella
Category: Jewelry
Area: Sydney
Address: Level 9, Ste 10, 428 George St
Sydney New South Wales
Phone: 1300 988 470

#258
Sneakerboy
Category: Shoe Store
Area: Sydney
Address: 3 Temperance Lane Sydney
New South Wales
Phone: +61 3 9662 4447

#259
MACPAC
Category: Outdoor Gear
Area: Sydney
Address: Shop 42, Town Hall Arcade
464-480 Kent St Sydney
New South Wales
Phone: +61 2 9267 3510

#260
Jet Cycles
Category: Bikes
Area: Sydney
Address: 80 Clarence St Sydney
New South Wales
Phone: +61 2 9279 4200

#261
Leona Edmiston
Category: Women's Clothing
Average Price: Modest
Area: Sydney
Address: 195-195 Pitt St Sydney
New South Wales
Phone: +61 2 9221 7277

#262
Mary Holland - MET Centre
Category: Lingerie
Area: Sydney
Address: 273 George St Sydney
New South Wales
Phone: +61 2 9247 3494

#263
Zever Bead Shop
Category: Jewelry
Area: Sydney
Address: 250 Pitt Street Sydney
New South Wales
Phone: +61 2 9267 1654

#264
Optus World
Category: Mobile Phones
Area: Sydney
Address: Shop 9.36 World Square
Shopping Centre, 644 George St Sydney
New South Wales
Phone: +61 2 8215 6600

#265
Karen Millen
Category: Women's Clothing
Area: Sydney
Address: Shop 4018, Westfield Sydney
City, 188 Pitt Street Sydney
New South Wales
Phone: +61 2 9037 4081

#266
**Shoeologist - Barefoot
Running Specialists**
Category: Shoe Store, Outdoor Gear,
Sports Wear
Area: Sydney
Address: 505 Kent St Sydney
New South Wales
Phone: +61 2 8280 9000

#267
Only POS
Category: Office Equipment
Area: Sydney
Address: 33 York Street Sydney
New South Wales
Phone: 1300 887 672

#268
EB Games
Category: Electronics
Average Price: Modest
Area: Sydney
Address: The Galeries Vicotria,500
George St Sydney
New South Wales
Phone: +61 9 2644 149

#269
Cutler J H Pty Ltd
Category: Men's Clothing
Area: Sydney
Address: 12 O'Connell St Sydney
New South Wales
Phone: +61 2 9232 7122

#270
Courtesy of The Artist
Category: Jewelry
Area: Sydney
Address: The Strand Arcade, George St
Sydney New South Wales
Phone: +61 2 8354 1398

#271
Angus & Coote Repair Centre
Category: Jewelry
Area: Sydney
Address: Dymocks Bldg Lvl1/Shop 8
428 George St Sydney
New South Wales
Phone: +61 2 9223 6075

#272
Ben Sherman
Category: Men's Clothing
Area: Sydney
Address: 400 George St Sydney
New South Wales
Phone: +61 2 9222 1903

#273
Fashion By Farina
Category: Shopping
Average Price: Modest
Area: Sydney
Address: 428 George St Sydney
New South Wales
Phone: +61 2 9222 2933

#274
Cerrone Jewellers
Category: Jewelry
Area: Sydney
Address: 14 Martin Pl Sydney
New South Wales
Phone: +61 2 9232 6186

#275
Gucci
Category: Shopping
Area: Sydney
Address: 15 Martin Pl Sydney
New South Wales
Phone: +61 2 9232 7565

#276
Metcentre Pharmacy
Category: Drugstore
Area: Sydney
Address: Shop 39, Metcentre, 273
George St Sydney New South Wales
Phone: +61 2 9247 2045

#277
Kikki.K - Swedish Home
Category: Cards, Stationery
Address: Chifley Plaza Shop UG 10
Upper Ground 2 Chifley Sq Sydney
New South Wales
Phone: +61 2 8264 0128

#278
Audit & Fraud Software Pty
Category: Shopping
Area: Sydney
Address: Suite 604, 99 Bathurst St
Sydney New South Wales
Phone: +61 2 9229 8250

#279
Olympia Trophies Corporate
Category: Shopping
Area: Sydney
Address: 152 Pitt St Sydney
New South Wales
Phone: (300) 544-145

#280
Pandora
Category: Jewelry
Area: Sydney
Address: Shop 45 - 47, Queen Victoria
Building, 455 George St Sydney New
South Wales
Phone: +61 2 9283 7665

#281
Waldermar Jewellers
Category: Jewelry
Area: Sydney
Address: Suite 1003/ 155 King St
Sydney New South Wales
Phone: +61 2 9233 5284

#282
Ronald J. Crisp Pty Ltd
Category: Jewelry
Area: Sydney
Address: Suite 16, 3rd Floor, Dymocks
Bldg 424-428 George St Sydney
New South Wales
Phone: +61 2 9223 0372

#283
Breenspace Pty Ltd
Category: Art Gallery
Area: Sydney
Address: Level 3, 17/ 19 Alberta St
Sydney New South Wales
Phone: +61 2 9283 1113

#284
"Decora Homewares" Haymarket
Category: Home & Garden
Area: Sydney
Address: Shop 19a, Market City
Haymarket New South Wales
Phone: +61 2 9211 6663

#285
Intergy Consulting
Category: Shopping
Area: Sydney
Address: Level 3, Suite 3, 9- 13 Young
St Sydney New South Wales
Phone: +61 2 8090 7640

#286
Asadour's Fine Jewellery
Category: Jewelry
Area: Sydney
Address: Shop C54, Centrepoint
Westfield, 101 Castlereagh Street
Sydney New South Wales
Phone: +61 2 9223 7100

#287
Raymond's Jewellery
Category: Jewelry
Area: Sydney
Address: Shop 8, 80 Castlereagh Street,
St James Arcade Sydney
New South Wales
Phone: +61 2 9221 3313

#288
Harbourside Jewellers
Category: Jewelry
Area: Sydney
Address: Shop 133 Harbourside
Shopping Centre Sydney
New South Wales
Phone: +61 2 9281 5140

#289
Freedom Kitchens
Category: Kitchen & Bath
Area: Sydney
Address: The Galleries Victoria, Lvl 1,
500 George St Sydney New South Wales
Phone: +61 2 9261 4532

#290
The Footy Shop
Category: Sporting Goods
Area: Sydney
Address: Shop 219, Level 1,
Harbourside Shopping Centre Sydney
New South Wales
Phone: +61 2 9211 6861

#291
Imperial Arcade
Category: Shopping Center
Area: Sydney
Address: Pitt St Mall, Ctr Mgmt Office.
Suite 6-Level 1, 100 Market St Sydney
New South Wales
Phone: +61 2 9233 5662

#292
Time Connections - Watchmaker
Category: Watches
Area: Sydney
Address: Suite 210, Level 2, King
George Chambers, 375 George St
Sydney New South Wales
Phone: +61 2 9262 3485

#293
Jay Jays
Category: Fashion
Area: Sydney
Address: Shop R01-06 Glasshouse
On The Mall, 135 King St Sydney
New South Wales
Phone: +61 2 9235 0927

#294
Imperial Arcade
Category: Shopping Center
Area: Sydney
Address: Pitt St Mall, Ctr Mgmt Office.
Suite 6-Level 1, 100 Market St Sydney
New South Wales
Phone: +61 2 9233 5662

#295
The Florsheim Shoe Shops
Category: Shoe Store
Area: Sydney
Address: Shop MG22, Metcentre,
Cnr George & Margaret Sts Sydney
New South Wales
Phone: +61 2 9251 2987

#296
Watches of Switzerland
Category: Watches
Area: Sydney
Address: The Four Seasons Hotel, 199
George St Sydney New South Wales
Phone: +61 2 9251 0088

#297
Dymocks
Category: Bookstore
Area: Sydney
Address: Dymocks Head Office Level 6/
428 George St Sydney New South Wales
Phone: +61 2 9224 0411

#298
Sanity
Category: Music, DVDs
Area: Sydney
Address: Skygarden Building 162 Pitt St
Sydney Sydney New South Wales
Phone: +61 2 9223 8571

#299
Aesop
Category: Cosmetics, Beauty Supply
Area: Sydney
Address: 412-414 George Street
Sydney New South Wales
Phone: +61 2 9235 2353

#300
Australian Forms Office Choice
Category: Office Equipment
Area: Sydney
Address: 153 Phillip St Sydney
New South Wales
Phone: +61 2 9222 9666

#301
**Wheely Convenient Mobile
Bicycle Mechanics**
Category: Bikes, Bike Repair,
Maintenance
Area: Sydney
Address: 1 Martin Place Sydney
New South Wales
Phone: +61 4 3215 4550

#302
Priceline Pharmacy
Category: Drugstore
Area: Sydney
Address: 227 Elizabeth St Sydney
New South Wales
Phone: +61 2 9262 7700

#303
Ojay Pty Ltd
Category: Women's Clothing
Area: Sydney
Address: 413 George St Sydney
New South Wales
Phone: +61 2 9262 4500

#304
St James Pharmacy
Category: Drugstore
Area: Sydney
Address: 111 Elizabeth St Sydney
New South Wales
Phone: +61 2 9231 2662

#305
Officeworks
Category: Office Equipment, Cards,
Stationery,
Area: Sydney
Address: 151 Clarence St Sydney
New South Wales
Phone: +61 2 8297 4200

#306
Dymocks
Category: Bookstore
Area: Sydney
Address: 350 George St Sydney
New South Wales
Phone: +61 2 9223 5974

#307
Oscans Bulk Photo Scanning
Category: Photography Store, Services
Area: Sydney
Address: 66 King St Sydney
New South Wales
Phone: 1300 138 970

#308
David Benn Fine Jewellery
Category: Jewelry
Area: Sydney
Address: 64 Castlereagh St Sydney
New South Wales
Phone: +61 2 9233 4644

#309
**Australian Opal Jewellers
& Setters**
Category: Jewelry
Area: Sydney
Address: 3Rd Floor 295- 301 Pitt St
NSW New South Wales
Phone: +61 2 9264 1537

#310
Ilona Sophie Brow Specialist
Category: Cosmetics, Beauty Supply,
Eyelash Service
Area: Sydney
Address: Suite 813, Level 8, 160
Castlereagh St Sydney
New South Wales
Phone: +61 4 1073 6086

#311
Bill Hicks Jewellery Design
Category: Jewelry
Area: Sydney
Address: Suite 1005, 10Th Floor, Trust Building, 155 King St NSW New South Wales
Phone: +61 2 9231 0994

#312
Martin & Stein Antiques
Category: Antiques
Area: Sydney
Address: Shop 22, The Grand Walk, Queen Victoria Building 455 George St Sydney New South Wales
Phone: +61 2 9267 6628

#313
Pandora
Category: Jewelry
Area: Sydney
Address: Myer Sydney City, 436 George Street NSW New South Wales
Phone: +61 2 9238 9117

#314
Kenneth Mansergh
Category: Jewelry
Area: Sydney
Address: Ground Floor, 60-70 Elizabeth St Sydney New South Wales
Phone: +61 2 9233 1355

#315
Vendome
Category: Jewelry
Area: Sydney
Address: 12 Castlereagh St Sydney New South Wales
Phone: +61 2 9968 3582

#316
Jules Collins Jewellery
Category: Jewelry
Area: Sydney
Address: Shop P10, 61-101 Phillip St Sydney New South Wales
Phone: +61 2 9222 2798

#317
Dirt Cheap Cameras
Category: Books, Mags, Music, Video
Area: Sydney
Address: Queen Victoria Building New South Wales 1230
Phone: +61 2 9232 2744

#318
Itap Wynyard Pty Ltd
Category: Computers
Area: Sydney
Address: Hunter Connection, Shop H11, 7-13 Hunter St Sydney New South Wales
Phone: +61 2 9221 9947

#319
Dirt Cheap Stores Pty Ltd
Category: Photography Store, Services
Area: Sydney
Address: 32 York St Sydney New South Wales
Phone: +61 2 9299 9985

#320
The Florsheim Shoe Shops
Category: Shoe Store
Area: Sydney
Address: Shop MG22, Metcentre, Cnr George & Margaret Sts Sydney New South Wales
Phone: +61 2 9251 2987

#321
Watches of Switzerland
Category: Watches
Area: Sydney
Address: The Four Seasons Hotel, 199 George St Sydney New South Wales
Phone: +61 2 9251 0088

#322
Leap Legal Software Pty
Category: Shopping
Area: Sydney
Address: Level 8, 207 Kent St Sydney New South Wales
Phone: +61 2 8273 7544

#323
ECCO Shoes
Category: Shoe Store
Area: Sydney
Address: Wesfield Sydney, Shop 23G, Cnr Pitt St Mall And Market St Sydney New South Wales
Phone: +61 2 9232 8734

#324
Altmann & Cherny
Category: Jewelry
Area: Sydney
Address: 18 Pitt St Sydney New South Wales
Phone: +61 2 9251 9477

#325
Dove Diamonds
Category: Jewelry
Area: Sydney
Address: Ste111/ 222 Pitt St Sydney
New South Wales
Phone: +61 2 9269 0061

#326
Telstra Store
Category: Mobile Phones
Area: Sydney
Address: 400 George St Sydney
New South Wales

#327
Anthony Squires
Category: Men's Clothing
Area: Sydney
Address: 4 Bligh St Sydney
New South Wales
Phone: +61 2 9230 0519

#328
**City Stationery Office
Choice Market Street**
Category: Office Equipment
Area: Sydney
Address: 28 Market Street Sydney
New South Wales
Phone: +61 2 9262 4189

#329
POP Caps
Category: Hats
Area: Sydney
Address: Sydney
New South Wales
Phone: +61 2 4258 5684

#330
Kent Street Studio
Category: Women's Clothing
Area: Sydney
Address: 435A-437 Kent St Sydney
New South Wales
Phone: +61 2 9260 9727

#331
Mitchells Adventure
Category: Outdoor Gear
Area: Sydney
Address: 81 York St Sydney
New South Wales
Phone: +61 2 9299 6321

#332
Esteem Designz
Category: Arts, Crafts, Education
Area: Sydney
Address: Sydney
New South Wales
Phone: +61 2 9523 7297

#333
Gucci
Category: Shopping
Area: Sydney
Address: 136 George St The Rocks
New South Wales
Phone: +61 2 9252 1663

#334
Prada Australia Pty
Category: Women's Clothing
Area: Sydney
Address: 7/ 15 Castlereagh St NSW
New South Wales
Phone: +61 2 9223 1688

#335
Ermenegildo Zegna Boutique
Category: Men's Clothing
Area: Sydney
Address: Cnr Castlereagh & King St
Sydney
New South Wales
Phone: +61 2 9222 9355

#336
Cerrone Jewellers
Category: Jewelry
Area: Sydney
Address: 14 Martin Pl Sydney
New South Wales
Phone: +61 2 9232 6186

#337
Gay Exchange
Category: Adult
Area: Sydney
Address: 44 Park St Sydney
New South Wales
Phone: +61 2 9264 1020

#338
Mountain Equipment
Category: Outdoor Gear
Area: Sydney
Address: 491 Kent St Sydney
New South Wales
Phone: +61 2 9264 5888

#339
J. H. Cutler
Category: Men's Clothing
Address: 12 O'connell St Sydney
New South Wales
Phone: +61 2 9232 7122

#340
Roz La Kelin Bridal Avenue
Category: Bridal
Area: Sydney
Address: 428 George St Sydney
New South Wales
Phone: 1300 274 337

#341
Hardy Brothers Jewellers
Category: Jewelry
Area: Sydney
Address: 60 Castlereagh Street Sydney
New South Wales
Phone: +61 2 9232 2422

#342
Looksmart Alterations
Category: Women's Clothing
Area: Sydney
Address: 428 George Street, Level 9,
Suite 15 Dymocks Building Shopping
Centre Sydney
New South Wales
Phone: +61 2 9223 0111

#343
Marbo Shirt
Category: Fashion
Area: Sydney
Address: Shop 115 Strand Arcade 412-
414 George St NSW New South Wales
Phone: +61 2 9221 6644

#344
Im Boutique
Category: Lingerie
Area: Sydney
Address: Shop 3018 Sydney Westfield
Sydney New South Wales
Phone: +61 2 9232 0088

#345
Telstra Store Sydney
Category: Mobile Phones
Area: Sydney
Address: Shop 9.35, World Square
Shopping Centre, 644 George St Sydney
New South Wales
Phone: +61 2 8576 5574

#346
Mchugh's Shoes
Category: Shoe Store
Area: Sydney
Address: Shop 19, St James Centre,
107-111 Elizabeth Street Sydney
New South Wales
Phone: +61 2 9231 3039

#347
Office Choice
Category: Shopping
Area: Sydney
Address: 299 Elizabeth St Sydney
New South Wales
Phone: +61 2 9267 8627

#348
Sunlite Hardware
Category: Hardware Store
Area: Sydney
Address: 74 Pitt St Sydney
New South Wales
Phone: +61 2 9233 7698

#349
TOWANDA
Category: Women's Clothing
Area: Sydney
Address: Shop 40, Level 1, Queen
Victoria Building, 455 George St Sydney
New South Wales
Phone: +61 2 9283 4848

#350
Beqoo Sydney
Category: Accessories, Formal Wear
Area: Sydney
Address: 7-13 Hunter St Sydney
New South Wales
Phone: +61 2 9235 3881

#351
Fairfax & Roberts Jewellers
Category: Jewelry
Area: Sydney
Address: 11 Castlereagh St Sydney
New South Wales
Phone: +61 2 9232 8510

#352
General Pants Co.
Category: Fashion
Area: Sydney
Address: 197 Pitt St Sydney
New South Wales
Phone: +61 2 8275 5155

#353
Leonidas-Cocoa Bean
Category: Flowers, Gifts
Area: Sydney
Address: Shop 14, Chifley Plaza, 2
Chifley Square Sydney
New South Wales
Phone: +61 2 9222 1230

#354
A Diamond Wholesaler
Category: Jewelry
Area: Sydney
Address: Suite 1307, 87-89 Liverpool
Street (World Tower) Sydney
New South Wales
Phone: +61 2 9283 6096

#355
Absolute World Connections
Category: Mobile Phones
Area: Sydney
Address: Shop 9.25, World Square
Shopping Centre, 644 George St Sydney
New South Wales
Phone: +61 2 9267 6800

#356
Diamond Events
Category: Jewelry
Area: Sydney
Address: Level 57 MLC Centre 19-21
Martin Pl Sydney New South Wales
Phone: 1300 880 152

#357
Leap Legal Software Pty
Category: Shopping
Area: Sydney
Address: Level 8, 207 Kent St Sydney
New South Wales
Phone: +61 2 8273 7544

#358
Bettina Liano
Category: Women's Clothing
Area: Sydney
Address: Shop 74-78, Level 1 Strand
Arcade, Pitt St Sydney New South Wales
Phone: +61 2 9223 3511

#359
Attik Clothing
Category: Women's Clothing
Area: Sydney
Address: Shp 32b/ 275 Pitt St Sydney
New South Wales
Phone: +61 2 9266 0601

#360
Anthony Squires
Category: Men's Clothing
Area: Sydney
Address: Market St Sydney
New South Wales
Phone: +61 2 9266 5261

#361
Solar Chargers
Category: Mobile Phones
Area: Sydney
Address: 171 Clarence St Sydney
New South Wales
Phone: +61 2 9420 2388

#362
Rebel
Category: Sporting Goods
Area: Sydney
Address: 77 King St Sydney
New South Wales
Phone: +61 2 9221 8633

#363
Magic Gardening Sydney
Category: Gardeners, Nursery,
Gardening, Furniture Store
Average Price: Modest
Area: Sydney
Address: Kent St 414 Sydney
New South Wales
Phone: +61 2 8310 4050

#364
Typo
Category: Cards, Stationery,
Art Supplies
Area: Sydney
Address: 644 George St Sydney
New South Wales
Phone: +44 29 283 3742

#365
Bijoux Box
Category: Accessories, Jewelry
Area: Sydney
Address: 1 Martin Pl, GPO Buidling,
Ground Floor Sydney New South Wales
Phone: +61 2 9229 7703

#366
Abrisham
Category: Women's Clothing
Area: Sydney
Address: 299/298-304 Sussex St
Sydney New South Wales
Phone: +61 2 8958 9377

#367
Kalmar Antiques Pty
Category: Antiques
Area: Sydney
Address: Level 1, Shop 47 Queen
Victoria Building, George St NSW
New South Wales
Phone: +61 2 9264 0696

#368
GMQ
Category: Jewelry
Area: Sydney
Address: 155 King St Sydney
New South Wales
Phone: +61 4 1187 6198

#369
Bizoffice Furniture
Category: Furniture Store
Area: Sydney
Address: 1 Farrer Pl, Governor Phillip
Tower Sydney New South Wales
Phone: 1300 137 968

#370
Portmans
Category: Women's Clothing
Area: Sydney
Address: Pitt St Sydney
New South Wales
Phone: +61 2 9223 1726

#371
Armani Exchange
Category: Shopping
Area: Sydney
Address: 107 King St Sydney
New South Wales
Phone: +61 2 9231 0047

#372
Stockland Piccadilly
Category: Shopping Center
Area: Sydney
Address: 210 Pitt St Sydney
New South Wales
Phone: +61 2 9267 0722

#373
Regal Watches & Jewellery
Category: Jewelry
Area: Sydney
Address: George St Sydney
New South Wales
Phone: +61 2 9267 7265

#374
Victoria Buckley Jewellery
Category: Jewelry
Area: Sydney
Address: 412 George St Sydney
New South Wales
Phone: +61 2 9231 5571

#375
Studio Fabrics
Category: Bridal
Area: Sydney
Address: 12 O'Connell St Sydney
New South Wales
Phone: +61 2 9231 0068

#376
Country Road Clothing Pty
Category: Women's Clothing
Area: Sydney
Address: 144 Pitt St Sydney
New South Wales
Phone: +61 2 9394 1818

#377
Face Shop
Category: Cosmetics, Beauty Supply
Area: Sydney
Address: 572 George St Sydney
New South Wales
Phone: +61 2 9264 8622

#378
Gorman
Category: Men's Clothing
Average Price: Expensive
Area: Sydney
Address: 412-414 George St Sydney
New South Wales
Phone: +61 2 9232 1997

#379
Veronika Maine
Category: Women's Clothing
Area: Sydney
Address: 273 George St Sydney
New South Wales 2148
Phone: +61 2 8065 7571

#380
City Pharmacy - MLC Centre
Category: Drugstore
Area: Sydney
Address: Shop 609 Mlc Center Sydney
New South Wales
Phone: +61 2 9233 1338

#381
Uggs On Sydney
Category: Home & Garden
Area: Sydney
Address: Shop 14, 501 George St NSW
New South Wales
Phone: +61 2 9807 8922

#382
Vodafone
Category: Mobile Phones
Area: Sydney
Address: 285 George St Sydney
New South Wales
Phone: 1300 650 410

#383
MC Cyclery
Category: Bikes
Area: Sydney
Address: 230 Clarence St Sydney
New South Wales
Phone: +61 2 9349 2154

#384
Equip
Category: Accessories
Area: Sydney
Address: Queen Victoria Building Shop
64, 455 George Street Sydney
New South Wales
Phone: +61 2 9283 3213

#385
Karisma
Category: Accessories
Area: Sydney
Address: Shop B2, 2A Bligh St Sydney
New South Wales
Phone: +61 2 9221 7711

#386
Eze IT
Category: Computers
Area: Sydney
Address: Level 57, MLC Centre,
19 - 29 Martin Pl Sydney
New South Wales
Phone: +61 2 9238 6641

#387
General Pants Co.
Category: Fashion
Area: Sydney
Address: Shop 10.14 World Square
Shopping Centre, 644 George St Sydney
New South Wales
Phone: +61 2 8275 5159

#388
The Flower Man
Category: Florist
Area: Sydney
Address: 225 George St Sydney
New South Wales
Phone: +61 2 9251 4000

#389
Hifidelity Lounge
Category: Music, DVDs
Area: Sydney
Address: Shop 421 Harbourside
Shopping Center Darling Harbour
New South Wales
Phone: +61 2 9281 2102

#390
Elly Rab Academy of Singing
Category: Musical Instruments
Area: Sydney
Address: 250 Pitt Street Suite 403 /
Level 4 Sydney New South Wales
Phone: +61 2 9264 5042

#391
ECCO Shoes SYDNEY
Category: Shoe Store
Area: Sydney
Address: Wesfield Sydney, Shop 23G,
Cnr Pitt St Mall And Market St Sydney
New South Wales
Phone: +61 2 9232 8734

#392
Sky Garden
Category: Shopping Center
Area: Sydney
Address: Pitt St Mall, Level 1, 100
Market St Sydney New South Wales
Phone: +61 2 9233 5662

#393
Karen Millen
Category: Women's Clothing
Area: Sydney
Address: Myer Sydney City 436 George
St Sydney New South Wales
Phone: +61 2 9037 4141

#394
The Footy Shop
Category: Sporting Goods
Area: Sydney
Address: Shop 219, Level 1,
Harbourside Shopping Centre Sydney
New South Wales
Phone: +61 2 9211 6861

#395
Bettina Liano
Category: Women's Clothing
Area: Sydney
Address: Shop 74-78, Level 1 Strand
Arcade, Pitt St Sydney New South Wales
Phone: +61 2 9223 3511

#396
Akira Boutique
Category: Women's Clothing
Area: Sydney
Address: The Strand Arcade, Level 2,
412-414 George St Sydney
New South Wales
Phone: +61 2 9232 1078

#397
Attik Clothing
Category: Women's Clothing
Area: Sydney
Address: Shp 32b/ 275 Pitt St Sydney
New South Wales
Phone: +61 2 9266 0601

#398
Karen Millen
Category: Women's Clothing
Area: Sydney
Address: Shop 4018, Westfield Sydney
City, 188 Pitt Street Sydney

New South Wales
Phone: +61 2 9037 4081

#399
Sky Garden
Category: Shopping Center
Area: Sydney
Address: Pitt St Mall, Level 1, 100
Market St Sydney New South Wales
Phone: +61 2 9233 5662

#400
Australian Diamond Exchange
Category: Jewelry
Area: Sydney
Address: 262 Pitt St Sydney
New South Wales
Phone: +61 2 9252 2388

#401
BESTBUY Pharmacy Wynyard
Category: Drugstore
Area: Sydney
Address: Shop W14, Wynyard Station
Sydney New South Wales
Phone: +61 2 9299 1327

#402
Telstra Store
Category: Mobile Phones
Area: Sydney
Address: Shop 9.35 World Square
Shopping Centre, 644 George St Sydney
New South Wales
Phone: 1800 724 945

#403
Sydney Wedding Dresses
Category: Women's Clothing
Area: Sydney
Address: 2/428 George St Sydney
New South Wales
Phone: +61 2 9222 2678

#404
Victoria & Albert Antiques
Category: Antiques
Area: Sydney
Address: Shop 17, The Strand Arcade
412 - 414 George St Sydney
New South Wales
Phone: +61 2 9221 7198

#405
No. 1 Martin Place
Category: Shopping Center
Area: Sydney
Address: 1 Martin Pl Sydney
New South Wales
Phone: +61 2 9221 5073

#406
Coty Australia Pty Limited
Category: Cosmetics, Beauty Supply
Area: Sydney
Address: 1 Market St Sydney
New South Wales
Phone: +61 2 8263 9960

#407
Mywalit
Category: Luggage
Area: Sydney
Address: Level 2, Shops 34-36,
455 George St Sydney
New South Wales
Phone: +61 2 9266 0064

#408
Germanicos Tailors
Category: Men's Clothing
Area: Sydney
Address: 147 King St Sydney
New South Wales
Phone: (300) 824-567

#409
Politix
Category: Men's Clothing
Area: Sydney
Address: Shp33/ 455 George St Sydney
New South Wales
Phone: +61 2 9264 9812

#410
Cue
Category: Women's Clothing
Area: Sydney
Address: George St Sydney
New South Wales
Phone: +61 2 9231 4433

#411
Urbanews
Category: Newspapers & Magazines
Area: Sydney
Address: 1 Harbour St Sydney
New South Wales
Phone: +61 2 9266 0889

#412
Starluxe
Category: Jewelry
Area: Sydney
Address: 109 Pitt St Sydney
New South Wales
Phone: 1800 201 141

#413
Saba
Category: Women's Clothing,
Accessories, Men's Clothing
Area: Sydney
Address: Shop 6G, Sydney Central
Plaza Sydney New South Wales
Phone: +61 2 9232 4666

#414
Blush Flowers
Category: Florist
Area: Sydney
Address: Lobby, 227 Elizabeth St
Sydney New South Wales
Phone: +61 2 9283 1212

#415
Antique & Modern Clock Repairs
Category: Shopping
Area: Sydney
Address: Shop 2/ 2 Bridge St Sydney
New South Wales
Phone: +61 2 9247 5119

#416
Equip
Category: Accessories
Area: Sydney
Address: Mid City Centre Shop 64, 197
Pitt Street Sydney New South Wales
Phone: +61 2 9232 4705

#417
Itap Group Pty
Category: Computers
Area: Sydney
Address: Level 8/ 35 Clarence Street
Sydney New South Wales
Phone: 1300 669 889

#418
General Pants Co.
Category: Fashion
Area: Sydney
Address: Level 1 Shop 1014, Westfield
Shopping Centre, Cnr Pitt St Mall &
Market St Sydney New South Wales
Phone: +61 2 8275 5160

#419
Fairfax & Roberts Jewellers
Category: Jewelry
Area: Sydney
Address: 44 Martin Pl Sydney
New South Wales
Phone: +61 2 9232 8511

#420
Utopia Records
Category: Music, DVDs
Area: Sydney
Address: Lower Ground Floor,
511 Kent St Sydney
New South Wales
Phone: +61 2 9571 6662

#421
Bettaprint Rubber Stamps
Category: Shopping
Area: Sydney
Address: Level 8, Dymocks Building,
428 George St Sydney
New South Wales
Phone: 1300 782 677

#422
Intergy Consulting
Category: Shopping
Area: Sydney
Address: Level 3, Suite 3, 9- 13 Young
St Sydney New South Wales
Phone: +61 2 8090 7640

#423
Homemaker City
Category: Shopping Center
Area: Sydney
Address: Level 52, MLC Centre, 19
Martin Place Sydney New South Wales
Phone: +61 2 8239 3555

#424
The Footy Shop Pty
Category: Sporting Goods
Area: Sydney
Address: Shop 219, Level 1,
Harbourside Shopping Ctre Darling
Harbour New South Wales
Phone: +61 2 9211 6861

#425
Akira Boutique
Category: Women's Clothing
Area: Sydney
Address: The Strand Arcade, Level 2,
412-414 George St Sydney
New South Wales
Phone: +61 2 9232 1078

#426
Homemaker City
Category: Shopping Center
Area: Sydney
Address: Level 52, MLC Centre,
19 Martin Place Sydney
New South Wales
Phone: +61 2 8239 3555

#427
The Footy Shop Pty Ltd
Category: Sporting Goods
Area: Sydney
Address: Shop 219, Level 1,
Harbourside Shopping Ctre Darling
Harbour New South Wales
Phone: +61 2 9211 6861

#428
Time Connections - Watchmaker
Category: Watches
Area: Sydney
Address: Suite 210, Level 2, King
George Chambers, 375 George St
Sydney New South Wales
Phone: +61 2 9262 3485

#429
Bettaprint Rubber Stamps
Category: Shopping
Area: Sydney
Address: Level 8, Dymocks Building,
428 George St Sydney New South Wales
Phone: 1300 782 677

#430
Telstra Store
Category: Mobile Phones
Area: Sydney
Address: 231 Elizabeth St Sydney
New South Wales

#431
Telstra Store
Category: Mobile Phones
Area: Sydney
Address: Shop 5020, Westfield Sydney,
188 Pitt St Sydney New South Wales

#432
Telstra Store
Category: Mobile Phones
Area: Sydney
Address: Shop G2, 245 Pitt St Sydney
New South Wales

#433
**City Stationery Office Choice
Elizabeth Street**
Category: Office Equipment
Area: Sydney
Address: 299 Elizabeth Street Sydney
New South Wales
Phone: +61 2 9283 7753

#434
Sofia Furniture
Category: Furniture Store
Area: Sydney
Address: 320 Sussex St Sydney
New South Wales
Phone: +61 2 8355 4643

#435
Best Gardener Sydney
Category: Gardeners, Nursery,
Gardening, Furniture Store
Average Price: Modest
Area: Sydney
Address: Castlereagh St 164 Sydney
New South Wales
Phone: +61 2 8103 4115

#436
Botanics Florist Sydney
Category: Florist
Area: Sydney
Address: 26 Sussex St Sydney
New South Wales
Phone: +61 2 9279 1389

#437
Blockout
Category: Women's Clothing
Area: Sydney
Address: 455 George St Sydney
New South Wales
Phone: +61 2 9286 3625

#438
Patagonia
Category: Sports Wear
Area: Sydney
Address: 93 Bathurst St Sydney
New South Wales
Phone: +61 2 9267 7666

#439
Zaeger Diamonds & Watches
Category: Watches, Jewelry
Area: Sydney
Address: St 815, 160 Castlereagh St
Sydney New South Wales
Phone: +61 4 3146 4163

#440
J4U Makeup Studio
Category: Makeup Artists, Cosmetics,
Beauty Supply, Eyelash Service
Area: Sydney
Address: 1216D Level12 World Tower
Sydney New South Wales
Phone: +61 4 1653 5767

#441
Inski
Category: Outdoor Gear
Area: Sydney
Address: 46 York St Sydney
New South Wales
Phone: +61 2 9233 3200

#442
Larry Adler Ski & Outdoor
Category: Sporting Goods
Area: Sydney
Address: 497 Kent St Sydney
New South Wales
Phone: +61 2 9264 2500

#443
Officeworks
Category: Office Equipment,
Electronics, Cards, Stationery
Area: Sydney
Address: 242 Pitt St Sydney
New South Wales
Phone: +61 2 8267 5300

#444
Beauty Grace
Category: Cosmetics, Beauty Supply
Area: Sydney
Address: 273 George St Sydney
New South Wales
Phone: +61 2 9266 3200

#445
Carla Zampatti
Category: Shopping
Area: Sydney
Address: Myer, Market St Sydney
New South Wales
Phone: +61 2 9238 9501

#446
MC Cycles + Giant
Category: Bikes
Area: Sydney
Address: 230 Clarence St Sydney
New South Wales
Phone: +61 2 8021 5669

#447
Tresors
Category: Antiques, Jewelry
Area: Sydney
Address: The Strand Arcade Sydney
New South Wales
Phone: +61 2 9222 1848

#448
The Corner Shop
Category: Women's Clothing
Average Price: Exclusive
Address: 412-414 George St Sydney
New South Wales
Phone: +61 2 9221 1788

#449
Morning Glory
Category: Office Equipment, Toy Store
Average Price: Modest
Address: 22 Goulburn Street Haymarket
New South Wales
Phone: +61 2 9267 7899

#450
Kings Comics
Category: Comic Books
Average Price: Expensive
Area: Sydney
Address: 310 Pitt St Sydney
New South Wales
Phone: +61 2 9267 5615

#451
LUSH Botanical Arrangement
Category: Florist
Area: Sydney
Address: 301 George St Sydney
New South Wales
Phone: +61 2 9299 3992

#452
**Karen Deakin Antique
& Vintage Jewellery**
Category: Jewelry
Area: Sydney
Address: Level 4 Dymocks Bldg
428 George St Sydney New South Wales
Phone: +61 2 9221 1404

#453
Gabreil Jewellers
Category: Jewelry
Area: Sydney
Address: 155 King St Sydney
New South Wales
Phone: +61 2 9233 8319

#454
Fastflowers.Com.Au Sydney
Category: Florist
Area: Sydney
Address: 38 College St Sydney
New South Wales
Phone: +61 2 9331 7174

#455
Hipster
Category: Women's Clothing
Area: Sydney
Address: 109 Pitt St Sydney
New South Wales
Phone: +61 2 9223 2504

#456
Phillips IT
Category: Computers
Area: Sydney
Address: 222 Sussex St Sydney
New South Wales
Phone: +61 2 8262 9900

#457
Babushkas
Category: Toy Store
Average Price: Expensive
Area: Sydney
Address: Shp313/ Harbourside Shopng
Cntr Darling Harbour New South Wales
Phone: +61 2 9212 1810

#458
The Shirt Shop
Category: Fashion
Area: Sydney
Address: The Colonial Centre 20
Elizabeth St Sydney New South Wales
Phone: +61 2 9233 2886

#459
Land Beyond Beyond
Category: Bookstore
Area: Sydney
Address: 583 George St Sydney
New South Wales
Phone: +61 2 9267 6279

#460
Gospel Pianos Pty
Category: Musical Instruments
Area: Sydney
Address: 156 Castlereagh St NSW
New South Wales
Phone: +61 2 9264 0007

#461
Frameworks
Category: Framing
Area: Sydney
Address: 184 Elizabeth St Sydney
New South Wales
Phone: +61 2 9211 1270

#462
P & L Pascale Holdings Pty
Category: Discount Store
Area: Sydney
Address: 238 Pitt St Sydney
New South Wales
Phone: +61 2 9261 1773

#463
Costello's of
Category: Jewelry
Area: Sydney
Address: 280 George St Sydney
New South Wales
Phone: +61 2 9232 1011

#464
Mahler Trading Pty
Category: Jewelry
Area: Sydney
Address: 70 Castlereagh St Sydney
New South Wales
Phone: +61 2 9232 0450

#465
Rodd Gunn & Logan
Category: Men's Clothing
Area: Sydney
Address: 155 George St Sydney
New South Wales
Phone: +61 2 9252 9373

#466
Laura Ashley Australia Pty
Category: Women's Clothing
Area: Sydney
Address: Centrepoint Sydney
New South Wales
Phone: +61 2 9232 2829

#467
Collections Design
Category: Fashion
Area: Sydney
Address: 37 Bligh St Sydney
New South Wales
Phone: +61 2 9558 8200

#468
Bevisco Commercial Interiors
Category: Office Equipment
Area: Sydney
Address: 63 Sussex St Sydney
New South Wales
Phone: +61 2 9279 2244

#469
Tancredi Jewellers
Category: Jewelry
Area: Sydney
Address: 184 Pitt St Sydney
New South Wales
Phone: +61 2 9221 8100

#470
T & H Dream Pty
Category: Bookstore
Area: Sydney
Address: 26A Lime St Sydney
New South Wales
Phone: +61 2 9299 3556

#471
Covers
Category: Shopping
Area: Sydney
Address: 131 Elizabeth St Sydney
New South Wales
Phone: +61 2 9266 5377

#472
Dymocks Stationery Superstore
Category: Cards, Stationery, Bookstore
Area: Sydney
Address: 430 George St Sydney
New South Wales
Phone: +61 2 9235 2677

#473
Sock Drawer
Category: Lingerie
Area: Sydney
Address: Darling Harbour Sydney
New South Wales
Phone: +61 2 9212 7766

#474
Wynyard Tobacconist
Category: Tobacco Shop
Area: Sydney
Address: 301 George St Sydney
New South Wales
Phone: +61 2 9299 6547

#475
Macquarie Street Pharmacy
Category: Drugstore
Area: Sydney
Address: 195 Macquarie St Sydney
New South Wales
Phone: +61 2 9221 1622

#476
Caviglia
Category: Men's Clothing
Area: Sydney
Address: 64 Castlereagh St Sydney
New South Wales
Phone: +61 2 9233 1997

#477
Ojay Pty
Category: Women's Clothing
Area: Sydney
Address: 450 George St Sydney
New South Wales
Phone: +61 2 9232 8355

#478
Sassy 14
Category: Women's Clothing
Area: Sydney
Address: Castlereagh St Sydney
New South Wales
Phone: +61 2 9222 1746

#479
Woolford
Category: Women's Clothing
Area: Sydney
Address: Sydney Central Plaza Shop
29 G 450 George St NSW
New South Wales
Phone: +61 2 9232 0008

#480
Billy Hyde Music
Category: Musical Instruments
Area: Sydney
Address: 222 Clarence St Sydney
New South Wales
Phone: +61 2 9269 9600

#481
Perry Madison Designs
Category: Florist
Area: Sydney
Address: 201 Elizabeth St Sydney
New South Wales
Phone: +61 2 9283 8800

#482
Jonathan Marks Photography
Category: Art Gallery
Area: Sydney
Address: George St Sydney
New South Wales
Phone: +61 2 9267 6808

#483
Twinkle Imp-Ex P/ L
Category: Jewelry
Area: Sydney
Address: Suite 11, Level 9, 250 Pitt St
Sydney New South Wales
Phone: +61 2 9261 5005

#484
Watch World Australia
Category: Watches
Area: Sydney
Address: K1.08 Market City Haymarket
New South Wales
Phone: +61 2 9211 3238

#485
Calibre Clothing Pty
Category: Men's Clothing
Area: Sydney
Address: 139 Elizabeth St Sydney
New South Wales
Phone: +61 2 9267 9321

#486
Picolo Gifts & Souvenirs
Category: Shopping
Area: Sydney
Address: 333 George St Sydney
New South Wales
Phone: +61 2 9262 6219

#487
Gerrards Jewellers Pty
Category: Jewelry
Area: Sydney
Address: 155 King St Sydney
New South Wales
Phone: +61 2 9232 4882

#488
Office Fitout Sydney Pty
Category: Office Equipment
Area: Sydney
Address: Clarence St Sydney
New South Wales
Phone: +61 2 8078 6988

#489
De Stoop Brothers Diamond
Category: Jewelry
Area: Sydney
Address: 295-301 Pitt St Sydney
New South Wales
Phone: +61 2 9261 2442

#490
Jayson Brunsdon
Category: Women's Clothing
Area: Sydney
Address: 412 George St Sydney
New South Wales
Phone: +61 2 9233 8891

#491
Nicholls Price
Category: Shopping
Area: Sydney
Address: Suite 1605 Level 1B, 33 Bligh
St Sydney New South Wales
Phone: +61 2 9222 9155

#492
Val Parks Shirt Shop
Category: Men's Clothing
Area: Sydney
Address: 72 Pitt St Sydney
New South Wales
Phone: +61 2 9231 2001

#493
John W Thompson Engravers
Category: Jewelry
Area: Sydney
Address: Ste 1,Lvl 4,Dymocks Building,
428 George St Sydney New South Wales
Phone: +61 2 9233 3520

#494
Diamond Traders City
Category: Jewelry
Area: Sydney
Address: 250 Pitt St Sydney
New South Wales
Phone: +61 2 9267 7133

#495
**Great Australian Jumper
Company Pty**
Category: Women's Clothing
Area: Sydney
Address: 350 Kent St Sydney
New South Wales
Phone: +61 2 9299 3388

#496
Havana Express Sydney
Category: Tobacco Shop
Area: Sydney
Address: 1 Martin Pl Sydney
New South Wales
Phone: +61 2 9223 9700

#497
Cartier Head Office
Category: Jewelry
Area: Sydney
Address: 420 George St Sydney
New South Wales
Phone: 1800 130 000

#498
Quality Selections IMP Aust
Category: Home Decor
Area: Sydney
Address: 152-156 Clarence St NSW
New South Wales
Phone: +61 2 9290 1222

#499
Hunter-Taylor Gallery Aust
Category: Art Gallery
Area: Sydney
Address: 259 Pitt St Sydney
New South Wales
Phone: +61 2 9261 4417

#500
Pharmeasy
Category: Drugstore
Area: Sydney
Address: 28 Margaret St Sydney
New South Wales
Phone: +61 2 8270 1100

TOP 500 RESTAURANTS

The Most Recommended by Locals & Trevelers

(From #1 to #500)

#1
Din Tai Fung
Cuisines: Chinese, Taiwanese
Average Price: Modest
Area: Sydney
Address: 644 George St Sydney
New South Wales
Phone: +61 2 9264 6010

#2
Rockpool Bar & Grill
Cuisines: Bar, Australian, Australian
Average Price: Exclusive
Area: Sydney
Address: 66 Hunter St Sydney
New South Wales
Phone: +61 2 8078 1900

#3
Tetsuya's Restaurant
Cuisines: Seafood, Asian Fusion
Average Price: Exclusive
Area: Sydney
Address: 529 Kent St Sydney
New South Wales
Phone: +61 3 9267 2900

#4
Bourke Street Bakery
Cuisines: Café, Bakery
Average Price: Inexpensive
Area: Surry Hills
Address: 633 Bourke St Sydney
New South Wales 2010
Phone: +61 2 9699 1011

#5
Home Thai Restaurant
Cuisines: Thai
Average Price: Modest
Area: Sydney
Address: 299 Sussex St Sydney
New South Wales
Phone: +61 2 9261 5058

#6
Mr Wong
Cuisines: Chinese, Asian Fusion
Average Price: Expensive
Area: Sydney
Address: 3 Bridge Ln Sydney
New South Wales
Phone: +61 2 9240 3000

#7
Bar Tapavino
Cuisines: Spanish, Bar
Average Price: Expensive
Area: Sydney
Address: 6 Bulletin Pl Sydney
New South Wales
Phone: +61 2 9247 3221

#8
Sydney Madang
Cuisines: Korean
Average Price: Modest
Area: Sydney
Address: 371 Pitt St Sydney
New South Wales
Phone: +61 2 9264 7010

#9
Snag Stand
Cuisines: Fast Food, Hot Dogs
Average Price: Inexpensive
Area: Sydney
Address: 188 Pitt Street Sydney
New South Wales
Phone: +61 2 9221 9600

#10
Gumshara Ramen
Cuisines: Japanese
Average Price: Inexpensive
Area: Haymarket
Address: 25-29 Dixon St Sydney
New South Wales
Phone: +61 4 1025 3180

#11
Oiden
Cuisines: Japanese
Average Price: Inexpensive
Area: Sydney
Address: 537-551 George St Sydney
New South Wales
Phone: +61 2 9267 1368

#12
Chat Thai
Cuisines: Thai
Average Price: Modest
Area: Haymarket
Address: 20 Campbell St Sydney
New South Wales
Phone: +61 2 9211 1808

#13
Three Williams
Cuisines: Café
Average Price: Modest
Area: Redfern
Address: 613a Elizabeth St Sydney
New South Wales 2016
Phone: +61 2 9698 1111

#14
Berta
Cuisines: Italian
Area: Sydney
Address: 17-19 Alberta St Sydney
New South Wales
Phone: +61 2 9264 6133

#15
Menya Japan Noodle Bar City
Cuisines: Japanese
Average Price: Inexpensive
Area: Sydney
Address: 1 Market St Sydney
New South Wales
Phone: +61 2 9267 4649

#16
Hana Hana
Cuisines: Japanese
Average Price: Inexpensive
Area: Haymarket
Address: 5/209 Thomas St Sydney
New South Wales
Phone: +61 2 9280 1570

#17
Chefs Gallery Townhall
Cuisines: Chinese
Average Price: Modest
Area: Sydney
Address: Regent Place G/F 501 George
St Sydney New South Wales
Phone: +61 2 9267 8877

#18
Din Tai Fung Dumpling Bar
Cuisines: Dim Sum
Average Price: Modest
Area: Sydney
Address: 188 Pitt St Sydney
New South Wales
Phone: +61 2 8246 7032

#19
Pendolino
Cuisines: Italian
Average Price: Expensive
Area: Sydney
Address: Shop 100-102, Level 2,
412-414 George St Sydney
New South Wales
Phone: +61 2 9231 6117

#20
Makoto
Cuisines: Japanese, Sushi Bar
Average Price: Inexpensive
Area: Sydney
Address: 119 Liverpool St Sydney
New South Wales
Phone: +61 2 9283 6767

#21
Ippudo Sydney
Cuisines: Japanese
Average Price: Modest
Area: Sydney
Address: 188 Pitt St Sydney
New South Wales
Phone: +61 2 8078 7020

#22
Menya Mappen
Cuisines: Japanese
Average Price: Inexpensive
Area: Sydney
Address: 537-551 George St Sydney
New South Wales
Phone: +61 2 9283 5525

#23
Malay Chinese Takeaway
Cuisines: Malaysian, Chinese
Average Price: Inexpensive
Area: Sydney
Address: 50-58 Hunter St Sydney
New South Wales
Phone: +61 2 9231 6788

#24
Bodhi Bar
Cuisines: Vegan, Vegetarian, Chinese
Average Price: Modest
Area: Sydney
Address: 4 College St Sydney
New South Wales
Phone: +61 2 9360 2523

#25
Jamie's Italian
Cuisines: Italian
Average Price: Modest
Area: Sydney
Address: 107 Pitt St Sydney
New South Wales
Phone: +61 2 8240 9000

#26
Sea Bay Restaurant
Cuisines: Chinese
Average Price: Inexpensive
Area: Sydney
Address: 372 Pitt St Sydney
New South Wales
Phone: +61 2 9267 4855

#27
Klink
Cuisines: Café, Coffee, Tea
Average Price: Inexpensive
Area: Sydney
Address: 281 Clarence Street Sydney
New South Wales
Phone: +61 4 1511 8505

#28
Grill'd Healthy Burgers
Cuisines: Burgers
Average Price: Inexpensive
Area: Sydney
Address: Level 2, Harbourside Shopping
Ctr Sydney New South Wales
Phone: +61 2 9281 5121

#29
Fix St James
Cuisines: Wine Bar, Italian, Australian
Average Price: Expensive
Area: Sydney
Address: 111 Elizabeth St Sydney
New South Wales
Phone: +61 2 9232 2767

#30
Momofuku Seiobo
Cuisines: Korean, Asian Fusion
Average Price: Exclusive
Area: Pyrmont
Address: 80 Pyrmont St Sydney
New South Wales 2009
Phone: +61 2 9777 9000

#31
Nazimi
Cuisines: Japanese
Average Price: Modest
Area: Sydney
Address: 141 York St Sydney
New South Wales
Phone: +61 2 9283 2990

#32
The Rook
Cuisines: Bar, Burgers
Average Price: Modest
Area: Sydney
Address: 56-58 York St Sydney
New South Wales
Phone: +61 2 9262 2505

#33
Goodgod Small Club
Cuisines: Bar, American, Music Venues
Average Price: Inexpensive
Area: Sydney
Address: 55 Liverpool St Sydney
New South Wales
Phone: +61 8 0840 587

#34
Big Bite On Pitt
Cuisines: Sandwiches
Average Price: Inexpensive
Area: Sydney
Address: 250 Pitt St Sydney
New South Wales
Phone: +61 2 9283 4700

#35
Opera Kitchen
Cuisines: Nightlife, Burgers
Average Price: Modest
Area: Sydney
Address: Bennelong Pt Sydney
New South Wales
Phone: +61 4 5009 9888

#36
Ichiban Boshi
Cuisines: Japanese
Average Price: Inexpensive
Area: Sydney
Address: 500 George St Sydney
New South Wales
Phone: +61 2 9262 7677

#37
**Bambini Trust Cafe
& Wine Room**
Cuisines: Café, European, Wine Bar
Average Price: Expensive
Area: Sydney
Address: 185 Elizabeth St Sydney
New South Wales
Phone: +61 2 9283 7098

#38
Chat Thai
Cuisines: Thai
Average Price: Inexpensive
Area: Sydney
Address: 500 George Street Sydney
New South Wales
Phone: +61 2 9264 7109

#39
Hana Hana
Cuisines: Japanese
Average Price: Inexpensive
Area: Sydney
Address: 339 Sussex St Sydney
New South Wales
Phone: +61 2 9268 0410

#40
**Dragon Boy Japanese
Noodle Bar**
Cuisines: Japanese
Average Price: Inexpensive
Area: Sydney
Address: 123 Liverpool St Sydney
New South Wales
Phone: +61 2 9264 8880

#41
Saké
Cuisines: Japanese, Bar
Average Price: Expensive
Area: The Rocks
Address: 12 Argyle St Sydney
New South Wales
Phone: +61 2 9259 5656

#42
Rabbit Hole Bar & Dining
Cuisines: Australian, Cocktail Bar
Average Price: Expensive
Area: Sydney
Address: 82 Elizabeth St Sydney
New South Wales
Phone: +61 2 8084 2505

#43
Loaf & Devotion
Cuisines: Breakfast & Brunch
Average Price: Inexpensive
Area: Sydney
Address: 57-59 York St Sydney
New South Wales
Phone: +61 4 1962 7527

#44
Marlowe's Way
Cuisines: Café
Average Price: Inexpensive
Area: Sydney
Address: Cnr Tank Stream Way &
Bridge Ln Sydney New South Wales
Phone: +61 4 3248 7598

#45
Searock Grill
Cuisines: Seafood, Steakhouse
Average Price: Expensive
Area: Sydney
Address: 5 Macquarie St Sydney
New South Wales
Phone: +61 2 9252 0777

#46
BLACK By Ezard
Cuisines: Australian, Steakhouse
Average Price: Exclusive
Area: Pyrmont
Address: 80 Pyrmont St Sydney
New South Wales 2009
Phone: +61 2 9657 9109

#47
Stitch Bar
Cuisines: Burgers, Hot Dogs,
Cocktail Bar
Average Price: Expensive
Area: Sydney
Address: 61 York St Sydney
New South Wales
Phone: +61 2 9279 0380

#48
Bistro Papillon
Cuisines: French
Average Price: Exclusive
Area: Sydney
Address: 98 Clarence St Sydney
New South Wales
Phone: +61 2 9262 2402

#49
Lynn Shanghai Cuisine
Cuisines: Shanghainese
Average Price: Modest
Area: Sydney
Address: 199 Castlereagh St Sydney
New South Wales
Phone: +61 2 9267 7780

#50
Ladurée
Cuisines: Desserts, French
Average Price: Modest
Area: Sydney
Address: 100 Market St Sydney
New South Wales
Phone: +61 2 9231 0491

#51
One Six One Rotisserie
Cuisines: French, Coffee, Tea,
Breakfast & Brunch
Area: Sydney
Address: 161 Castlereagh St Sydney
New South Wales
Phone: +61 2 9283 0161

#52
Felix Bistro & Bar
Cuisines: French
Average Price: Expensive
Area: Sydney
Address: 2 Ash St Sydney
New South Wales
Phone: +61 2 9240 3000

#53
Medusa Greek Taverna
Cuisines: Greek
Average Price: Expensive
Area: Sydney
Address: 2 Market St Sydney
New South Wales
Phone: +61 2 9267 0799

#54
Fish At The Rocks
Cuisines: Restaurant
Average Price: Expensive
Area: Millers Point
Address: Cnr Argyle & Kent Sts Sydney
New South Wales
Phone: +61 2 9252 4614

#55
ARIA Restaurant Sydney
Cuisines: Australian
Average Price: Exclusive
Area: Sydney
Address: 1 Macquarie St Sydney
New South Wales
Phone: +61 2 9252 2555

#56
La Rosa
Cuisines: Pizza, Italian, Wine Bar
Average Price: Modest
Area: Sydney
Address: 193 Pitt St Sydney
New South Wales
Phone: +61 2 9223 1674

#57
The Woods
Cuisines: Australian
Average Price: Expensive
Area: Sydney
Address: 199 George St Sydney
New South Wales
Phone: +61 2 9250 3100

#58
3 Wise Monkeys Pub
Cuisines: Pub, Gastropub
Average Price: Modest
Area: Sydney
Address: 555 George St Sydney
New South Wales
Phone: +61 2 9283 5855

#59
Spice Temple
Cuisines: Chinese
Average Price: Expensive
Area: Sydney
Address: 10 Bligh St Sydney
New South Wales
Phone: +61 2 8078 1888

#60
Glass
Cuisines: Brasseries
Average Price: Expensive
Area: Sydney
Address: 488 George St Sydney
New South Wales
Phone: +61 2 9265 6068

#61

Encasa
Cuisines: Spanish, Tapas
Average Price: Modest
Area: Haymarket
Address: 423 Pitt St Sydney
New South Wales
Phone: +61 2 9211 4257

#62

Redoak Boutique Beer Cafe
Cuisines: Pub, Australian, Beer Bar
Average Price: Modest
Area: Sydney
Address: 201 Clarence St Sydney
New South Wales
Phone: +61 2 9262 3303

#63

Chinta Ria
Cuisines: Malaysian, Fast Food,
Asian Fusion
Average Price: Modest
Area: Sydney
Address: 201 Sussex Street Sydney
New South Wales
Phone: +61 2 9264 3211

#64

Two Black Sheep
Cuisines: Coffee, Tea, Café
Average Price: Inexpensive
Area: Sydney
Address: 580 George St Sydney
New South Wales
Phone: +61 4 9700 3211

#65

Est Restaurant
Cuisines: European
Average Price: Exclusive
Area: Sydney
Address: 252 George St Sydney
New South Wales
Phone: +61 2 9240 3000

#66

Misschu
Cuisines: Vietnamese
Average Price: Modest
Area: Sydney
Address: 501 George St Sydney
New South Wales
Phone: +61 2 9283 0357

#67

Little Vienna
Cuisines: Sandwiches
Average Price: Inexpensive
Area: Sydney
Address: 20 Hunter St Sydney
New South Wales
Phone: +61 2 9232 0033

#68

Yebisu Izakaya
Cuisines: Japanese, Bar, Sushi Bar
Average Price: Modest
Area: Sydney
Address: 501 George St Sydney
New South Wales
Phone: +61 2 9266 0301

#69

Sydney Cove Oyster Bar
Cuisines: Seafood, Breakfast & Brunch
Average Price: Modest
Area: Sydney
Address: Lot 1 Circular Quay E Sydney
New South Wales
Phone: +61 2 9247 2937

#70

Ipoh On York
Cuisines: Malaysian,
Breakfast & Brunch
Average Price: Inexpensive
Area: Sydney
Address: 89 York St Sydney
New South Wales
Phone: +61 2 9299 0001

#71

Chilli Cha Cha
Cuisines: Thai, Australian
Average Price: Inexpensive
Area: Haymarket
Address: 40-50 Campbell St Sydney
New South Wales
Phone: +61 2 9211 2025

#72

Madame Nhu
Cuisines: Vietnamese, Fast Food
Average Price: Inexpensive
Area: Sydney
Address: 500 George Street Sydney
New South Wales
Phone: +61 2 9283 3355

#73
Diethnes Greek Restaurant
Cuisines: Restaurant
Average Price: Expensive
Area: Sydney
Address: 336 Pitt St Sydney
New South Wales
Phone: +61 2 9267 8956

#74
Swine & Co.
Cuisines: Deli
Average Price: Inexpensive
Area: Sydney
Address: 16 O'Connell St Sydney
New South Wales
Phone: +61 2 9009 0990

#75
Braza Churrascaria
Cuisines: Brazilian
Average Price: Expensive
Area: Sydney
Address: 1-25 Harbour St Sydney
New South Wales
Phone: +61 2 9286 3733

#76
I'm Angus Steak House
Cuisines: Seafood, Steakhouse
Average Price: Expensive
Area: Sydney
Address: The Promenade Sydney
New South Wales
Phone: 1300 989 989

#77
O Bal Tan
Cuisines: Korean
Average Price: Expensive
Area: Sydney
Address: 363A Pitt St Sydney
New South Wales
Phone: +61 2 9269 0299

#78
Chat Thai Westfield Sydney
Cuisines: Restaurant
Average Price: Modest
Area: Sydney
Address: 188 Pitt St Sydney
New South Wales
Phone: +61 2 9221 0600

#79
Encasa Deli
Cuisines: Delicatessen, Café
Average Price: Inexpensive
Area: Sydney
Address: 135 Bathurst St Sydney
New South Wales
Phone: +61 2 9283 4277

#80
The Foxhole
Cuisines: Bar, Café
Average Price: Modest
Area: Sydney
Address: 68A Erskine Street Sydney
New South Wales
Phone: +61 2 9279 4969

#81
Hyde Park Barracks Cafe
Cuisines: Café
Average Price: Modest
Area: Sydney
Address: Queens Square Macquarie St
Sydney New South Wales
Phone: +61 2 9222 1815

#82
Vapiano
Cuisines: Italian
Average Price: Modest
Area: Sydney
Address: Corner King And York St
Sydney New South Wales
Phone: +61 2 9299 0079

#83
Panzerotti Cafe
Cuisines: Café
Area: Sydney
Address: 2 York St Sydney
New South Wales
Phone: +61 2 9290 1119

#84
B.B.Q. King Restaurant
Cuisines: Restaurant
Average Price: Modest
Area: Sydney
Address: 18 Goulburn St Sydney
New South Wales
Phone: +61 2 9267 2586

#85
360 Bar And Restaurant
Cuisines: Bar, European
Average Price: Exclusive
Area: Sydney
Address: Reception Level 4, Sydney
Westfield Centre Sydney
New South Wales
Phone: +61 2 8223 3883

#86
Kiroran Silk Road Uygur
Cuisines: Chinese
Average Price: Modest
Area: Sydney
Address: 6 Dixon St Sydney
New South Wales
Phone: +61 2 9283 0998

#87
Super Bowl Chinese Restaurant
Cuisines: Chinese
Average Price: Modest
Area: Haymarket
Address: 41 Dixon St Sydney
New South Wales
Phone: +61 2 9281 2462

#88
Chophouse
Cuisines: Steakhouse
Average Price: Expensive
Area: Sydney
Address: 25 Bligh St Sydney
New South Wales
Phone: 1300 246 748

#89
Rockpool
Cuisines: Australian
Average Price: Exclusive
Area: Sydney
Address: 11 Bridge St Sydney
New South Wales
Phone: +61 2 9252 1888

#90
Sabbaba
Cuisines: Fast Food, Middle Eastern
Average Price: Inexpensive
Area: Sydney
Address: 77 Castlereagh Street Sydney
New South Wales
Phone: +61 2 9223 3315

#91
Drunken Rice
Cuisines: Korean
Average Price: Inexpensive
Area: Sydney
Address: 8 Central St Sydney
New South Wales
Phone: +61 2 9261 0111

#92
Cafe Cre Asion
Cuisines: Café, Desserts, Sandwiches
Average Price: Inexpensive
Area: Sydney
Address: 21 Alberta St Sydney
New South Wales
Phone: +61 4 0494 1528

#93
Prime Steak Restaurant
Cuisines: French, Steakhouse
Average Price: Exclusive
Area: Sydney
Address: Lower Ground Floor 1 Martin
Pl Sydney New South Wales
Phone: +61 2 9229 7777

#94
Coffee Trails
Cuisines: Café, Coffee, Tea
Average Price: Inexpensive
Area: Haymarket
Address: Henry Deane Plaza, 2 Lee St
Sydney New South Wales
Phone: +61 2 9211 6555

#95
Alpha Restaurant
Cuisines: Greek
Average Price: Exclusive
Area: Sydney
Address: 238 Castlereagh St Sydney
New South Wales
Phone: +61 2 9098 1111

#96
My Sweet Memory
Cuisines: Office Equipment, Café
Average Price: Inexpensive
Area: Sydney
Address: 95 Bathurst St Sydney
New South Wales
Phone: +61 2 8971 7465

#97
Cantina Bar & Grill
Cuisines: Bar, American
Area: Balmain
Address: 350 Darling Street Sydney
New South Wales 2041
Phone: +61 2 9357 3033

#98
Yama Japanese Cafe Restaurant
Cuisines: Restaurant
Area: Sydney
Address: 455 George St Sydney
New South Wales
Phone: +61 2 9269 0080

#99
The Macquarie Hotel
Cuisines: Pub, Pub Food, Beer Bar,
Jazz, Blues, Brewerie
Area: Surry Hills
Address: 40-44 Wentworth Ave Sydney
New South Wales
Phone: +61 2 8262 8888

#100
Wok Station
Cuisines: Thai
Average Price: Modest
Area: Pyrmont
Address: 2/135 Harris Street Sydney
New South Wales 2009
Phone: +61 2 9518 8188

#101
Miso Japanese Restaurant
Cuisines: Japanese
Average Price: Modest
Area: Sydney
Address: 123 Liverpool St Sydney
New South Wales
Phone: +61 2 9283 9686

#102
King Street Brewhouse
Cuisines: Sports Bar, Restaurant
Average Price: Modest
Area: Sydney
Address: 22 The Promenade Sydney
New South Wales
Phone: +61 2 8270 7901

#103
The Cuban Place
Cuisines: Cuban, Music Venues, Bar
Average Price: Expensive
Area: Sydney
Address: 125 York St Sydney
New South Wales
Phone: +61 2 9264 4224

#104
Eat Love Pizza
Cuisines: Pizza, Italian
Average Price: Expensive
Area: Sydney
Address: 31 Wheat Road Sydney
New South Wales
Phone: +61 2 8267 3666

#105
Taste Baguette
Cuisines: Vietnamese, Coffee,
Tea, Bakery, Café
Average Price: Inexpensive
Area: Sydney
Address: 68 Market St Sydney
New South Wales
Phone: +61 2 9233 7778

#106
Suminoya Japanese Restaurant
Cuisines: Japanese
Average Price: Expensive
Area: Sydney
Address: 1 Hosking Pl Sydney
New South Wales
Phone: +61 2 9231 2177

#107
Caffe Tiamo
Cuisines: Coffee, Tea,
Breakfast & Brunch
Average Price: Inexpensive
Area: Sydney
Address: 374 Pitt St Sydney
New South Wales
Phone: +61 4 0402 5525

#108
Cafe Sopra
Cuisines: Italian
Average Price: Expensive
Area: Sydney
Address: 11 Bridge St Sydney
New South Wales
Phone: +61 2 8298 2700

#109
The Arthouse Hotel
Cuisines: Bar, Music Venues, Australian
Average Price: Expensive
Area: Sydney
Address: 275 Pitt St Sydney
New South Wales
Phone: +61 2 9284 1200

#110
Fratelli Fresh-Bridge St
Cuisines: Deli, Italian
Average Price: Modest
Area: Sydney
Address: 11 Bridge St Sydney
New South Wales
Phone: +61 2 8298 2700

#111
Pancakes On The Rocks
Cuisines: Crêperie, Desserts
Average Price: Modest
Area: Sydney
Address: 229/230 Harbourside
Shopping Centre Sydney New South
Wales
Phone: +61 9 2803 791

#112
Blancharu
Cuisines: French, Asian Fusion
Average Price: Expensive
Area: Elizabeth Bay
Address: Shop 1, 21 Elizabeth Bay Rd
Sydney
New South Wales 2011
Phone: +61 2 9360 3555

#113
Bungalow 8
Cuisines: Bar, Austrian, Dance Club
Average Price: Modest
Area: Sydney
Address: 3 Lime St Sydney
New South Wales
Phone: +61 2 9299 4660

#114
Georges
Cuisines: Mediterranean, Greek
Average Price: Expensive
Area: Sydney
Address: 17 Lime St Sydney
New South Wales
Phone: +61 2 9295 5066

#115
The Tilbury Hotel
Cuisines: Pub, Australian
Average Price: Expensive
Area: Woolloomooloo
Address: 12-18 Nicholson St Sydney
New South Wales 2011
Phone: +61 2 9368 1955

#116
Sanctuary Hotel
Cuisines: Venues, Event Space,
Pub, European
Average Price: Modest
Area: Sydney
Address: 545 Kent Street Sydney
New South Wales
Phone: +61 2 9264 1119

#117
The Naughty Chef
Cuisines: Vietnamese
Average Price: Inexpensive
Area: Sydney
Address: Shop H04, Hunter Arcade
Sydney New South Wales
Phone: +61 2 9262 3373

#118
Kazbah
Cuisines: Turkish, Middle Eastern
Average Price: Expensive
Area: Sydney
Address: The Promenade, Harbourside
Shopping Centre Sydney
New South Wales
Phone: +61 2 9555 7067

#119
The Flynn
Cuisines: Australian
Average Price: Modest
Area: Sydney
Address: 2A Bligh St Sydney
New South Wales
Phone: +61 2 9223 0037

#120
Nandos Sydney
Cuisines: Restaurant
Average Price: Modest
Area: Sydney
Address: 332 Kent St Sydney
New South Wales
Phone: +61 2 9262 3384

#121
Hotel Sweeney's
Cuisines: Thai, Beer Gardens, Pub
Average Price: Inexpensive
Area: Sydney
Address: 236 Clarence St Sydney
New South Wales
Phone: +61 2 9267 1116

#122
Shinara Grill & Lounge
Cuisines: Korean
Average Price: Modest
Area: Sydney
Address: Shp 1/ 338 Pitt St Sydney
New South Wales
Phone: +61 2 9262 9218

#123
Bangbang
Cuisines: Café, Coffee, Tea
Average Price: Modest
Area: Surry Hills
Address: 113 Reservoir Street Sydney
New South Wales 2010
Phone: +61 2 9281 0018

#124
Bavarian Bier Cafe
Cuisines: German, Beer Bar
Average Price: Modest
Area: Sydney
Address: 24 York St Sydney
New South Wales
Phone: +61 2 8297 4111

#125
Guillaume At Bennelong
Cuisines: French
Average Price: Exclusive
Area: Sydney
Address: Bennelong Point Sydney
New South Wales
Phone: +61 2 9241 1999

#126
Bluebird Coffee
Cuisines: Coffee, Tea, Breakfast &
Brunch
Average Price: Inexpensive
Area: Sydney
Address: 501 George St Sydney
New South Wales
Phone: +61 4 1766 2477

#127
Miro Tapas Bar
Cuisines: Spanish, Tapas
Average Price: Modest
Area: Sydney
Address: 76 Liverpool St Sydney
New South Wales
Phone: +61 2 9267 3126

#128
The Morrison Bar & Oyster Room
Cuisines: Bar, Seafood
Average Price: Modest
Area: Sydney
Address: 225 George St Sydney
New South Wales
Phone: +61 2 9247 6744

#129
Kingsleys Australian Steakhouse
Cuisines: Steakhouse
Average Price: Expensive
Area: Sydney
Address: 29A King St Sydney
New South Wales
Phone: +61 2 9295 5080

#130
Bar Pronto
Cuisines: Café
Area: Sydney
Address: Shp2/ 72 Pitt St Sydney
New South Wales
Phone: +61 2 9238 0611

#131
Ho's Dim Sim Kitchen
Cuisines: Dim Sum
Average Price: Inexpensive
Area: Haymarket
Address: 429a Pitt Street Sydney
New South Wales
Phone: +61 2 9281 2725

#132
Old Town Hong Kong Cuisine
Cuisines: Cantonese
Average Price: Modest
Area: Sydney
Address: 10A Dixon St Sydney
New South Wales
Phone: +61 2 9426 4888

#133
Le Pain Quotidien
Cuisines: Café, Coffee, Tea, Bakery
Average Price: Modest
Area: Sydney
Address: Pitt St Mall And Market St
Sydney New South Wales
Phone: +61 2 8246 9213

#134
Baker Bros
Cuisines: Salad, Café, Sandwiches
Average Price: Inexpensive
Area: Sydney
Address: 56-58 York St Sydney
New South Wales
Phone: +61 2 9262 3884

#135
Pakwaan
Cuisines: Indian
Average Price: Inexpensive
Area: Sydney
Address: 2 Darling Drv Sydney
New South Wales
Phone: +61 2 9211 9165

#136
North Sandwiches
Cuisines: Burgers, Sandwiches
Average Price: Modest
Area: Sydney
Address: 2 Bridge St Sydney
New South Wales
Phone: +61 2 9251 6111

#137
Contrabando
Cuisines: Café
Area: Sydney
Address: 21 Bent St Sydney
New South Wales
Phone: +61 9 2310 049

#138
Capitan Torres Spanish Restaurant
Cuisines: Spanish
Average Price: Expensive
Area: Sydney
Address: 73 Liverpool St Sydney
New South Wales
Phone: +61 2 9264 5574

#139
Le Grand Cafe By Becasse
Cuisines: Café, French
Average Price: Inexpensive
Area: Sydney
Address: 257 Clarence St Sydney
New South Wales
Phone: +61 2 9267 1755

#140
Verandah Main Bar & BBQ
Cuisines: Bar, Gastropub
Average Price: Modest
Area: Sydney
Address: 55 - 65 Elizabeth St Sydney
New South Wales
Phone: +61 2 9239 5888

#141
Sakae
Cuisines: Japanese
Area: Sydney
Address: 116 Liverpool St Sydney
New South Wales
Phone: +61 2 9269 0990

#142
Coast
Cuisines: Mediterranean
Average Price: Exclusive
Area: Sydney
Address: The Roof Terrace, Cockle Bay
Wharf Sydney New South Wales 1026
Phone: +61 2 9267 6700

#143
Cyren Restaurant & Bar
Cuisines: Seafood
Average Price: Modest
Area: Sydney
Address: 197 Waterfront Sydney
New South Wales
Phone: 1300 989 989

#144
Charlie & Co
Cuisines: Burgers
Average Price: Modest
Area: Sydney
Address: Cnr Market & Castlereagh St
Sydney New South Wales
Phone: +61 2 8072 7777

#145
CQ Cafe
Cuisines: Café, European
Average Price: Modest
Area: Sydney
Address: 1 Macquarie PL Sydney
New South Wales
Phone: +61 2 9241 3979

#146
Sydney Tower Sky Lounge
Cuisines: Venues, Event Space,
Australian
Average Price: Expensive
Area: Sydney
Address: 100 Market St Sydney
New South Wales
Phone: +61 2 8223 3800

#147
Brooklyn Hide Bagels
Cuisines: American, Bakery
Average Price: Modest
Area: Surry Hills
Address: 226 Commonwealth St Sydney
New South Wales 2010
Phone: +61 2 9211 6448

#148
Low 302
Cuisines: Tapas, Lounge
Average Price: Modest
Area: Darlinghurst
Address: 302 Crown St, Sydney
New South Wales 2010
Phone: +61 2 9368 1548

#149
Machiavelli Ristorante Italiano
Cuisines: Restaurant
Average Price: Expensive
Area: Sydney
Address: 123 Clarence St Sydney
New South Wales
Phone: +61 2 9299 3748

#150
Crane
Cuisines: Japanese
Average Price: Expensive
Area: Potts Point
Address: 32 Bayswater Rd Sydney
New South Wales 2011
Phone: +61 2 9357 3414

#151
Condor Japanese Noodle Restaurant
Cuisines: Restaurant
Average Price: Inexpensive
Area: Sydney
Address: 5 York St Sydney
New South Wales
Phone: +61 2 9299 8686

#152
The Malaya Restaurant
Cuisines: Malaysian
Average Price: Expensive
Area: Sydney
Address: 39 Lime St Sydney
New South Wales
Phone: +61 2 9279 1170

#153
Sushi Tei
Cuisines: Japanese
Average Price: Modest
Area: Sydney
Address: 127a Liverpool St Sydney
New South Wales
Phone: +61 2 9283 7889

#154
Macchiato Restaurant
Cuisines: Café
Average Price: Modest
Area: Sydney
Address: Cnr Pitt & Liverpool Sts,
Shop 2/ 338 Pitt St Sydney
New South Wales
Phone: +61 2 9262 9525

#155
Cargo Bar / Lounge
Cuisines: Lounge, Restaurant,
Social Club
Average Price: Expensive
Area: Sydney
Address: Lime Street 21 Sydney
New South Wales
Phone: +61 2 9262 1777

#156
Noodle Mee
Cuisines: Fast Food
Average Price: Inexpensive
Area: Sydney
Address: 289 George St Sydney
New South Wales
Phone: +61 2 9299 8840

#157
Umami
Cuisines: Sushi Bar, Japanese
Average Price: Modest
Area: Sydney
Address: 73 Bathurst St Sydney
New South Wales
Phone: +61 2 9267 5878

#158
Bona Fides
Cuisines: Café, Coffee, Tea,
Breakfast & Brunch
Average Price: Modest
Area: Sydney
Address: 70 Druitt St Sydney
New South Wales
Phone: +61 2 9264 1929

#159
The Ship Inn
Cuisines: Pub, Restaurant
Average Price: Modest
Area: Sydney
Address: Corner Alfred & Pitt Streets
Sydney New South Wales
Phone: +61 2 9241 2433

#160
Streets of Saigon
Cuisines: Vietnamese, Asian Fusion
Average Price: Modest
Area: Sydney
Address: Shop 5004, Level 5 Sydney
New South Wales
Phone: +61 2 8072 7050

#161
The Passage
Cuisines: European, Tapas, Bar
Average Price: Modest
Area: Darlinghurst
Address: 231A Victoria St Sydney
New South Wales 2010
Phone: +61 2 9358 6116

#162
Uighur Cuisine
Cuisines: Restaurant
Average Price: Modest
Area: Sydney
Address: Shop 1/ 8 Dixon St Sydney
New South Wales
Phone: +61 2 9267 8555

#163
Pie Face
Cuisines: Fast Food
Average Price: Inexpensive
Area: Sydney
Address: World Square Shopping
Centre, 644/680 George Street Sydney
NSW 2 Sydney New South Wales
Phone: +61 2 9261 3111

#164
Portobello Caffe
Cuisines: Café
Area: Sydney
Address: 3 East Circular Quay Sydney
New South Wales
Phone: +61 2 9247 8548

#165
Georgie's Spuds & Snags
Cuisines: Hot Dogs, Salad, Potatoes
Average Price: Inexpensive
Area: Sydney
Address: Harbourside Shopping Ct
Sydney New South Wales
Phone: +61 2 9211 0082

#166
Nok Nok Thai Eating House
Cuisines: Thai
Average Price: Modest
Area: Sydney
Address: Shop 9/1 Harbour Street,
Darling Walk Sydney
New South Wales
Phone: +61 2 9267 7992

#167
Wagamama Bridge Street
Cuisines: Japanese
Average Price: Modest
Area: Sydney
Address: 38 Bridge St Sydney
New South Wales
Phone: +61 2 9252 8696

#168
Subsolo
Cuisines: Spanish
Average Price: Expensive
Area: Sydney
Address: 161 King St Sydney
New South Wales
Phone: +61 2 9223 7000

#169
QVB Gourmet Seafood
Cuisines: Seafood
Area: Sydney
Address: QVB 455 George St Sydney
New South Wales
Phone: +61 2 9267 4050

#170
Méjico
Cuisines: Mexican
Average Price: Expensive
Area: Sydney
Address: 105 Pitt St Sydney
New South Wales
Phone: +44 29 230 0119

#171
Hokkaido
Cuisines: Japanese
Area: Sydney
Address: 20 Loftus St Sydney
New South Wales
Phone: +61 2 9251 8280

#172
Summit Restaurant
Cuisines: Australian
Average Price: Expensive
Area: Sydney
Address: 264 George St Sydney
New South Wales
Phone: +61 2 9247 9777

#173
Golden Century Seafood Restaurant
Cuisines: Chinese
Average Price: Exclusive
Area: Haymarket
Address: 393 Sussex St Sydney
New South Wales
Phone: +61 2 9212 3901

#174
David Jones Oyster Bar
Cuisines: Seafood
Area: Sydney
Address: 65-77 Market Street Sydney
New South Wales
Phone: +61 2 9266 5544

#175
Le Pain Quotidien
Cuisines: French, Bakery
Average Price: Modest
Area: The Rocks
Address: 127 George St Sydney
New South Wales 2043
Phone: +61 2 9252 3840

#176
Lovebite Cafe
Cuisines: Café
Average Price: Inexpensive
Area: Sydney
Address: Grnd Flr/ 66 Goulburn St
Sydney New South Wales
Phone: +61 2 9269 0353

#177
Mother Chu's Vegetarian Kitchen
Cuisines: Vegetarian
Average Price: Modest
Area: Sydney
Address: 367 Pitt St Sydney
New South Wales
Phone: +61 2 9283 2828

#178
Takeru Japanese Cuisine
Cuisines: Restaurant
Average Price: Modest
Area: Sydney
Address: 339-345 Sussex St Sydney
New South Wales
Phone: +61 2 9283 3975

#179
Cafe Tramezzini
Cuisines: Café
Area: Sydney
Address: Shop 3, Corner Bathurst Street
& Pitt Square Sydney New South Wales
Phone: +61 2 9264 4110

#180
The Hudson
Cuisines: Bar, Australian
Area: Sydney
Address: 49 Lime St Sydney
New South Wales
Phone: +61 2 9279 3379

#181
1912 Dining Bar
Cuisines: Japanese, Jazz,
Blues, Asian Fusion
Average Price: Modest
Area: Haymarket
Address: 27-33 Goulburn St Sydney
New South Wales
Phone: +61 2 8970 5813

#182
The Lab Cafe
Cuisines: Café, Coffee, Tea
Average Price: Modest
Area: Sydney
Address: 109 Pitt St Sydney
New South Wales
Phone: +61 4 5103 8795

#183
Samosorn Thai
Cuisines: Thai
Average Price: Inexpensive
Area: Sydney
Address: 450 George St Sydney
New South Wales
Phone: +61 2 9280 2227

#184
Bistro Fax
Cuisines: Restaurant
Average Price: Expensive
Area: Sydney
Address: Pitt St Cnr O'Connell & Hunter
Sts Sydney New South Wales
Phone: +61 2 8214 0400

#185
Piatto Di Pasta
Cuisines: Italian, Fast Food
Average Price: Inexpensive
Area: Haymarket
Address: 2 Lee St Sydney
New South Wales
Phone: +61 2 8040 5845

#186
Pure Platinum
Cuisines: Adult Entertainment,
Restaurant
Area: Sydney
Address: 252 Pitt St Sydney
New South Wales
Phone: +61 2 9267 4454

#187
Devine Food & Wine
Cuisines: Wine Bar, Italian, European
Average Price: Expensive
Area: Sydney
Address: 32 Market Street Sydney
New South Wales
Phone: +61 2 9262 6906

#188
Alice's Makan
Cuisines: Malaysian
Average Price: Inexpensive
Area: Sydney
Address: 580 George St Sydney
New South Wales
Phone: +61 2 9262 7771

#189
Goshu Ramen Tei
Cuisines: Japanese
Average Price: Modest
Area: Sydney
Address: 5 York St Sydney
New South Wales
Phone: +61 2 9290 3745

#190
The Spice Cellar
Cuisines: Dance Club, Tapas, Wine Bar
Average Price: Modest
Area: Sydney
Address: 58 Elizabeth St Sydney
New South Wales
Phone: +61 2 9223 5585

#191
The Canopy
Cuisines: Italian, Café, Australian
Average Price: Modest
Area: Sydney
Address: 157 Liverpool St Sydney
New South Wales
Phone: +61 2 9264 3007

#192
Vessel Italian & Bar
Cuisines: Italian
Average Price: Modest
Area: Sydney
Address: 1 Shelley Street Sydney
New South Wales
Phone: +61 2 9295 5070

#193
Guzman Y Gomez Mexican Taqueria
Cuisines: Restaurant
Average Price: Inexpensive
Area: Sydney
Address: Square Food Court, Shop 404, 364 George St Sydney New South Wales
Phone: +61 2 9247 4422

#194
Sedap
Cuisines: Malaysian
Average Price: Modest
Area: Sydney
Address: Shop 10, 501 George St Sydney New South Wales
Phone: +61 2 9262 7979

#195
Senyai
Cuisines: Thai
Average Price: Modest
Area: Sydney
Address: 486 Kent St Sydney New South Wales
Phone: +61 2 9283 8686

#196
Le Pain Quotidien Sydney Westfield
Cuisines: Café, Bakery
Average Price: Modest
Area: Sydney
Address: 188 Pitt St Sydney New South Wales
Phone: +61 2 8246 9213

#197
Bistroteque
Cuisines: Café
Area: Sydney
Address: The Met Cntr Shp MG14/ 23 Jamison St Sydney New South Wales
Phone: +61 2 9241 3123

#198
Sakuratei Japanese Restaurant
Cuisines: Australian
Average Price: Exclusive
Area: Sydney
Address: 202 Clarence St Sydney New South Wales
Phone: +61 2 9267 4552

#199
Waterfront Restaurant
Cuisines: Seafood, Australian
Average Price: Exclusive
Area: The Rocks
Address: 27 Circular Quay W Sydney New South Wales
Phone: 1300 115 116

#200
The Brewery Espresso Bar
Cuisines: Café
Area: Sydney
Address: 64 Erskine St Sydney New South Wales
Phone: +61 4 3537 8690

#201
Shancheng Hot Pot King
Cuisines: Chinese
Average Price: Modest
Area: Sydney
Address: 8A/363 Sussex St Sydney New South Wales
Phone: +61 2 9267 6366

#202
Kozy Restaurants
Cuisines: Korean
Area: Sydney
Address: 7 Wilmot St Sydney New South Wales
Phone: +61 2 9267 3533

#203
Grill'd Healthy Burgers
Cuisines: Burgers, Vegetarian
Average Price: Modest
Area: Sydney
Address: 644 George Street Sydney New South Wales
Phone: +61 2 9261 4900

#204
Suzy Spoon's Vegetarian Butcher
Cuisines: Café, Vegan, Vegetarian
Average Price: Modest
Area: Newtown
Address: 22-24 King St Sydney New South Wales 2042
Phone: +61 2 9557 9762

#205
GPO Pizza By Wood
Cuisines: Pizza
Average Price: Modest
Area: Sydney
Address: 1 Martin Pl Sydney
New South Wales
Phone: +61 2 9229 7722

#206
My Selection
Cuisines: Vietnamese
Area: Sydney
Address: Basement, 7-13 Hunter St
Sydney New South Wales
Phone: +61 4 3999 8276

#207
Delima Restaurant
Cuisines: Indonesian
Average Price: Modest
Area: Sydney
Address: 1 Dixon St Sydney
New South Wales
Phone: +61 2 9267 7045

#208
China Lane
Cuisines: Chinese
Average Price: Expensive
Area: Sydney
Address: 1 Angel Pl Sydney
New South Wales
Phone: +61 2 9231 3939

#209
Steersons Steakhouse
Cuisines: Steakhouse
Average Price: Expensive
Area: Sydney
Address: 17 Lime St Sydney
New South Wales
Phone: +61 2 9295 5060

#210
Olivo
Cuisines: Italian
Average Price: Expensive
Area: Sydney
Address: 2-10 Darling Drive Sydney
New South Wales
Phone: +61 2 9280 4200

#211
Shipleys
Cuisines: European
Area: Haymarket
Address: 68 Harbour Street Sydney
New South Wales
Phone: +61 2 9291 0258

#212
Reuben & Moore
Cuisines: American
Average Price: Modest
Area: Sydney
Address: Market & Castlereagh St
Sydney New South Wales
Phone: +61 4 2344 1220

#213
Bluestone Cafe
Cuisines: Café
Average Price: Modest
Area: Sydney
Address: 28-34 O'Connell St Sydney
New South Wales
Phone: +61 2 9221 1841

#214
Jet Bar Cafe
Cuisines: Café, Bar
Average Price: Modest
Area: Sydney
Address: Shop 55, 455 George Street
Sydney New South Wales
Phone: +61 2 9283 5004

#215
Vivo Cafe
Cuisines: Café
Average Price: Modest
Area: Sydney
Address: 388 George St Sydney
New South Wales
Phone: +61 2 9221 1169

#216
The Sydney Cove Oyster Bar
Cuisines: Restaurant, Bar
Area: Sydney
Address: East Circular Quay 1 Sydney
New South Wales
Phone: +61 9 2472 937

#217
Peace Harmony
Cuisines: Thai, Vegetarian
Area: Sydney
Address: 27 King St Sydney
New South Wales
Phone: +61 2 9299 0419

#218
Oy
Cuisines: Thai
Average Price: Inexpensive
Area: Elizabeth Bay
Address: Macleay Street 71a Sydney
New South Wales 2011
Phone: +61 2 9361 4498

#219
Fairmont Restaurant
At The Hotel Occidental
Cuisines: Steakhouse
Area: Sydney
Address: 43 York St Sydney
New South Wales
Phone: +61 2 9299 7180

#220
Sydney Mint Cafe
Cuisines: Café
Area: Sydney
Address: 10 Macquarie St Sydney
New South Wales
Phone: +61 2 9233 3337

#221
Mums Thai
Cuisines: Thai
Area: Pyrmont
Address: 1/233 Harris Street Sydney
New South Wales 2009
Phone: +61 9 5719 988

#222
Cockle Bay Wharf
Cuisines: Restaurant, Social Club,
Local Flavor
Average Price: Modest
Area: Sydney
Address: 201 Sussex St Sydney
New South Wales
Phone: +61 2 9269 9800

#223
Top Choice Sizzling And Hot Pot
Cuisines: Fast Food
Area: Haymarket
Address: 401 Sussex St Sydney
New South Wales
Phone: +61 2 9212 1580

#224
Made In Italy
Cuisines: Food Delivery Services, Pizza
Area: Sydney
Address: 37 York Ln Sydney
New South Wales
Phone: +61 2 9299 0900

#225
Foyer Cafe
Cuisines: Café
Average Price: Modest
Area: Sydney
Address: 207 Kent Street Sydney
New South Wales
Phone: +61 2 9252 9556

#226
Bar Anonimo
Cuisines: Café, Italian
Average Price: Inexpensive
Area: Pyrmont
Address: 104 Miller St Sydney
New South Wales 2009
Phone: +61 4 0138 3232

#227
Izote
Cuisines: Mexican
Average Price: Modest
Area: Sydney
Address: King St 6 Sydney
New South Wales 2001
Phone: +61 2 8084 9651

#228
Home Cafè
Cuisines: Coffee, Tea, Thai
Average Price: Modest
Area: Sydney
Address: 39 Liverpool St Sydney
New South Wales
Phone: +61 9 2613 011

#229
La Bora Pizzeria Ristorante
Cuisines: Restaurant
Area: Sydney
Address: 9A Barrack St Sydney
New South Wales
Phone: +61 2 9233 5296

#230
Wolfies
Cuisines: Steakhouse, Australian
Average Price: Expensive
Area: The Rocks
Address: 27 Circular Quay West Sydney
New South Wales
Phone: 1300 115 116

#231
Sofitel Wentworth Sydney Lounge
Cuisines: Lounge, Café
Average Price: Modest
Area: Sydney
Address: 101 Phillip St Sydney
New South Wales
Phone: +61 2 9228 9188

#232
Casa Di Nico Italian Restaurant
Cuisines: Italian
Average Price: Expensive
Area: Sydney
Address: King Street Wharf Sydney
New South Wales
Phone: +61 2 9279 4115

#233
FORTYTWO Restaurant/Cafe
Cuisines: Italian, Café
Area: Newtown
Address: 134a Sydney
New South Wales 2042
Phone: +61 2 8068 8959

#234
Rossini Australia Square
Cuisines: Restaurant
Area: Sydney
Address: 264 George St Sydney
New South Wales
Phone: +61 2 9247 3040

#235
Arisun
Cuisines: Korean
Average Price: Modest
Area: Sydney
Address: 1 Dixon St Sydney
New South Wales
Phone: +61 2 9264 1588

#236
Hole In The Wall: Sandwich Factory
Cuisines: Café
Average Price: Inexpensive
Area: Sydney
Address: 229 Macquarie St Sydney
New South Wales
Phone: +61 2 9222 1755

#237
Stacks Taverna
Cuisines: Mediterranean, Bar, Greek
Average Price: Modest
Area: Sydney
Address: 1-25 Harbour St Sydney
New South Wales
Phone: 1300 989 989

#238
Work In Progress
Cuisines: Thai
Area: Sydney
Address: 50 King St Sydney
New South Wales
Phone: +61 2 9240 3000

#239
Ogalo City
Cuisines: Portuguese
Average Price: Inexpensive
Area: Sydney
Address: 127 Liverpool St Sydney
New South Wales
Phone: +61 2 9264 0660

#240
Wine Odyssey Australia
Cuisines: Bar, Australian
Area: The Rocks
Address: Argyle Street 39 Sydney
New South Wales
Phone: 1300 136 498

#241
Uno Expresso Cafe
Cuisines: Café
Average Price: Inexpensive
Area: Sydney
Address: 60 Park St Sydney
New South Wales
Phone: +61 2 9264 2229

#242
Burgerlicious
Cuisines: Fast Food, Burgers
Average Price: Modest
Area: Sydney
Address: 130 Liverpool St Sydney
New South Wales
Phone: +61 2 9264 4446

#243
Jimmy's Recipe Malaysia
Cuisines: Malaysian
Average Price: Inexpensive
Area: Sydney
Address: 17-19 Bridge St Sydney
New South Wales
Phone: +61 2 9252 3380

#244
Oz Turk Pizza's & Kebabs
Cuisines: Fast Food, Café
Average Price: Inexpensive
Area: Haymarket
Address: 704 George St Sydney
New South Wales
Phone: +61 2 9280 1310

#245
Capital Grill
Cuisines: Bar, Café, European
Area: Sydney
Address: 1 Macquarie Place Sydney
Sydney New South Wales
Phone: +61 2 9247 4445

#246
**Happy Chef Seafood
& Noodles Restaurant**
Cuisines: Chinese, Malaysian, Seafood
Average Price: Inexpensive
Area: Haymarket
Address: 401 Sussex St Sydney
New South Wales
Phone: +61 2 9281 5832

#247
City Slice
Cuisines: Pizza
Average Price: Modest
Area: Sydney
Address: 35 Erskine St Sydney
New South Wales
Phone: +61 2 9299 0082

#248
Insomnia Kebab And Pizza
Cuisines: Middle Eastern,
Fast Food, Pizza
Area: Sydney
Address: 46 Park Street Sydney
New South Wales
Phone: +61 9 2648 433

#249
Postales
Cuisines: Spanish, Tapas
Area: Sydney
Address: 1 Martin Pl Sydney
New South Wales
Phone: +61 2 9229 7700

#250
Buns & Balls
Cuisines: Burgers
Average Price: Modest
Area: Potts Point
Address: 33 Bayswater Rd Sydney
New South Wales 2011
Phone: +61 9 3269 054

#251
Arc Cafe
Cuisines: Café, Sandwiches
Average Price: Modest
Area: Sydney
Address: 3 Macquarie Street Sydney
New South Wales
Phone: +61 2 8274 7900

#252
Cafe La Rosa
Cuisines: Coffee, Tea, Café
Area: Sydney
Address: 117 Liverpool Street Sydney
New South Wales
Phone: +353 29 2690059

#253
Sassy's Red Cafe
Cuisines: Malaysian
Average Price: Modest
Area: Sydney
Address: 188 Pitt St Sydney
New South Wales
Phone: +61 2 8072 8072

#254
678 Korean Bbq
Cuisines: Korean
Average Price: Modest
Area: Haymarket
Address: 1/ 396 Pitt St Sydney
New South Wales
Phone: +61 2 9267 7334

#255
Tokkuri Saki & Wine Bar
Cuisines: Japanese, Wine Bar
Area: Sydney
Address: 273 George St Sydney
New South Wales
Phone: +61 2 9252 6345

#256
Alfredo Authentic Italian Restaurant
Cuisines: Italian
Average Price: Expensive
Area: Sydney
Address: 16 Bulletin Pl Sydney
New South Wales
Phone: +61 2 9251 2929

#257
Saap Thai
Cuisines: Thai
Average Price: Inexpensive
Area: Sydney
Address: 378 Pitt St Sydney
New South Wales
Phone: +61 2 9267 9604

#258
PER KILO
Cuisines: Buffet, Latin American, Vegetarian
Average Price: Inexpensive
Area: Sydney
Address: 35 Erskine St Sydney
New South Wales
Phone: +61 4 1883 5103

#259
Cafe Nice
Cuisines: French, Italian
Average Price: Expensive
Area: Sydney
Address: 2 Phillip St Sydney
New South Wales
Phone: +61 2 8248 9600

#260
Bello Cafe
Cuisines: Restaurant, Pub
Area: Sydney
Address: 22 Loftus St Sydney
New South Wales
Phone: +61 2 9251 0105

#261
Sakura
Cuisines: Japanese
Average Price: Inexpensive
Area: Sydney
Address: 325 Pitt St Sydney
New South Wales
Phone: +61 2 9261 0711

#262
Rossini Restaurants
Cuisines: Restaurant
Average Price: Inexpensive
Area: Sydney
Address: Alfred St Sydney
New South Wales
Phone: +61 2 9247 8026

#263
Taiwan Ganbei
Cuisines: Taiwanese
Average Price: Inexpensive
Area: Sydney
Address: 52 Dixon St Sydney
New South Wales
Phone: +61 2 9212 2220

#264
Vermicelli
Cuisines: Fast Food, Vietnamese
Area: Sydney
Address: 63 King St Sydney
New South Wales
Phone: +61 2 9279 0030

#265
Giovanni's Restaurant & Pizzeria
Cuisines: Restaurant
Average Price: Modest
Area: The Rocks
Address: 225 George St, Cnr Harrington & Essex Sts Sydney New South Wales
Phone: +61 2 9251 8808

#266
Mad Mex
Cuisines: Mexican
Average Price: Inexpensive
Area: Sydney
Address: 450 George St, Shop 1 Sydney New South Wales
Phone: +61 2 9222 1700

#267
Parliament On King
Cuisines: Australian
Average Price: Inexpensive
Area: Erskineville
Address: 632 King St Sydney New South Wales 2043
Phone: +61 4 1423 5325

#268
Ito's Malaysian
Cuisines: Malaysian
Average Price: Inexpensive
Area: Sydney
Address: 201 Elizabeth St Sydney New South Wales
Phone: +61 2 9264 9001

#269
Globe Bar & Brasserie
Cuisines: Brasseries, Bar, Tea Room
Average Price: Expensive
Area: Millers Point
Address: 115 Kent St Sydney New South Wales
Phone: +61 2 8248 5252

#270
Caysorn
Cuisines: Thai
Average Price: Inexpensive
Area: Haymarket
Address: Shop 106 Sydney New South Wales
Phone: +61 9 2115 749

#271
Avenue On Chifley
Cuisines: Restaurant
Average Price: Modest
Area: Sydney
Address: 2 Chifley Sq Sydney New South Wales
Phone: +61 2 9221 7599

#272
Bridge St Garage
Cuisines: Latin American, Burgers
Area: Sydney
Address: 17 Bridge St Sydney New South Wales
Phone: +61 2 9251 9392

#273
The Coffee Club - Park Street
Cuisines: Café
Area: Sydney
Address: 27 Park St Sydney New South Wales
Phone: +61 2 9264 9676

#274
T2B
Cuisines: Café, Coffee, Tea, Specialty Food
Average Price: Inexpensive
Area: Sydney
Address: Westfield Sydney, 450 George Street Sydney New South Wales
Phone: +61 2 9230 0022

#275
Kura 3
Cuisines: Japanese
Average Price: Inexpensive
Area: Sydney
Address: 1/6 Dixon St Sydney New South Wales
Phone: +61 2 9268 0016

#276
Marketa Espresso Cafe
Cuisines: Breakfast & Brunch, Café
Area: Sydney
Address: 464-480 Kent St Sydney New South Wales
Phone: +61 2 9261 1455

#277
Pie Face
Cuisines: Australian
Average Price: Inexpensive
Area: Sydney
Address: 171 Castlereagh St Sydney
New South Wales
Phone: +61 2 9267 3470

#278
Feast Restaurant
Sheraton On The Park
Cuisines: Seafood, Australian
Average Price: Exclusive
Area: Sydney
Address: 161 Elizabeth Street Sydney
New South Wales
Phone: +61 2 9286 6000

#279
Iberico Spanish Cuisine
Cuisines: Spanish, Tapas
Area: Sydney
Address: 88 Liverpool St Sydney
New South Wales
Phone: +61 2 9267 5993

#280
Chop Chop
Cuisines: Vietnamese, Fast Food
Area: Sydney
Address: 36 York Street Sydney
New South Wales
Phone: +61 2 9290 2106

#281
Saigon Pho
Cuisines: Vietnamese
Area: Haymarket
Address: 401-403 Sussex St Sydney
New South Wales
Phone: +61 2 9212 5387

#282
Saladworks
Cuisines: Health Market, Sandwiches
Area: Sydney
Address: 133-145 Castlereagh Street
Sydney New South Wales
Phone: +61 2 9264 0071

#283
Spice Room @ The Malaya
Cuisines: Malaysian
Area: Sydney
Address: 39 Lime Street Sydney
New South Wales
Phone: +61 9 2791 170

#284
Pizza Da Noi
Cuisines: Pizza, Italian
Area: Glebe
Address: Shop 4, 198 - 206 St Johns Rd
Sydney New South Wales 2037
Phone: +61 2 9552 3995

#285
The Bridge Room
Cuisines: Restaurant
Area: Sydney
Address: 44 Bridge St Sydney
New South Wales
Phone: +61 2 9247 7000

#286
Mordeo Pasta & Panini Bar
Cuisines: Italian
Area: Sydney
Address: 126 Phillip St Sydney
New South Wales
Phone: +61 2 9232 4789

#287
Max Brenner
Cuisines: Restaurant
Area: Darlinghurst
Address: Oxford Street Sydney
New South Wales 2029
Phone: +61 2 9389 0088

#288
Glider
Cuisines: Café, Asian Fusion
Average Price: Modest
Area: Potts Point
Address: 197 Victoria St Sydney
New South Wales 2011
Phone: +44 4109 92354

#289
Pavel & Co.
Cuisines: Delicatessen, Sandwiches
Average Price: Inexpensive
Area: Sydney
Address: 222 Kent St Sydney
New South Wales
Phone: +61 2 9146 0716

#290
Mosaic Restaurant
Cuisines: Restaurant
Area: Sydney
Address: 1 Martin Pl Sydney
New South Wales
Phone: +61 2 8223 1110

#291
Eleven Kitchen & Cellar
Cuisines: European
Average Price: Modest
Area: Sydney
Address: 11 Lime St Sydney
New South Wales
Phone: +61 2 9290 3533

#292
Corn Exchange Restaurant
Cuisines: Restaurant
Average Price: Expensive
Area: Sydney
Address: 161 Sussex St Sydney
New South Wales
Phone: +61 2 9290 4760

#293
Pho 88
Cuisines: Vietnamese, Food
Average Price: Modest
Area: Newtown
Address: 343 King St Sydney
New South Wales 2042
Phone: +61 2 9519 4972

#294
Galileo
Cuisines: French, Specialty Food
Average Price: Expensive
Area: Sydney
Address: The Observatory Hotel 89-113
Sydney New South Wales
Phone: +61 2 8248 5252

#295
Jazz City BBQ
Cuisines: American
Area: Surry Hills
Address: 200 Goulburn St Sydney
New South Wales 2010
Phone: +61 2 8354 1776

#296
Bertoni Casalinga
Cuisines: Café
Average Price: Inexpensive
Area: Sydney
Address: 262 Kent St Sydney
New South Wales
Phone: +61 2 9262 5845

#297
Bavarian Bier Cafe
Cuisines: German, Beer Bar
Area: Sydney
Address: 16 O'Connell St Sydney
New South Wales
Phone: +61 2 9221 0100

#298
Kansai
Cuisines: Japanese
Area: Sydney
Address: 70 Pitt Street Sydney
New South Wales
Phone: +61 2 9232 5785

#299
The Emperor's Choice King
Cuisines: Restaurant
Average Price: Modest
Area: Sydney
Address: 147 King St Sydney
New South Wales
Phone: +61 2 9232 1881

#300
Bar Fiori
Cuisines: Café
Area: Sydney
Address: 155 Castlereagh St Sydney
New South Wales
Phone: +61 2 9261 8846

#301
Ragu Pasta & Wine Bar
Cuisines: Italian
Average Price: Inexpensive
Area: Sydney
Address: Cnr Pitt St Mall & Market St
Sydney New South Wales
Phone: +61 2 8072 8005

#302
Little Haveli
Cuisines: Indian
Average Price: Inexpensive
Area: Chippendale
Address: 153 Broadway Sydney
New South Wales 2007
Phone: +61 2 9212 2471

#303
Mr B's Hotel
Cuisines: Chinese, Pub, Asian Fusion
Average Price: Modest
Area: Haymarket
Address: 396 Pitt St, Sydney
New South Wales
Phone: +61 2 8080 7777

#304
Tom N Tom's Coffee
Cuisines: Café
Average Price: Inexpensive
Area: Sydney
Address: 97 Bathurst St Sydney
New South Wales
Phone: +61 2 9267 9989

#305
Spice Chopsticks
Cuisines: Korean
Area: Sydney
Address: 379 Pitt St Sydney
New South Wales
Phone: +61 2 9266 0797

#306
Mad Mex
Cuisines: Mexican
Average Price: Inexpensive
Area: Haymarket
Address: 815 George Street Sydney
New South Wales
Phone: +61 2 9211 6449

#307
T2
Cuisines: Coffee, Tea,
Specialty Food, Café
Average Price: Modest
Area: Sydney
Address: 450 George Street Sydney
New South Wales
Phone: +44 29 261 5040

#308
Pondo-Selera Indonesian & Malaysian Food
Cuisines: Restaurant
Area: Haymarket
Address: 413 Sussex St Sydney
New South Wales
Phone: +61 2 9281 8206

#309
Blancharu By Yomo
Cuisines: Asian Fusion
Area: Elizabeth Bay
Address: 1/21 Elizabeth Bay Rd Sydney
New South Wales 2011
Phone: +61 2 9360 3555

#310
Nandos World Square
Cuisines: Fast Food
Average Price: Inexpensive
Area: Sydney
Address: 680 George St Sydney
New South Wales
Phone: +61 2 9283 6444

#311
Just Pure Bistro, JPB
Cuisines: Bar, Bistros
Average Price: Expensive
Area: Sydney
Address: 68 Market St Sydney
New South Wales
Phone: +61 2 9238 8888

#312
Janus Sydney
Cuisines: Italian
Area: Sydney
Address: Westfield Sydney, 188 Pitt St
Sydney New South Wales
Phone: +61 2 8072 9140

#313
Tamayaki
Cuisines: Japanese
Average Price: Modest
Area: Sydney
Address: 1 Dixon St Sydney
New South Wales
Phone: +61 4 5029 0190

#314
Espresso On York
Cuisines: Coffee, Tea,
Breakfast & Brunch
Area: Sydney
Address: Cnr York & Market St Sydney
New South Wales
Phone: +61 4 1749 4437

#315
Tawandang
Cuisines: Thai
Average Price: Modest
Area: Haymarket
Address: 702 George St Sydney
New South Wales
Phone: +61 2 9211 0138

#316
Modus Caffe
Cuisines: Coffee, Tea,
Breakfast & Brunch, Italian
Area: Sydney
Address: 9 Castlereagh St Sydney
New South Wales
Phone: +61 2 9223 9131

#317
Mr Mekong
Cuisines: Thai
Average Price: Inexpensive
Area: Sydney
Address: 201 Kent St, Maritime Trade
Towers Sydney New South Wales
Phone: +61 2 8964 7607

#318
Quadrant Restaurant
Cuisines: Restaurant
Average Price: Expensive
Area: Sydney
Address: 61 Macquarie St Sydney
New South Wales
Phone: +61 2 9256 4000

#319
Casa Asturiana
Spanish Restaurant
Cuisines: Spanish
Average Price: Modest
Area: Sydney
Address: 77 Liverpool St Sydney
New South Wales
Phone: +61 2 9264 1010

#320
Mizuya
Cuisines: Japanese, Karaoke
Average Price: Modest
Area: Sydney
Address: 614 George St Sydney
New South Wales
Phone: +61 2 9266 0866

#321
LNC Dessert House
Cuisines: Chinese, Desserts
Average Price: Inexpensive
Area: Sydney
Address: 339 Sussex St Sydney
New South Wales
Phone: +61 2 9283 3823

#322
Pino Latte
Cuisines: Coffee, Tea, Café
Area: Sydney
Address: 122 Castlereagh St Sydney
New South Wales
Phone: +61 2 9267 6830

#323
Ichiban Boshi Express
Cuisines: Japanese
Area: Sydney
Address: 500 George St Sydney
New South Wales
Phone: +61 2 9264 7780

#324
Park Cafe On Chalmers
Cuisines: Coffee, Tea, Fast Food
Area: Redfern
Address: 51 Chalmers St Sydney
New South Wales 2195
Phone: +61 2 8399 0661

#325
Athenian Greek Restaurant
Cuisines: Greek
Average Price: Expensive
Area: Sydney
Address: 11 Barrack St Sydney
New South Wales
Phone: +61 2 9262 2624

#326
Bica Coffee Lounge
Cuisines: Café
Area: Sydney
Address: 19 Lime Street Sydney
New South Wales
Phone: +61 2 9290 3278

#327
Peace Harmony Vegetarian Thai Restaurant
Cuisines: Vegetarian
Average Price: Inexpensive
Area: Sydney
Address: 44 Erskine St Sydney
New South Wales
Phone: +61 2 9262 2247

#328
Malacca Straits Thai
Cuisines: Fast Food
Area: Sydney
Address: 303 Pitt St Sydney
New South Wales
Phone: +61 2 9267 5454

#329
Kushiyaki Azuma
Cuisines: Teppanyaki
Average Price: Modest
Area: Sydney
Address: 501 George St Sydney
New South Wales
Phone: +61 2 9267 7775

#330
Steel Bar & Grill
Cuisines: Restaurant
Average Price: Exclusive
Area: Sydney
Address: 60 Carrington St Sydney
New South Wales
Phone: +61 2 9299 9997

#331
Steersons Steakhouse
Cuisines: Restaurant
Area: Sydney
Address: 7 Bridge St Sydney
New South Wales
Phone: +61 2 9295 5099

#332
GPO Cheese & Wine Room
Cuisines: Wine Bar, Cheese Shop, Australian
Average Price: Expensive
Area: Sydney
Address: 1 Martin Pl Sydney
New South Wales
Phone: +61 2 9229 7701

#333
Charr
Cuisines: Steakhouse
Average Price: Expensive
Area: Sydney
Address: 11 Jamison St Sydney
New South Wales
Phone: +61 2 9696 2500

#334
Bar Fredo
Cuisines: Café, Coffee, Tea, Breakfast & Brunch
Average Price: Modest
Area: Millers Point
Address: Shop 9, Pier 8/9, 23 Hickson Rd Sydney New South Wales
Phone: +61 2 9241 1248

#335
Palings Kitchen And Bar
Cuisines: European
Average Price: Modest
Area: Sydney
Address: 330 George St Sydney
New South Wales
Phone: +61 9 2403 000

#336
Saladworks
Cuisines: Fast Food
Average Price: Inexpensive
Area: Sydney
Address: 17 Hunter St Sydney
New South Wales
Phone: +61 2 9223 0677

#337
Sepia
Cuisines: European
Average Price: Exclusive
Area: Sydney
Address: 201 Sussex St Sydney
New South Wales
Phone: +61 2 9283 1990

#338
O Organic Produce
Cuisines: Café, Gluten-Free
Average Price: Inexpensive
Area: Sydney
Address: 7 Hunter St Sydney
New South Wales
Phone: +61 2 9223 8806

#339
Forbes Hotel
Cuisines: Hotel, Restaurant
Average Price: Modest
Area: Sydney
Address: 30 York St Sydney
New South Wales
Phone: +61 2 9299 3703

#340
Crust Gourmet Pizza Bar
Cuisines: Pizza
Average Price: Modest
Area: Sydney
Address: Cnr Pitt St Mall And Market St
Sydney New South Wales
Phone: +61 2 8246 9085

#341
Valencia Sandwich Bar
Cuisines: Fast Food, Sandwiches
Average Price: Inexpensive
Area: Sydney
Address: 299 Kent St Sydney
New South Wales
Phone: +61 2 9299 1096

#342
Orient Hotel Restaurant
Cuisines: Venues, Event Space,
Restaurant, Pub
Average Price: Modest
Area: The Rocks
Address: 89 George St Sydney
New South Wales
Phone: +61 2 9251 5631

#343
Espresso Bianco
Cuisines: Café, Coffee, Tea
Average Price: Modest
Area: Sydney
Address: 383 Kent St Sydney
New South Wales
Phone: +61 2 9262 1717

#344
Umi Sushi & Udon
Cuisines: Japanese
Average Price: Modest
Area: Sydney
Address: 1-25 Harbour St Sydney
New South Wales
Phone: +61 2 9283 2006

#345
Batch Sandwich & Espresso Bar
Cuisines: Coffee, Tea,
Breakfast & Brunch
Average Price: Inexpensive
Area: Sydney
Address: 70 Pitt St Sydney
New South Wales
Phone: +61 2 9231 4672

#346
Baia The Italian
Cuisines: Italian
Average Price: Modest
Area: Sydney
Address: Cockle Bay Whrf Sydney
New South Wales
Phone: +61 2 9283 3434

#347
Bentley Restaurant & Bar
Cuisines: Australian
Average Price: Exclusive
Area: Sydney
Address: 27 O'Connell St Sydney
New South Wales
Phone: +61 2 8214 0505

#348
Queens Square Coffee
Cuisines: Café, Coffee, Tea
Average Price: Modest
Area: Sydney
Address: 173 King Street Sydney
New South Wales
Phone: +61 2 8227 1300

#349
Mazzaro Restaurant
Cuisines: Restaurant
Average Price: Expensive
Area: Sydney
Address: Hyde Park Inn 279 Elizabeth
St Sydney New South Wales
Phone: +61 2 9267 0605

#350
Macchiato
Cuisines: Café
Average Price: Expensive
Area: Sydney
Address: 338 Pitt St Sydney
New South Wales
Phone: +61 2 9262 9525

#351
Guzman Y Gomez
Cuisines: Mexican, Food Court
Average Price: Inexpensive
Area: Sydney
Address: MLC Centre, Martin Pl Sydney
New South Wales
Phone: +61 2 9221 1777

#352
Xic Lo Vietnamese Restaurant
Cuisines: Vietnamese
Average Price: Inexpensive
Area: Haymarket
Address: Thomas St 215A Sydney
New South Wales
Phone: +61 2 9280 1678

#353
Essence Restaurant & Wharf Bar
Cuisines: European
Average Price: Expensive
Area: Sydney
Address: 11 Lime Street Sydney
New South Wales
Phone: +61 2 9290 3500

#354
Bistro Cbd
Cuisines: French
Average Price: Modest
Area: Sydney
Address: 52 King Street Level 1 Sydney
New South Wales
Phone: +61 2 8297 7010

#355
China Republic
Cuisines: Chinese
Average Price: Expensive
Area: Sydney
Address: 680 George St Sydney
New South Wales
Phone: +61 2 8081 0888

#356
Reantong Thai Restaurant
Cuisines: Thai
Average Price: Inexpensive
Area: Pyrmont
Address: 233 Harris St Sydney
New South Wales 2009
Phone: +61 2 9571 9988

#357
Saladplus
Cuisines: Salad
Average Price: Inexpensive
Area: Sydney
Address: 83 Clarence St Sydney
New South Wales
Phone: +61 2 9299 4458

#358
Kobe Jones Sydney
Cuisines: Japanese
Average Price: Exclusive
Area: Sydney
Address: 29 Lime St Sydney
New South Wales
Phone: +61 2 9299 5290

#359
Max Brenner
Cuisines: Desserts, Café
Average Price: Inexpensive
Area: Sydney
Address: 273 George Street Sydney
New South Wales
Phone: +61 2 9251 7788

#360
Little Rumour
Cuisines: Bar, Burgers, Pizza
Average Price: Modest
Area: Sydney
Address: 4 Castlereagh St Sydney
New South Wales
Phone: +61 2 9232

#361
Mecca Espresso King St
Cuisines: Café
Average Price: Inexpensive
Area: Sydney
Address: 67 King St Sydney
New South Wales
Phone: +61 2 9299 8828

#362
Wagamama
Cuisines: Asian Fusion
Average Price: Modest
Area: Sydney
Address: 500 George Street Sydney
New South Wales
Phone: +61 2 9261 0292

#363
Nonya By Ginger & Spice
Cuisines: Nyonya
Average Price: Modest
Area: Sydney
Address: 1 Dixon St Sydney
New South Wales
Phone: +61 9 2837 022

#364
Cyril's Delicatessen
Cuisines: Deli
Average Price: Modest
Area: Haymarket
Address: 181 Hay St Sydney
New South Wales
Phone: +61 2 9211 0994

#365
The Botanica Brasserie
Cuisines: Seafood, Buffet
Average Price: Expensive
Area: Sydney
Address: 161 Elizabeth Street Level 1,
Sydney New South Wales
Phone: +61 2 9286 6650

#366
Shoyu
Cuisines: Japanese, Korean
Average Price: Inexpensive
Area: Sydney
Address: 515 Kent St Sydney
New South Wales
Phone: +61 2 9264 7470

#367
Neptune Palace Restaurant
Cuisines: Chinese, Halal, Malaysian
Average Price: Modest
Area: Sydney
Address: Corner of Pitt And Alfred
Streets Sydney New South Wales
Phone: +61 2 9241 3338

#368
The Fox Hole
Cuisines: Bar, Café
Average Price: Inexpensive
Area: Sydney
Address: 68A Erskine St Sydney
New South Wales
Phone: +61 2 9279 4369

#369
Subterranean Greek Bar & Grill
Cuisines: Mediterranean, Greek
Average Price: Modest
Area: Sydney
Address: 1 Martin Pl Sydney
New South Wales
Phone: +61 2 9229 7700

#370
Presse Cafe
Cuisines: Café
Average Price: Inexpensive
Area: Sydney
Address: 20 Martin Place, Sydney
New South Wales
Phone: +61 2 9231 2277

#371
New York Metro Cafe
Cuisines: Coffee, Tea,
Breakfast & Brunch, Café
Average Price: Modest
Area: Sydney
Address: Shop 15-16, Town Hall Square
Sydney New South Wales
Phone: +61 2 9264 7198

#372
Cafe Opera
Cuisines: Australian, Buffet
Average Price: Expensive
Area: Sydney
Address: Macquarie St 117 Sydney
New South Wales
Phone: +61 2 9253 9000

#373
Cafe Rosso Espresso
Cuisines: Coffee, Tea,
Breakfast & Brunch
Average Price: Modest
Area: Sydney
Address: 500 George St, Sydney
New South Wales
Phone: +61 2 9266 0771

#374
Deli De Lite
Cuisines: Sandwiches,
Coffee, Tea, Café
Average Price: Inexpensive
Area: Sydney
Address: 39 Martin Pl Sydney
New South Wales
Phone: +61 2 9232 1705

#375
Harbourkitchen Bar
Cuisines: Specialty Food,
Mediterranean
Average Price: Expensive
Area: The Rocks
Address: Hickson Rd 7 Sydney
New South Wales
Phone: +61 2 9256 1661

#376
Akaneya Japanese Restaurant
Cuisines: Restaurant
Average Price: Modest
Area: Sydney
Address: 347 Kent St Sydney
New South Wales
Phone: +61 2 9279 1141

#377
Sourdough Panini Bakery Bar
Cuisines: Bakery, Café
Average Price: Inexpensive
Area: Sydney
Address: 85 Liverpool St Sydney
New South Wales
Phone: +61 2 9299 2380

#378
Ajisen Ramen
Cuisines: Restaurant
Average Price: Inexpensive
Area: Sydney
Address: 85 Liverpool St Sydney
New South Wales
Phone: +61 2 9267 8816

#379
Ramen Zundo
Cuisines: Japanese
Average Price: Modest
Area: Sydney
Address: 644 George St Sydney
New South Wales
Phone: +61 2 9264 6113

#380
Yanagi
Cuisines: Japanese
Average Price: Inexpensive
Area: Sydney
Address: 76 Clarence St Sydney
New South Wales
Phone: +61 9 2993 232

#381
Arima Sushi
Cuisines: Restaurant
Average Price: Inexpensive
Area: Sydney
Address: 106 Bathurst St Sydney
New South Wales
Phone: +61 2 9267 3588

#382
Good Co
Cuisines: Café, Coffee, Tea
Average Price: Modest
Area: Sydney
Address: 255 George St Sydney
New South Wales
Phone: +61 2 9293 2551

#383
Pepper Lunch
Cuisines: Japanese
Average Price: Inexpensive
Area: Sydney
Address: 537-551 George St Sydney
New South Wales
Phone: +61 2 9283 2017

#384
Adria Rybar & Grill
Cuisines: Mediterranean
Average Price: Expensive
Area: Sydney
Address: The Promenade Sydney
New South Wales
Phone: 1300 989 989

#385
Relish
Cuisines: Fast Food, Desserts,
Health Market
Average Price: Inexpensive
Area: Glebe
Address: 1 Bay St Sydney
New South Wales 2007
Phone: +61 2 9211 3377

#386
Maximus Cafe
Cuisines: Café
Average Price: Inexpensive
Area: Sydney
Address: No. 1 Martin Pl Sydney
New South Wales
Phone: +61 2 9229 7700

#387
Spilling The Beans Cafe
Cuisines: Café
Average Price: Inexpensive
Area: Sydney
Address: 215 Clarence St Sydney
New South Wales
Phone: +61 2 9299 7371

#388
Mero Mero
Cuisines: Café, Salad
Average Price: Modest
Area: Sydney
Address: 500 George Street Sydney
New South Wales
Phone: +61 4 2154 8927

#389
Guzman Y Gomez
Cuisines: Mexican
Average Price: Inexpensive
Area: Sydney
Address: Shop 10.31, 680 George St
Sydney New South Wales
Phone: +61 2 9191 0909

#390
The Macquarie Street Gourmet
Cuisines: Fast Food
Average Price: Modest
Area: Sydney
Address: 225 Macquarie St Sydney
New South Wales
Phone: +61 2 9221 5043

#391
Lizë + Bath
Cuisines: Café, Gluten-Free
Average Price: Inexpensive
Area: Sydney
Address: 227 Elizabeth St Sydney
New South Wales
Phone: +61 2 9261 8221

#392
Cafe Connection
Cuisines: Café, Coffee, Tea
Average Price: Modest
Area: Sydney
Address: Shp2/ 37 York St Sydney
New South Wales
Phone: +61 2 9262 2826

#393
Indochine Cafe
Cuisines: Vietnamese
Average Price: Modest
Area: Sydney
Address: 111 Elizabeth St Sydney
New South Wales
Phone: +61 2 9233 1088

#394
Flyover Bar
Cuisines: Australian
Average Price: Modest
Area: Sydney
Address: 275 Kent St Sydney
New South Wales
Phone: +61 2 9262 1988

#395
Sharak
Cuisines: Japanese
Average Price: Modest
Area: Sydney
Address: 371 Pitt St Sydney
New South Wales
Phone: +61 2 8084 3341

#396
T2 - T2B
Cuisines: Café, Coffee, Tea,
Specialty Food
Average Price: Inexpensive
Area: Sydney
Address: Shop LG99, 455 George St
Sydney New South Wales
Phone: +61 2 9283 3926

#397
Qv Bar Cafe
Cuisines: Café, Coffee, Tea
Average Price: Modest
Area: Sydney
Address: 455 George St Sydney
New South Wales
Phone: +61 2 9267 1122

#398
GPO Sydney
Cuisines: Venues, Event Space,
Restaurant, Bar
Average Price: Expensive
Area: Sydney
Address: 1 Martin Pl Sydney
New South Wales
Phone: +61 2 9229 7700

#399
Taste of Shanghai
Cuisines: Chinese
Average Price: Modest
Area: Sydney
Address: 644 George St Sydney
New South Wales
Phone: +61 2 9261 8832

#400
Hyde Park Cafe
Cuisines: Café
Average Price: Modest
Area: Sydney
Address: Cnr Elizabeth & Liverpool
Street Sydney New South Wales
Phone: +61 2 9264 8751

#401
Sugarbean Cafe
Cuisines: Fast Food, Café
Average Price: Inexpensive
Area: Sydney
Address: 50 Hunter St Sydney
New South Wales
Phone: +61 2 9232 2002

#402
THR1VE
Cuisines: Juice Bar, Gluten-Free
Average Price: Modest
Area: Sydney
Address: 19-29 Martin Pl Sydney
New South Wales
Phone: +61 2 9221 3885

#403
Holy Basil
Cuisines: Thai, Laos
Average Price: Modest
Area: Sydney
Address: 127 Liverpool St Sydney
New South Wales
Phone: +61 2 9283 8284

#404
Lindt Chocolat Café
Cuisines: Venues, Event Space, Café
Average Price: Modest
Area: Sydney
Address: 53 Martin Pl Sydney
New South Wales
Phone: +61 2 8257 1600

#405
Table For 20
Cuisines: Italian
Average Price: Expensive
Area: Darlinghurst
Address: 182 Campbell Street Sydney
New South Wales 2010
Phone: +61 4 1609 6916

#406
Bar Fresh
Cuisines: Coffee, Tea, Café
Average Price: Modest
Area: Sydney
Address: 346 Kent St Sydney
New South Wales
Phone: +61 2 9279 0840

#407
Ichi-Ban Boshi
Cuisines: Japanese
Average Price: Inexpensive
Area: Sydney
Address: 500 George St Sydney
New South Wales
Phone: +61 2 9262 7677

#408
Mcdonald's
Cuisines: Fast Food, Burgers
Average Price: Exclusive
Area: Sydney
Address: 377 George St Sydney
New South Wales
Phone: +61 2 9299 8203

#409
Settlement On Quay
Cuisines: Café
Average Price: Modest
Area: Sydney
Address: 33 Alfred St Sydney
New South Wales
Phone: +61 2 9241 4010

#410
Sosumi Sushi Train
Cuisines: Sushi Bar, Japanese
Average Price: Exclusive
Area: Sydney
Address: 1 Martin Pl Sydney
New South Wales
Phone: +61 2 9229 7710

#411
Bezzini King Street Wharf
Cuisines: Café
Average Price: Inexpensive
Area: Sydney
Address: 12 Shelley St Sydney
New South Wales
Phone: +61 2 9299 3620

#412
Yogurberry
Cuisines: Café, Ice Cream, Desserts
Average Price: Inexpensive
Area: Sydney
Address: 644 George St Sydney
New South Wales
Phone: +61 2 9283 1193

#413
Sydney Fish Market
Cuisines: Seafood Market,
Seafood, Fish & Chips
Average Price: Modest
Area: Pyrmont
Address: Bank St Pyrmont
New South Wales 2009
Phone: +61 2 9004 1100

#414
Corn Exchange Restaurant
Cuisines: Seafood, Buffet
Average Price: Modest
Area: Sydney
Address: Sussex Street 161 Sydney
New South Wales
Phone: +61 2 9290 4851

#415
Workshop Espresso
Cuisines: Café, Coffee, Tea
Average Price: Inexpensive
Area: Sydney
Address: 500 George St Sydney
New South Wales
Phone: +61 2 9264 8836

#416
Palace Chinese Restaurant
Cuisines: Chinese
Average Price: Modest
Area: Sydney
Address: 133 -145 Castlereigh St
Sydney New South Wales
Phone: +61 2 9283 6288

#417
Lime St Cafe
Cuisines: Mediterranean
Average Price: Modest
Area: Sydney
Address: 60 Lime St Sydney
New South Wales
Phone: +61 2 9299 6006

#418
The Tearoom QVB
Cuisines: Restaurant
Average Price: Modest
Area: Sydney
Address: 455 George St Sydney
New South Wales
Phone: +61 2 9283 7279

#419
Laksa King
Cuisines: Malaysian
Average Price: Modest
Area: Sydney
Address: 41/43 Erskine Street Sydney
New South Wales
Phone: +61 2 9290 3680

#420
Thai Tree
Cuisines: Fast Food
Average Price: Modest
Area: Sydney
Address: 259 George St Sydney
New South Wales
Phone: +61 2 9252 0881

#421
Mamak
Cuisines: Malaysian, Ethnic Food
Average Price: Modest
Area: Haymarket
Address: 15 Goulburn St Haymarket
New South Wales
Phone: +61 2 9211 1668

#422
Porteno
Cuisines: Argentine
Average Price: Expensive
Area: Surry Hills
Address: 358 Cleveland St Surry Hills
New South Wales 2010
Phone: +61 2 8399 1440

#423
The Royal George
Cuisines: Bar, Pub Food
Average Price: Modest
Area: Sydney
Address: 330 George St Sydney
New South Wales
Phone: +61 2 9254 8002

#424
Maya Da Dhaba
Cuisines: Indian
Average Price: Modest
Area: Redfern
Address: 431 Cleveland St Surry Hills
New South Wales 2010
Phone: +61 2 8399 3785

#425
The Little Marionette On The Dale
Cuisines: Café, Coffee, Tea
Average Price: Modest
Area: Annandale
Address: 18 Trafalgar St Annandale
New South Wales 2038
Phone: +61 2 9557 8337

#426
Rossini Cafe
Cuisines: Café
Average Price: Modest
Area: Sydney
Address: Shop 5f, 1 O'Connell St
Sydney New South Wales
Phone: +61 2 9247 8882

#427
Acqua Pazza
Cuisines: Restaurant
Average Price: Expensive
Area: Sydney
Address: 1 Bent St Sydney
New South Wales
Phone: +61 2 9247 0851

#428
Quay
Cuisines: European
Average Price: Exclusive
Area: The Rocks
Address: Overseas Passenger Terminal
The Rocks New South Wales
Phone: +61 2 9251 5600

#429
The Lord Nelson Brewery Hotel
Cuisines: Pub, Beer Bar, Australian
Average Price: Modest
Area: Millers Point
Address: 19 Kent St The Rocks
New South Wales
Phone: +61 2 9251 4044

#430
Buffalo Dining Club
Cuisines: Italian
Average Price: Modest
Area: Darlinghurst
Address: 116 Surrey St Darlinghurst
New South Wales 2010
Phone: +61 2 9332 4052

#431
The Local Taphouse
Cuisines: Pub, Australian, Beer Bar
Average Price: Modest
Area: Darlinghurst
Address: 122 Flinders St Darlinghurst
New South Wales 2010
Phone: +61 2 9360 0088

#432
Zest Salad & Juices
Cuisines: Fast Food, Salad
Average Price: Inexpensive
Area: Sydney
Address: 50 Bridge St Sydney
New South Wales
Phone: +61 2 9233 5071

#433
Musashi
Cuisines: Japanese
Average Price: Modest
Area: Haymarket
Address: 5/447 Pitt St Haymarket
New South Wales
Phone: +61 2 9280 0377

#434
Fat Buddha Restaurant
Cuisines: Chinese
Average Price: Modest
Area: Sydney
Address: 455 George St Sydney
New South Wales
Phone: +61 2 9264 9558

#435
Single Origin Roasters
Cuisines: Coffee, Tea,
Breakfast & Brunch, Café
Average Price: Modest
Area: Surry Hills
Address: 60-64 Reservoir St Surry Hills
New South Wales 2010
Phone: +61 2 9211 0665

#436
Mr Crackles
Cuisines: Sandwiches,
Hot Dogs, Fast Food
Average Price: Inexpensive
Area: Darlinghurst
Address: 155 Oxford St Darlinghurst
New South Wales 2010
Phone: +61 2 8068 2832

#437
Chinese Noodle Restaurant
Cuisines: Chinese
Average Price: Inexpensive
Area: Haymarket
Address: 8 Quay St Haymarket
New South Wales
Phone: +61 2 9281 9051

#438
Sydney Tower Restaurants
Cuisines: Restaurant
Average Price: Exclusive
Area: Sydney
Address: 100 Market St Sydney
New South Wales
Phone: +61 2 8223 3800

#439
Sushi Rio
Cuisines: Japanese
Average Price: Modest
Area: Sydney
Address: 339 Sussex St Sydney
New South Wales
Phone: +61 2 9261 2388

#440
The Rocks Cafe
Cuisines: Australian
Average Price: Modest
Area: The Rocks
Address: 99 George St The Rocks
New South Wales
Phone: +61 2 9247 3089

#441
Nomad
Cuisines: Wine Bar, Australian
Average Price: Expensive
Area: Surry Hills
Address: 16 Foster St Surry Hills
New South Wales 2010
Phone: +61 9 2803 395

#442
Chefs Gallery Jamison
Cuisines: Chinese
Average Price: Modest
Area: Sydney
Address: Metcentre G/F 273 George St
Sydney New South Wales
Phone: +61 2 9247 8888

#443
Crazy Wings
Cuisines: Restaurant
Average Price: Inexpensive
Area: Sydney
Address: 1 Dixon St Sydney
New South Wales
Phone: +61 2 9267 8862

#444
Min Sok Chon
Cuisines: Korean
Average Price: Modest
Area: Sydney
Address: 1/116 Liverpool St Sydney
New South Wales
Phone: +61 2 9267 7798

#445
Makanai
Cuisines: Ethnic Food, Sushi Bar,
Japanese
Average Price: Modest
Area: Sydney
Address: 239 Pitt St Sydney
New South Wales
Phone: +61 2 9222 9077

#446
Mecca Espresso CQ
Cuisines: Café
Average Price: Inexpensive
Area: Sydney
Address: 1 Alfred St Sydney
New South Wales
Phone: +61 2 9252 7668

#447
Mary's
Cuisines: Bar, Burgers, American
Average Price: Modest
Area: Newtown
Address: 6 Mary St Newtown
New South Wales 2042
Phone: +61 2 4995 9550

#448
Harry's Café De Wheels
Cuisines: Café, Hot Dogs, Fast Food
Average Price: Inexpensive
Area: Woolloomooloo
Address: Cowper Wharf Rd
Woolloomooloo
New South Wales 2011
Phone: +61 2 9357 3074

#449
Petaling Street
Cuisines: Malaysian
Average Price: Inexpensive
Area: Haymarket
Address: 760 George St Haymarket
New South Wales
Phone: +61 2 9280 1006

#450
Le Monde Cafe
Cuisines: Café, Breakfast & Brunch
Average Price: Modest
Area: Surry Hills
Address: 83 Foveaux St Surry Hills
New South Wales 2010
Phone: +61 2 9211 3568

#451
Lucky Tsotsi Shebeen & Bar
Cuisines: Bar, African
Average Price: Modest
Area: Darlinghurst
Address: 245 Oxford St Darlinghurst
New South Wales 2010
Phone: +61 2 8354 1306

#452
Brewtown Newtown
Cuisines: Café
Average Price: Modest
Area: Newtown
Address: 6-8 O'connell St Newtown
New South Wales 2042
Phone: +61 2 9519 2920

#453
Intermezzo Ristorante
Cuisines: Italian, Café
Average Price: Modest
Area: Sydney
Address: No. 1 Martin Pl Sydney
New South Wales
Phone: +61 2 9229 7788

#454
Fratelli Paradiso
Cuisines: Italian
Average Price: Modest
Area: Potts Point
Address: 16 Challis Ave Potts Point
New South Wales 2011
Phone: +61 2 9357 1744

#455
Chur Burger
Cuisines: Burgers
Average Price: Modest
Area: Surry Hills
Address: 48 Albion St Surry Hills
New South Wales 2010
Phone: +61 2 9212 3602

#456
Kabuki Shoroku Japanese Restaurant
Cuisines: Japanese
Average Price: Expensive
Area: Sydney
Address: 202 Clarence St Sydney
New South Wales
Phone: +61 2 9267 4552

#457
Ms. G's
Cuisines: Bar, Asian Fusion, Vietnamese
Average Price: Expensive
Area: Potts Point
Address: 155 Victoria St Potts Point
New South Wales 2011
Phone: +61 2 9240 3000

#458
Pony Lounge & Dining
Cuisines: Restaurant
Average Price: Expensive
Area: The Rocks
Address: 10 Playfair St The Rocks
New South Wales
Phone: +61 2 9252 7797

#459
A Tavola
Cuisines: Italian
Average Price: Exclusive
Area: Darlinghurst
Address: 348 Victoria St Darlinghurst
New South Wales 2010
Phone: +61 2 9331 7871

#460
**Masuya Japanese Seafood
Restaurant**
Cuisines: Japanese
Average Price: Expensive
Area: Sydney
Address: 14 O'Connell St Sydney
New South Wales
Phone: +61 2 9235 2717

#461
Spice I Am
Cuisines: Thai
Average Price: Modest
Area: Surry Hills
Address: 90 Wentworth Ave Surry Hills
New South Wales 2010
Phone: +61 2 9280 0928

#462
Doppio Espresso
Cuisines: Café
Average Price: Modest
Area: Sydney
Address: 284 Pitt St Sydney
New South Wales
Phone: +61 2 9286 3367

#463
Darlie Laundromatic
Cuisines: Café, Lounge, Gastropub
Average Price: Modest
Area: Darlinghurst
Address: 304A Palmer St Darlinghurst
New South Wales 2010
Phone: +61 2 8095 0129

#464
Robocog
Cuisines: Café
Average Price: Modest
Area: Surry Hills
Address: 249 Riley St Surry Hills
New South Wales 2010
Phone: +61 2 9281 2880

#465
Asagao
Cuisines: Fast Food
Average Price: Modest
Area: Haymarket
Address: 9-13 Hay St Sydney
New South Wales
Phone: +61 2 9281 3050

#466
Mammas
Cuisines: Australian
Average Price: Modest
Area: Sydney
Address: 57 Liverpool St Sydney
New South Wales
Phone: +61 2 9264 5841

#467
Hari's Vegetarian
Cuisines: Vegetarian, Vegan
Average Price: Inexpensive
Area: Ultimo
Address: 157 Broadway Sydney
New South Wales 2007
Phone: +61 2 9212 1010

#468
Different Drummer
Cuisines: Lounge, Spanish
Average Price: Expensive
Area: Glebe
Address: 185 Glebe Point Rd Glebe
New South Wales 2037
Phone: +61 2 9552 3406

#469
Ananas
Cuisines: French, Mediterranean
Average Price: Expensive
Area: The Rocks
Address: 18 Argyle St The Rocks
New South Wales
Phone: +61 2 9259 5668

#470
The Pie Tin
Cuisines: Café, Bakery, Desserts
Average Price: Inexpensive
Area: Newtown
Address: 1A Brown St Newtown
New South Wales 2042
Phone: +61 2 9519 7880

#471
Bloodwood
Cuisines: Australian
Average Price: Expensive
Area: Newtown
Address: 416 King Street Newtown
New South Wales 2042
Phone: +61 2 9557 7699

#472
Sailors Thai, Ivy
Cuisines: Thai
Average Price: Expensive
Area: Sydney
Address: 330 George St Sydney
New South Wales
Phone: +61 2 9240 3000

#473
Lucio Pizzeria
Cuisines: Italian, Pizza
Average Price: Modest
Area: Darlinghurst
Address: 248 Palmer St Darlinghurst
New South Wales 2010
Phone: +61 2 9332 3766

#474
Sushi On Stanley
Cuisines: Sushi Bar
Average Price: Inexpensive
Area: Darlinghurst
Address: 85 Stanley St Darlinghurst
New South Wales 2010
Phone: +61 2 9357 6465

#475
**The Commons Local
Eating House**
Cuisines: Breakfast & Brunch,
Mediterranean, Cocktail Bar
Average Price: Modest
Area: Darlinghurst
Address: 32 Burton St Darlinghurst
New South Wales 2010
Phone: +61 2 9358 1487

#476
Gumption By Coffee Alchemy
Cuisines: Café, Coffee, Tea
Average Price: Inexpensive
Area: Sydney
Address: 412-414 George St Sydney
New South Wales
Phone: +61 2 9232 4199

#477
The Apollo
Cuisines: Greek, Australian
Average Price: Expensive
Area: Elizabeth Bay
Address: 44 Macleay St Elizabeth Bay
New South Wales 2011
Phone: +61 2 8354 0888

#478
Le Pelican
Cuisines: Restaurant
Average Price: Expensive
Area: Surry Hills
Address: 411 Bourke St Surry Hills
New South Wales 2010
Phone: +61 2 9380 2622

#479
Galileo Restaurant
Cuisines: European
Average Price: Exclusive
Area: Millers Point
Address: 89 Kent St Sydney
New South Wales
Phone: +61 2 9256 5220

#480
India Quay
Cuisines: Restaurant
Average Price: Exclusive
Area: Sydney
Address: 2 Phillip St Sydney
New South Wales
Phone: +61 2 9251 7722

#481
The Alfred Cafe
Cuisines: Café
Average Price: Modest
Area: Newtown
Address: 100 Carillon Avenue Sydney
New South Wales 2050
Phone: +61 2 9550 6100

#482
Four In Hand
Cuisines: Gastropub
Average Price: Expensive
Area: Paddington
Address: 105 Sutherland St Paddington
New South Wales 2021
Phone: +61 2 9326 2254

#483
Longrain
Cuisines: Wine Bar, Thai, Lounge
Average Price: Expensive
Area: Surry Hills
Address: 85 Commonwealth St Surry
Hills New South Wales 2010
Phone: +61 2 9280 2888

#484
Rosso Pomodoro
Cuisines: Italian, Pizza
Average Price: Modest
Area: Balmain
Address: Shop 90-91/24 Buchanan St
Balmain New South Wales 2041
Phone: +61 2 9555 5924

#485
The Fine Food Store & Café
Cuisines: Shopping, Coffee,
Tea, Café, Deli
Average Price: Modest
Area: The Rocks
Address: Cnr Mill Lane & Kendall Lane
The Rocks New South Wales
Phone: +61 2 9252 1196

#486
Kingsleys Steak & Crabhouse
Cuisines: Seafood, Steakhouse
Average Price: Expensive
Area: Woolloomooloo
Address: 6 Cowper Wharf Rd
Woolloomooloo New South Wales 2011
Phone: 1300 546 475

#487
Spicy Sichuan Restaurant
Cuisines: Chinese
Average Price: Modest
Area: Glebe
Address: 1-9 Glebe Point Rd Glebe
New South Wales 2037
Phone: +61 2 9660 8200

#488
Revolver
Cuisines: Café, Breakfast & Brunch
Average Price: Modest
Area: Annandale
Address: 291 Annandale Street
Annandale New South Wales 2038
Phone: +61 2 9555 4727

#489
Bills
Cuisines: Breakfast & Brunch,
Australian
Average Price: Modest
Area: Darlinghurst
Address: 433 Liverpool St Darlinghurst
New South Wales 2010
Phone: +61 2 9360 9631

#490
Yoshii
Cuisines: Japanese
Average Price: Exclusive
Area: The Rocks
Address: 115 Harrington St The Rocks
New South Wales
Phone: +61 2 9247 2566

#491
Ramen Ikkyu
Cuisines: Japanese
Average Price: Inexpensive
Area: Haymarket
Address: 401 Sussex St Haymarket
New South Wales
Phone: +61 2 9281 0998

#492
Bar Adyar
Cuisines: Café
Average Price: Expensive
Area: Sydney
Address: 484 Kent Street Sydney
New South Wales
Phone: +61 2 9283 1443

#493
Serigo Espresso
Cuisines: Café, Coffee, Tea
Average Price: Modest
Area: Sydney
Address: 101 York St Sydney
New South Wales
Phone: +61 2 9279 3050

#494
4Fourteen
Cuisines: Gastropub
Average Price: Expensive
Area: Surry Hills
Address: 414 Bourke St Surry Hills
New South Wales 2010
Phone: +61 2 9331 5399

#495
Onde
Cuisines: Restaurant
Average Price: Expensive
Area: Darlinghurst
Address: 346 Liverpool St Darlinghurst
New South Wales 2010
Phone: +61 2 9331 8749

#496
Yok Yor Thai Food Factory
Cuisines: Thai
Average Price: Modest
Area: Haymarket
Address: 323 Castlereagh St Haymarket
New South Wales
Phone: +61 2 9280 0001

#497
Joe Black Cafe
Cuisines: Café, Coffee, Tea
Average Price: Modest
Area: Sydney
Address: 27 Commonwealth St Surry
Hills New South Wales 2010
Phone: +61 2 8097 8646

#498
Pastabella
Cuisines: Italian
Average Price: Modest
Area: Glebe
Address: 89 Glebe Point Rd Glebe
New South Wales 2037
Phone: +61 2 9566 4488

#499
Gnome
Cuisines: Coffee, Tea,
Breakfast & Brunch, Café
Average Price: Modest
Area: Surry Hills
Address: 536 Crown St Surry Hills
New South Wales 2010
Phone: +61 2 9332 3191

#500
The Original Maltese Cafe
Cuisines: Café
Average Price: Inexpensive
Area: Darlinghurst
Address: 310 Crown St Darlinghurst
New South Wales 2010
Phone: +61 2 9361 6942

TOP 450
ARTS & ENTERTAINMENT
Recommended by Locals & Trevelers
(From #1 to #450)

#1
Royal Botanic Gardens Sydney
Category: Park, Botanical Garden
Area: Sydney
Address: Mrs Macquaries Rd Sydney
New South Wales
Phone: +61 2 9231 8125

#2
Art Gallery of NSW
Category: Museum
Area: Sydney
Address: Art Gallery Rd Sydney
New South Wales
Phone: +61 2 9225 1744

#3
St George Open Air Cinema
Category: Cinema
Area: Sydney
Address: Fleet Steps Mrs Macquaries
Rd Sydney New South Wales
Phone: +61 300 366 649

#4
Sydney Theatre Company
Category: Performing Arts
Area: Dawes Point
Address: Pier 4, Hickson Rd Sydney
New South Wales
Phone: +61 2 9250 1777

#5
Australian Museum
Category: Museum
Area: Darlinghurst
Address: 6 College St Sydney
New South Wales
Phone: +61 2 9320 6000

#6
The Domain
Category: Botanical Garden,
Local Flavor, Park
Area: Sydney
Address: Art Gallery Road Sydney
New South Wales
Phone: +61 2 9231 8111

#7
Metro Theatre
Category: Music Venues
Average Price: Modest
Area: Sydney
Address: 624 George St Sydney
New South Wales
Phone: +61 2 9550 3666

#8
Sydney Tower Eye
Category: Arts, Entertainment
Area: Sydney
Address: 100 Market Street Sydney
New South Wales
Phone: +61 2 9333 9222

#9
The Cuban Place
Category: Cuban, Music Venues, Bar
Average Price: Expensive
Area: Sydney
Address: 125 York St Sydney
New South Wales
Phone: +61 2 9264 4224

#10
The Arthouse Hotel
Category: Bar, Music Venues, Australian
Average Price: Expensive
Area: Sydney
Address: 275 Pitt St Sydney
New South Wales
Phone: +61 2 9284 1200

#11
The Macquarie Hotel
Category: Pub, Pub Food, Beer Bar,
Jazz, Blues, Brewerie
Area: Surry Hills
Address: 40-44 Wentworth Ave Sydney
New South Wales
Phone: +61 2 8262 8888

#12
P.J.O'Brien's Irish Pub
Category: Pub, Sports Bar,
Music Venues
Average Price: Modest
Area: Sydney
Address: 57 King St Sydney
New South Wales
Phone: +61 2 9290 1811

#13
State Theatre
Category: Performing Arts
Area: Sydney
Address: 49 Market Street Sydney
New South Wales
Phone: +61 2 9373 6655

#14
Goodgod Small Club
Category: Bar, American, Music Venues
Average Price: Inexpensive
Area: Sydney
Address: 55 Liverpool St Sydney
New South Wales
Phone: +61 8 0840 587

#15
The Basement
Category: Jazz, Blues, Bar,
Music Venues
Average Price: Modest
Area: Sydney
Address: 7 Macquarie Place Sydney
New South Wales
Phone: +61 2 9251 2797

#16
Hoyts Broadway
Category: Cinema
Area: Glebe
Address: Broadway Shopping Center
Sydney New South Wales 2007
Phone: +61 2 9003 3820

#17
Government House
Category: Museum
Area: Sydney
Address: Macquarie St Sydney
New South Wales
Phone: +61 2 9931 5222

#18
Event Cinemas
Category: Cinema
Area: Sydney
Address: 05-525 George St Sydney
New South Wales
Phone: +61 2 9273 7300

#19
1912 Dining Bar
Category: Japanese, Jazz, Blues, Asian
Fusion
Average Price: Modest
Area: Haymarket
Address: 27-33 Goulburn St Sydney
New South Wales
Phone: +61 2 8970 5813

#20
Domain Express Walkway
Category: Parking, Arts, Entertainment
Area: Sydney
Address: Domain Car Park Sydney
New South Wales
Phone: +61 2 9232 6165

#21
Festival of Dangerous Ideas
Category: Festival
Area: Sydney
Address: 2 Macquarie Stree Sydney
New South Wales
Phone: +61 2 9250 7111

#22
Speaker's Corner
Category: Botanical Garden, Art Gallery
Area: Sydney
Address: The Domain Sydney
New South Wales
Phone: +61 2 9713 5780

#23
Madame Tussauds Sydney
Category: Art Gallery
Average Price: Modest
Area: Sydney
Address: Aquarium Pier Sydney
New South Wales
Phone: +61 800 205 851

#24
Manning Bar
Category: Music Venues, Pub
Average Price: Inexpensive
Area: Camperdown
Address: Manning Road Sydney
New South Wales 2006
Phone: +61 2 9563 6000

#25
St Andrew's Cathedral
Category: Landmark/Historical,
Music Venues, Church
Average Price: Inexpensive
Area: Sydney
Address: Corner of Bathurst And
George Streets Sydney
New South Wales
Phone: +61 2 9265 1661

#26
ANZAC War Memorial
Category: Museum, Landmark/Historical
Area: Haymarket
Address: Elizabeth Street Sydney
New South Wales
Phone: +61 2 9267 7668

#27
Justice & Police Museum
Category: Museum
Area: Sydney
Address: 8 Phillip St Sydney
New South Wales
Phone: +61 2 9252 1144

#28
Sydney Picture Hanging
Category: Art Gallery, Framing
Area: Potts Point
Address: 7 St Neot Ave Sydney
New South Wales 2011
Phone: +61 4 1025 8709

#29
Sydney Cricket Ground
Category: Stadium/Arena
Area: Paddington
Address: Moore Park Rd Sydney
New South Wales 2021
Phone: +61 2 9360 6601

#30
Art Equity Pty Ltd
Category: Art Gallery
Area: Sydney
Address: 66 King St Sydney
New South Wales
Phone: +61 2 9262 6660

#31
The Laugh Garage Comedi Club Pty
Category: Arts, Entertainment
Area: Sydney
Address: 60 Park St Sydney
New South Wales
Phone: +61 2 9264 1161

#32
Theatre Royal
Category: Performing Arts
Area: Sydney
Address: 108 King Street Sydney
New South Wales
Phone: +61 2 9224 8444

#33
Wildlife Photographer of The Year
Category: Art Gallery
Area: Darlinghurst
Address: 6 College Street Sydney
Sydney
New South Wales
Phone: +61 2 9320 6000

#34
Museum of Australian Currency Notes
Category: Museum
Area: Sydney
Address: 65 Martin Pl Sydney
New South Wales
Phone: +61 2 9551 9743

#35
Rugby Club
Category: Venues, Event Space, Social Club
Area: Sydney
Address: 31 Pitt St Sydney
New South Wales
Phone: +61 2 9247 3344

#36
Antique Print Room
Category: Antiques, Art Gallery
Area: Sydney
Address: Shop 7, Queen Victoria Building, 455 George St Sydney
New South Wales
Phone: +61 2 9267 4355

#37
The Spanish Club
Category: Music Venues, Spanish
Area: Sydney
Address: 88 Liverpool St Sydney
New South Wales
Phone: +61 2 9267 8440

#38
City Tattersalls Club
Category: Social Club, Bar
Area: Sydney
Address: 198 Pitt St Sydney
New South Wales
Phone: +61 2 9267 9421

#39
Sydney Entertainment Centre
Category: Stadium/Arena
Area: Sydney
Address: 35 Harbour Street Sydney
New South Wales
Phone: +61 2 9320 4200

#40
**The Metropolitan Museum
of Art Store**
Category: Jewelry, Art Gallery,
Home Decor
Area: Sydney
Address: 455 George St Sydney
New South Wales
Phone: +61 2 9283 3799

#41
John Chen Gallery
Category: Art Gallery
Area: Sydney
Address: George St Sydney
New South Wales
Phone: +61 2 9267 0700

#42
Bowlers' Club of NSW
Category: Social Club
Area: Sydney
Address: 95 York St Sydney
New South Wales
Phone: +61 2 9290 1155

#43
NSW Leagues Club
Category: Social Club
Area: Sydney
Address: 165 Phillip St Sydney
New South Wales
Phone: +61 2 9232 2611

#44
The Japan Foundation, Sydney
Category: Libraries, Festival, Cinema
Area: Sydney
Address: Level 1, Chifley Plaza, 2
Chifley Square Sydney
New South Wales
Phone: +61 2 8239 0055

#45
Nippon Club
Category: Social Club
Area: Sydney
Address: 229 Macquarie St Sydney
New South Wales
Phone: +61 2 9232 2688

#46
Cockle Bay Wharf
Category: Restaurant, Social Club,
Local Flavor
Average Price: Modest
Area: Sydney
Address: 201 Sussex St Sydney
New South Wales
Phone: +61 2 9269 9800

#47
Sydney Opera House
Category: Venues, Event Space,
Performing Arts
Area: Sydney
Address: 2 Macquarie St Sydney
New South Wales
Phone: +61 2 9250 7111

#48
**4A Centre For Contemporary
Asian Art**
Category: Art Gallery
Area: Haymarket
Address: 181-187 Hay St Sydney
New South Wales
Phone: +61 2 9212 0380

#49
City of Sydney R.S.L
Category: Social Club
Area: Sydney
Address: 565 George St Sydney
New South Wales
Phone: +61 2 9264 6281

#50
THRILL - Events Team
Category: Venues, Event Space,
Street Art
Area: Sydney
Address: Sydney
New South Wales 2001
Phone: +61 4 5911 1129

#51
Coach Bar
Category: Bar, Cabaret, Indian
Area: Sydney
Address: 1 Martin Place Sydney
New South Wales
Phone: +61 2 9229 7700

#52
The Actor's Pulse
Category: Performing Arts,
Adult Education
Area: Redfern
Address: 103 Regent St Sydney
New South Wales 2016
Phone: +61 4 1447 5515

#53
Galaxy World
Category: Arcade
Area: Sydney
Address: 614 George St Sydney
New South Wales
Phone: +61 2 9261 5133

#54
Piermarq Art Advisory
Category: Art Gallery
Area: Pyrmont
Address: 26-32 Pirrama Rd Sydney
New South Wales 2009
Phone: +61 2 9660 7799

#55
Thrill Team Building Activities & Events, Sydney
Category: Arts, Entertainment
Area: Sydney
Address: 251 Elizabeth St Sydney
New South Wales
Phone: +61 2 9630 2222

#56
Wild At Art
Category: Arts, Entertainment
Area: Darlinghurst
Address: 77-83 William St Sydney
New South Wales 2010
Phone: +61 4 2293 3932

#57
Royal Automobile Club
Category: Social Club
Area: Sydney
Address: 89 Macquarie St Sydney
New South Wales
Phone: +61 2 8273 2300

#58
Monkey Baa Theatre Company
Category: Performing Arts
Area: Sydney
Address: 1-25 Harbour St Sydney
New South Wales
Phone: +61 2 8624 9341

#59
Event George Street
Category: Cinema
Area: Sydney
Address: 505 - 525 George St Sydney
New South Wales
Phone: +61 2 9273 7431

#60
Fideli's Bar & Restaurant
Category: Jazz, Blues, Food, Lounge
Area: Sydney
Address: 77 York St Sydney
New South Wales
Phone: +61 2 9262 3140

#61
Cello's
Category: Restaurant, Social Club
Area: Sydney
Address: 169 Castlereagh St Sydney
New South Wales
Phone: +61 2 9284 1000

#62
Breenspace Pty
Category: Art Gallery
Area: Sydney
Address: Level 3, 17/ 19 Alberta St
Sydney New South Wales
Phone: +61 2 9283 1113

#63
Australian National Maritime Museum
Category: Museum
Area: Sydney
Address: 2 Murray St Darling Harbour
New South Wales
Phone: +61 2 9298 3777

#64
The C.T.A Business Club Limited
Category: Social Club
Area: Sydney
Address: MLC Centre, Martin Pl Sydney
New South Wales
Phone: +61 2 9232 7344

#65
Event Cinemas
Category: Cinema
Area: Sydney
Address: Head Office Level 20, 227
Elizabeth St Sydney New South Wales
Phone: +61 2 9373 6600

#66
The Porter Sydney
Category: Social Club
Area: Sydney
Address: 1 O'Connell St Sydney
New South Wales
Phone: +61 2 8075 0930

#67
The American Club Sydney
Category: Social Club
Area: Sydney
Address: 131 Macquarie St Sydney
New South Wales
Phone: +61 2 9241 2020

#68
Soho Galleries Sydney
Category: Art Gallery
Area: Woolloomooloo
Address: 104 Cathedral St Sydney
New South Wales
Phone: +61 2 9326 9066

#69
**Shakespeare Globe Centre
Australia Inc**
Category: Arts, Entertainment
Area: Camperdown
Address: Old Teachers College
University Of Sydney, Sydney
New South Wales
Phone: +61 2 9351 5231

#70
Soho Galleries
Category: Art Gallery
Area: Surry Hills
Address: |Cnr Crown & Cathedral
Streets|Crown Street Sydney
New South Wales
Phone: +61 2 9326 9066

#71
Australian Music Centre
Category: Music Venues
Area: The Rocks
Address: 16 Mountain St Sydney
New South Wales 2007
Phone: +61 2 9935 7805

#72
Anna Schwartz Gallery
Category: Art Gallery
Area: Eveleigh
Address: 245 Wilson St Sydney
New South Wales
Phone: +61 2 8580 7002

#73
Bicycle New South Wales
Category: Social Club
Area: Chippendale
Address: 822 George St Sydney
New South Wales
Phone: +61 2 9218 5400

#74
Mori Gallery
Category: Art Gallery
Area: Sydney
Address: 168 Day St Sydney
New South Wales
Phone: +61 2 9283 2903

#75
CWM Galleries Pty
Category: Art Gallery
Area: Sydney
Address: 149 Sussex St Sydney
New South Wales
Phone: +61 2 9299 5004

#76
Asian Social Club
Category: Social Club
Area: Ultimo
Address: 330 Wattle St Sydney
New South Wales
Phone: +61 2 9217 9331

#77
Creation Development
Category: Art Gallery
Area: Sydney
Address: 281 Clarence St Sydney
New South Wales
Phone: +61 2 9283 4273

#78
Goon Yee Tong Incorporated
Category: Social Club
Area: Haymarket
Address: 50 Dixon St Sydney
New South Wales
Phone: +61 2 9281 7206

#79
Pendulum Gallery
Category: Art Gallery
Area: Sydney
Address: 203 Clarence St Sydney
New South Wales
Phone: +61 2 9262 4170

#80
D One Entertainment
Category: Art Gallery, Comedy Club
Area: Sydney
Address: 600 George St Sydney
New South Wales
Phone: +61 2 9547 2578

#81
York Conference & Function
Category: Social Club
Area: Sydney
Address: 95 York St Sydney
New South Wales
Phone: +61 2 9290 1155

#82
Club Grace
Category: Social Club
Area: Sydney
Address: 77 York Street Sydney
New South Wales
Phone: +61 2 9272 6685

#83
Jinta Desert Art Gallery
Category: Art Gallery
Area: Sydney
Address: 120 Clarence St Sydney
New South Wales
Phone: +61 2 9290 3639

#84
Tiy Loy
Category: Food, Social Club
Area: Haymarket
Address: 417 Sussex St Sydney
New South Wales
Phone: +61 2 9211 1945

#85
Thredbo Club Card Membership & Enquiries
Category: Social Club
Area: Sydney
Address: 49 Market St Sydney
New South Wales
Phone: +61 2 9373 6505

#86
Amber Gallery
Category: Art Gallery
Area: Sydney
Address: 428 George St Sydney
New South Wales
Phone: +61 2 9233 6654

#87
Hunter-Taylor Gallery Aust
Category: Art Gallery
Area: Sydney
Address: 259 Pitt St Sydney
New South Wales
Phone: +61 2 9261 4417

#88
N.S.W Rod Fishers Society
Category: Social Club
Area: Sydney
Address: 61 York St Sydney
New South Wales
Phone: +61 2 9299 1481

#89
Silks Club
Category: Social Club
Area: Sydney
Address: 202 Pitt St Sydney
New South Wales
Phone: +61 2 9267 9421

#90
N.S.W. Bookmakers Co-op
Category: Arts, Entertainment
Area: Sydney
Address: 198 Pitt St Sydney
New South Wales
Phone: +61 2 9267 7605

#91
Art Gallery By Roger Boreham
Category: Art Gallery
Area: Sydney
Address: 168 Pitt St Sydney
New South Wales
Phone: +61 2 9232 2334

#92
Catholic Club Limited
Category: Social Club
Area: Sydney
Address: 199 Castlereagh St Sydney
New South Wales
Phone: +61 2 9267 9725

#93
N.S.W. Masonic Club
Category: Social Club
Area: Sydney
Address: 169 Castlereagh St Sydney
New South Wales
Phone: +61 2 9284 1000

#94
Movie Blogbuster
Category: Cinema
Area: Sydney
Address: 1 Martin Pl Sydney
New South Wales
Phone: +61 2 8888 8888

#95
Club Albatross
Category: Social Club
Area: Sydney
Address: 155 Castlereagh St Sydney
New South Wales
Phone: +61 2 9283 5090

#96
Particle Temporal Exhibition Space
Category: Art Gallery
Area: Sydney
Address: 66 Goulburn St Sydney
New South Wales
Phone: +61 4 1512 5251

#97
Women's Club
Category: Social Club
Area: Sydney
Address: 179 Elizabeth St Sydney
New South Wales
Phone: +61 2 9264 5383

#98
Hellenic Club
Category: Social Club
Area: Sydney
Address: 251 Elizabeth St Sydney
New South Wales
Phone: +61 2 9264 5792

#99
Jonathan Marks Photography
Category: Art Gallery
Area: Sydney
Address: George St Sydney
New South Wales
Phone: +61 2 9267 6808

#100
Cinema On The Square
Category: Cinema
Area: Sydney
Address: George St Sydney
New South Wales
Phone: +61 2 9247 4197

#101
Sydney Jewish Museum
Category: Museum
Area: Darlinghurst
Address: 148 Darlinghurst Rd
Darlinghurst
New South Wales 2010
Phone: +61 2 9360 7999

#102
Gallery First Nighters Club
Category: Social Club
Area: Sydney
Address: 85 Castlereagh St Sydney
New South Wales
Phone: +61 2 9223 2840

#103
Australian Chamber Orchestra
Category: Music Venues
Area: Sydney
Address: 2 East Circular Quay Sydney
New South Wales
Phone: +61 2 8274 3800

#104
Evocative Management Australia
Category: Music Venues
Area: Sydney
Address: Sydney
New South Wales
Phone: +61 300 642 285

#105
Printfolio Gallery
Category: Art Gallery
Area: Sydney
Address: 60 Margaret St Sydney
New South Wales
Phone: +61 2 9247 6690

#106
NSW Sports Club
Category: Social Club
Area: Sydney
Address: 10 Hunter St Sydney
New South Wales
Phone: +61 2 9233 3899

#107
Country Rugby League of NSW
Category: Social Club
Area: Sydney
Address: 167 Phillip St Sydney
New South Wales
Phone: +61 2 9232 5868

#108
The Queen's Club
Category: Social Club
Area: Haymarket
Address: Elizabeth St Sydney
New South Wales
Phone: +61 2 9264 1171

#109
The Lowy Institute
Category: Cultural Center
Area: Sydney
Address: 31 Bligh St Sydney
New South Wales
Phone: +61 2 8238 9000

#110
The Gallery
At The Wentworth Pty
Category: Art Gallery
Area: Sydney
Address: 4 Bligh St Sydney
New South Wales
Phone: +61 2 9223 1700

#111
The Sydney Mint
Category: Museum
Area: Sydney
Address: The Mint 10 Macquarie St
Sydney New South Wales
Phone: +61 2 8239 2288

#112
Gallery At The Wentworth
Category: Art Gallery
Area: Sydney
Address: Wentworth Hotel 61 Phillip St
Sydney New South Wales
Phone: +61 2 9223 1700

#113
Aboriginal Dreamtime
Fine Art Gallery
Category: Art Gallery
Area: Sydney
Address: 199 George St Sydney
New South Wales
Phone: +61 2 9241 2953

#114
Australian Club
Category: Social Club
Area: Sydney
Address: 165 Macquarie St Sydney
New South Wales
Phone: +61 2 9229 0400

#115
University & Schools Club
Category: Social Club
Area: Sydney
Address: 60 Phillip St Sydney
New South Wales
Phone: +61 2 9247 1323

#116
Estonian Socy of Sydney
Category: Social Club
Area: Surry Hills
Address: 141 Campbell St Sydney
New South Wales
Phone: +61 2 9212 2373

#117
Harvard Club of
Category: Social Club
Area: Sydney
Address: 44 Bridge St Sydney
New South Wales
Phone: +61 2 9251 1616

#118
Helena Bischof Gallery
Category: Art Gallery
Area: Sydney
Address: Darling Hbr Sydney
New South Wales
Phone: +61 2 9281 2510

#119
Royal Exchange of Sydney
Category: Social Club
Area: Sydney
Address: Gresham St Sydney
New South Wales
Phone: +61 2 9247 4374

#120
Union Club
Category: Social Club
Area: Sydney
Address: Bent St Sydney
New South Wales
Phone: +61 2 9232 8266

#121
The Seymour Centre
Category: Festival
Area: Darlington
Address: Corner of City RD & Cleveland
St Sydney New South Wales 2008
Phone: +61 2 9351 7944

#122
Sydney Interactive Theatre
Category: Performing Arts
Area: The Rocks
Address: 143A George Street Sydney
New South Wales
Phone: +61 4 3300 0295

#123
Sheffer Gallery
Category: Art Gallery
Area: Darlington
Address: 38 Lander St Sydney
New South Wales
Phone: +61 2 9310 5683

#124
Museum of Contemporary Art
Category: Venues, Museum
Area: The Rocks
Address: 140 George Street The Rocks
New South Wales
Phone: +61 2 9245 2400

#125
Verona Cinema & Bar
Category: Cinema, Bar
Average Price: Modest
Area: Paddington
Address: 17 Oxford St Paddington
New South Wales 2021
Phone: +61 2 9360 6099

#126
The Art of Dr Seuss Woollahra
Category: Art Gallery
Average Price: Modest
Area: Paddington
Address: 8 Oxford St Woollahra
New South Wales 2025
Phone: +61 2 8964 9702

#127
Enmore Theatre
Category: Music Venues
Average Price: Modest
Area: Newtown
Address: 130 Enmore Rd Newtown
New South Wales 2042
Phone: +61 2 9550 3666

#128
Sydney Observatory
Category: Cultural Center
Area: Millers Point
Address: Watson Rd The Rocks
New South Wales
Phone: +61 2 9217 0341

#129
Powerhouse Museum
Category: Museum, Venues
Area: Ultimo
Address: 500 Harris St Ultimo
New South Wales 2007
Phone: +61 2 9217 0600

#130
IMAX Sydney
Category: Cinema
Address: 31 Wheat Rd Darling Harbour
New South Wales
Phone: +61 2 9281 3300

#131
The Vanguard
Category: Jazz, Blues, Music Venues
Average Price: Expensive
Address: 42 King St Newtown
New South Wales 2042
Phone: +61 2 9557 9409

#132
Cafe Lounge
Category: Café, Music Venues, Bar
Average Price: Modest
Area: Darlinghurst
Address: 277 Goulburn St Surry Hills
New South Wales 2010
Phone: +61 2 9016 3951

#133
Gaffa
Category: Art Gallery
Average Price: Modest
Area: Sydney
Address: 281 Clarence St Sydney
New South Wales
Phone: +61 2 9283 4273

#134
The Meat & Wine Co
Category: Steakhouse, Winery
Average Price: Expensive
Area: Sydney
Address: 31 Wheat Rd Darling Harbour
New South Wales
Phone: +61 2 9211 9888

#135
The World Bar
Category: Bar, Dance Club, Music
Venues
Average Price: Modest
Area: Potts Point
Address: 24 Bayswater Rd Potts Point
New South Wales 2011
Phone: +61 2 9357 7700

#136
Govinda's Restaurant
Category: Cinema, Indian, Vegetarian
Average Price: Modest
Area: Darlinghurst
Address: 112 Darlinghurst Rd
Darlinghurst
New South Wales 2010
Phone: +61 2 9380 5155

#137
Capitol Theatre
Category: Performing Arts
Area: Haymarket
Address: 13 Campbell St Haymarket
New South Wales
Phone: +61 2 9320 5000

#138
The Star
Category: Casino, Restaurant, Hotel
Average Price: Exclusive
Area: Pyrmont
Address: 80 Pyrmont St Pyrmont
New South Wales 2009
Phone: +61 800 700 700

#139
Brett Whiteley Studio
Category: Art Gallery
Area: Surry Hills
Address: 2 Raper St Surry Hills
New South Wales 2010
Phone: +61 2 9225 1881

#140
Sydney Festival
Category: Festival
Area: The Rocks
Address: 18 Hickson Rd The Rocks
New South Wales
Phone: +61 2 8248 6500

#141
Sydney Dance Lounge
Category: Café, Performing Arts
Average Price: Expensive
Area: Dawes Point
Address: 4-5 Hickson Road Walsh Bay
New South Wales
Phone: +61 2 9241 5021

#142
Museum of Sydney
Category: Museum, Venues,
Event Space
Area: Sydney
Address: Cnr Phillip & Bridge Sts NSW
New South Wales
Phone: +61 2 9251 5988

#143
Lo-Fi
Category: Lounge, Music Venues
Average Price: Modest
Area: Darlinghurst
Address: 383 Bourke St Darlinghurst
New South Wales 2010
Phone: +61 2 9331 6200

#144
Chauvel Cinema
Category: Cinema
Area: Paddington
Address: Cnr Oxford Street And Oatley
Road Paddington
New South Wales 2021
Phone: +61 2 9361 5398

#145
Paddington Bowling Club
Category: Dance Club, Social Club
Average Price: Modest
Area: Paddington
Address: 2 Quarry St Paddington
New South Wales 2021
Phone: +61 2 9363 1150

#146
Jazushi
Category: Japanese, Sushi Bar,
Jazz, Blues
Average Price: Expensive
Area: Surry Hills
Address: 145 Devonshire St Surry Hills
New South Wales 2010
Phone: +61 2 9699 8977

#147
Palace Cinemas
Category: Cinema
Area: Leichhardt
Address: 99 Norton St Leichhardt
New South Wales 2040
Phone: +61 2 9550 0122

#148
Blender Gallery
Category: Art Gallery, Musical
Instruments
Average Price: Exclusive
Area: Paddington
Address: 16 Elizabeth St Paddington
New South Wales 2021
Phone: +61 2 9380 7080

#149
Firstdraft
Category: Art Gallery
Average Price: Modest
Area: Surry Hills
Address: 116-118 Chalmers St Surry
Hills New South Wales 2010
Phone: +61 2 9698 3665

#150
Sydney Writers Festival
Category: Festival
Area: The Rocks
Address: Ground Floor 10 Hickson Rd
The Rocks New South Wales
Phone: +61 2 9252 7729

#151
Seymour Centre
Category: Performing Arts,
Music Venues
Average Price: Modest
Area: Darlington
Address: Corner of City Rd And
Cleveland St Chippendale
New South Wales 2008
Phone: +61 2 9351 7944

#152
Susannah Place Museum
Category: Museum
Area: The Rocks
Address: 64 Gloucester St The Rocks
New South Wales
Phone: +61 2 9241 1893

#153
Nicholson Museum
Category: Museum
Area: Camperdown
Address: University of Sydney,
Sydney New South Wales 2006
Phone: +61 2 9351 2812

#154
The Sydney Film Festival
Category: Festival
Area: Surry Hills
Address: 59 Marlborough St Surry Hills
New South Wales 2010
Phone: +61 2 9318 0999

#155
Griffin Theatre Co
Category: Arts, Entertainment
Area: Darlinghurst
Address: 13 Craigend St Kings Cross
New South Wales 2011
Phone: +61 2 9332 1052

#156
Palace Cinemas
Category: Cinema
Area: Paddington
Address: 17 Oxford Street Paddington
New South Wales 2021
Phone: +61 2 9360 6099

#157
The Rocks Discovery Museum
Category: Museum
Area: The Rocks
Address: Kendall Lane The Rocks
New South Wales
Phone: +61 2 9240 8680

#158
Punch Gallery
Category: Art Gallery, Jewelry
Average Price: Modest
Area: Balmain
Address: 209 Darling St Balmain
New South Wales 2041
Phone: +61 2 9810 1014

#159
Belvoir St Theatre
Category: Arts, Entertainment
Area: Surry Hills
Address: Belvoir St Surry Hills
New South Wales 2010
Phone: +61 2 9698 3344

#160
Oxford Art Factory
Category: Dance Club, Art Gallery
Average Price: Modest
Area: Surry Hills
Address: 36-42 Oxford St Darlinghurst
New South Wales 2010
Phone: +61 2 9332 3711

#161
New Theatre
Category: Performing Arts
Area: Newtown
Address: 542 King St Newtown
New South Wales 2042
Phone: +61 2 9519 3403

#162
The Standard
Category: Bar, Music Venues
Area: Darlinghurst
Address: 383 Bourke Street Darlinghurst
New South Wales 2010
Phone: +61 2 9552 6333

#163
Macleay Museum
Category: Museum
Area: Camperdown
Address: Gosper Lane Camperdown
New South Wales 2050
Phone: +61 2 9351 2274

#164
Australian Ballet
Category: Opera, Ballet
Area: The Rocks
Address: 10 Hickson Rd The Rocks
New South Wales
Phone: +61 2 9252 5500

#165
Hustle & Flow Bar
Category: Bar, Music Venues
Average Price: Modest
Area: Redfern
Address: 105 Regent St Redfern
New South Wales 2016
Phone: +61 2 9310 5593

#166
The Rocks Ghost Tours
Category: Arts, Entertainment
Area: The Rocks
Address: The Rocks
New South Wales
Phone: +61 300 731 971

#167
GT's Hotel
Category: Comedy Club,
Music Venues, Pub
Average Price: Modest
Area: Surry Hills
Address: 64 Devonshire St Surry Hills
New South Wales 2010
Phone: +61 2 9211 1687

#168
Sydney Lyric
Category: Arts, Entertainment
Area: Pyrmont
Address: Pirrama Rd Pyrmont
New South Wales 2009
Phone: +61 2 9509 3600

#169
The Lansdowne
Category: Pub, Music Venues,
Pub Food
Average Price: Inexpensive
Area: Chippendale
Address: 2 - 6 City Rd Chippendale
New South Wales 2008
Phone: +61 2 8218 2333

#170
Vivid Sydney
Category: Festival, Local Flavor
Area: Sydney
Address: 88 George St The Rocks
New South Wales
Phone: +61 2 8114 2400

#171
The Bourbon
Category: Bar, American, Jazz, Blues
Average Price: Modest
Area: Potts Point
Address: 22 Darlinghurst Rd Potts Point
New South Wales 2011
Phone: +61 2 9035 8888

#172
Spectrum
Category: Music Venues, Dance Club
Area: Surry Hills
Address: 34-44 Oxford Street
Darlinghurst New South Wales 2010
Phone: +61 2 9360 1375

#173
Queen Street Studio
Category: Art Gallery
Area: Chippendale
Address: 16 Queen Street Chippendale
New South Wales 2008
Phone: +61 4 1982 5895

#174
Mils Gallery
Category: Art Gallery
Area: Surry Hills
Address: 15 Randle St Surry Hills
New South Wales 2010
Phone: +61 4 2323 7663

#175
Town Hall Hotel
Category: Pub, Pizza, Music Venues
Average Price: Modest
Area: Newtown
Address: 326 King St Newtown
New South Wales 2042
Phone: +61 2 9557 1206

#176
The Commercial
Category: Art Gallery
Area: Redfern
Address: 148 Abercrombie St Redfern
New South Wales 2016
Phone: +61 2 8096 3292

#177
Work-Shop Makery
Category: Arts, Entertainment
Area: Darlinghurst
Address: 106 Oxford St Darlinghurst
New South Wales 2010
Phone: +61 4 0561 9923

#178
Ken Done Gallery
Category: Art Gallery
Average Price: Exclusive
Area: The Rocks
Address: 5 Hickson Rd The Rocks
New South Wales
Phone: +61 2 9247 2740

#179
National Art School Gallery
Category: Art Gallery
Area: Darlinghurst
Address: Forbes St Darlinghurst
New South Wales 2010
Phone: +61 2 9339 8744

#180
King Street Gallery
Category: Art Gallery
Area: Darlinghurst
Address: G01/ 177 Williams St
Darlinghurst New South Wales 2010
Phone: +61 2 9360 9727

#181
Lucio's
Category: Italian, Art Gallery
Area: Paddington
Address: 47 Windsor St Paddington
New South Wales 2021
Phone: +61 2 9380 5996

#182
Nashville Songwriters Association International
Category: Social Club,
Area: Balmain
Address: 255 Darling St Balmain
New South Wales 2041
Phone: +61 4 1103 7678

#183
Bang! Store
Category: Art Gallery, Home Decor
Area: Potts Point
Address: 115 Macleay Street Potts Point
New South Wales 2011
Phone: +61 2 9356 4319

#184
Dendy Cinema
Category: Cinema
Area: Newtown
Address: 261-263 King St Newtown
New South Wales 2042
Phone: +61 2 8594 9000

#185
Paddington Town Hall
Category: Performing Arts, Cinema
Area: Paddington
Address: 249 Oxford St Paddington
New South Wales 2021
Phone: +61 2 9265 9189

#186
Iain Dawson Gallery
Category: Art Gallery
Area: Paddington
Address: 443 Oxford St Paddington
New South Wales 2021
Phone: +61 2 9358 4337

#187
Bonham
Category: Art Gallery, Antiques
Area: Paddington
Address: 76 Paddington Street
Paddington New South Wales 2021
Phone: +61 2 8412 2222

#188
The Greek Film Festival
Category: Festival
Area: Leichhardt
Address: 99 Norton Street Leichhardt
New South Wales 2040
Phone: +61 300 306 776

#189
Galaxy World
Category: Photography Store, Arcade
Area: Haymarket
Address: 9-13 Hay Street Haymarket
New South Wales
Phone: +61 2 9281 4543

#190
**Kadmium Art Supplies
& Architectural Store**
Category: Art Supplies, Art Gallery
Average Price: Expensive
Area: Glebe
Address: 80b Bay St Broadway
New South Wales 2581
Phone: +61 2 9212 2669

#191
Redballoon Days
Category: Arts, Entertainment
Area: Pyrmont
Address: 179 Harris St Pyrmont
New South Wales 2009
Phone: +61 300 875 500

#192
Balmain Watch House
Category: Art Gallery, Local Flavor
Area: Balmain
Address: 179 Darling St Balmain
New South Wales 2041
Phone: +61 2 9818 1454

#193
Outré Gallery
Category: Art Gallery
Average Price: Expensive
Area: Surry Hills
Address: Shop 7, 285A Crown St Surry
Hills New South Wales 2010
Phone: +61 2 9332 2776

#194
New Hampton
Category: Cocktail Bar, Winery
Average Price: Inexpensive
Area: Potts Point
Address: 15 Bayswater Rd Potts Point
New South Wales 2011
Phone: +61 2 9331 1188

#195
Glass Artists' Gallery
Category: Art Gallery
Area: Glebe
Address: 70 Glebe Point Rd Glebe
New South Wales 2037
Phone: +61 2 9552 1552

#196
Star Poker
Category: Casino
Area: Pyrmont
Address: 80 Pyrmont Street Pyrmont
New South Wales 2009
Phone: +61 2 9657 8101

#197
Spirit Gallery
Category: Local Flavor, Art Gallery
Average Price: Expensive
Area: The Rocks
Address: Shop 8, The Rocks Centre
Argyle St The Rocks New South Wales
Phone: +61 2 9247 5961

#198
Mary St Cafe
Category: Art Gallery, Coffee, Tea
Area: Surry Hills
Address: 62 Mary St Surry Hills
New South Wales 2010
Phone: +61 4 0906 9430

#199
Newtown Theatre
Category: Arts, Entertainment
Address: Crn King & Bray St Newtown
New South Wales 2042
Phone: +61 2 9519 5081

#200
Galleryeight
Category: Art Gallery
Area: Millers Point
Address: 12 Argyle Place Millers Point
New South Wales
Phone: +61 2 9247 0010

#201
Sydney Symphony Box Office
Category: Music Venues
Area: The Rocks
Address: Corner Harrington & Argyle
Streets The Rocks New South Wales
Phone: +61 2 8215 4600

#202
The Artery At Darlinghurst
Category: Art Gallery
Average Price: Expensive
Area: Darlinghurst
Address: 221 Darlinghurst Rd
Darlinghurst New South Wales 2010
Phone: +61 2 9380 8234

#203
The Hughes Gallery
Category: Art Gallery, Museum
Average Price: Exclusive
Area: Surry Hills
Address: 270 Devonshire St Surry Hills
New South Wales 2010
Phone: +61 2 9698 3200

#204
Global Gallery
Category: Art Gallery
Area: Paddington
Address: 5 Comber Street Paddington
New South Wales 2021
Phone: +61 2 9360 5728

#205
Darlo Drama
Category: Arts, Entertainment
Area: Elizabeth Bay
Address: 19 Greenknowe Ave Elizabeth
Bay New South Wales 2011
Phone: +61 4 5237 2623

#206
Michael Commerford Gallery
Average Price: Expensive
Area: Darlinghurst
Address: 16 Mclachlan St Edgecliff
New South Wales 2027
Phone: +61 2 9331 3338

#207
Paragon Hotel
Category: Pub, Sports Bar,
Music Venues
Average Price: Modest
Area: Sydney
Address: Circular Quay
New South Wales
Phone: +61 2 9241 3522

#208
Newtown Festival
Category: Festival
Area: Camperdown
Address: Bound By St, Lennox St,
Church St And Federation Rd Newtown
New South Wales 2042
Phone: +61 2 9564 7333

#209
Artsite Gallery
Category: Art Gallery
Average Price: Expensive
Area: Camperdown
Address: 165 Salisbury Rd
Camperdown
New South Wales 2050
Phone: +61 2 8095 9678

#210
The Mint
Category: Venues, Museum
Area: Sydney
Address: 10 Macquarie St NSW
New South Wales
Phone: +61 2 8239 2288

#211
Butterfield Tate Gallery
Category: Antiques, Art Gallery,
Furniture Store
Area: Waterloo
Address: 30 Wellington Street Waterloo
New South Wales 2017
Phone: +61 4 0811 2819

#212
The Butler Goode Gallery
Category: Art Gallery
Area: Paddington
Address: 223 Glenmore Rd Paddington
New South Wales 2021
Phone: +61 2 9361 0937

#213
The Moose
Category: Jazz, Blues, Bar
Average Price: Expensive
Area: Newtown
Address: 530 King St Newtown
New South Wales 2042
Phone: +61 2 9557 0072

#214
Savill Galleries
Category: Art Gallery
Area: Paddington
Address: 156 Hargrave Street
Paddington New South Wales 2021
Phone: +61 2 9327 8311

#215
White Rabbit
Category: Art Gallery
Average Price: Modest
Area: Chippendale
Address: 30 Balfour St Chippendale
New South Wales 2008
Phone: +61 2 8399 2867

#216
Object Gallery
Category: Art Gallery
Area: Surry Hills
Address: 417 Bourke St Surry Hills
New South Wales 2010
Phone: +61 2 9361 4555

#217
Docks Hotel
Category: Dance Club, Music Venues
Area: Sydney
Address: Shop 225, Harbourside Darling
Harbour New South Wales
Phone: +61 2 9280 2270

#218
Salerno Gallery
Category: Art Gallery
Average Price: Modest
Area: Glebe
Address: 70 Glebe Point Rd Glebe
New South Wales 2037
Phone: +61 2 9660 0899

#219
NG Art Gallery
Category: Art Gallery
Area: Chippendale
Address: 3 Little Queen St Chippendale
New South Wales 2008
Phone: +61 2 9318 2992

#220
Pine Street Creative Arts Centre
Category: Leisure Center, Art Gallery
Area: Chippendale
Address: 64 Pine St Chippendale
New South Wales 2008
Phone: +61 2 9245 1503

#221
Transference Healing
Category: Beauty & Spa, Bookstore
Area: Chippendale
Address: 24-26 Cleveland Street
Chippendale New South Wales 2008
Phone: +61 2 9699 5567

#222
Hermann's Bar
Category: Music Venues, Pub
Area: Darlington
Address: Corner City Road & Butlin
Avenue University of Sydney
New South Wales 2006
Phone: +61 2 9563 6000

#223
Kudos Gallery
Category: Art Gallery
Average Price: Inexpensive
Area: Paddington
Address: 6 Napier St Paddington
New South Wales 2021
Phone: +61 2 9326 0034

#224
Annandale Gallery
Category: Art Gallery
Area: Annandale
Address: 110 Trafalgar Street
Annandale New South Wales 2038
Phone: +61 9 5521 699

#225
Hypnosis Fun
Category: Arts, Entertainment
Area: Pyrmont
Address: Pyrmont
New South Wales 2009
Phone: +61 4 1928 9791

#226
Alexandria-Erskineville Bowling Club
Category: Venues, Event Space, Bowling, Social Club
Area: Erskineville
Address: 1 Fox Ave Erskineville New South Wales 2043
Phone: +61 2 9557 5749

#227
Beehive Gallery
Category: Art Gallery
Average Price: Modest
Area: Newtown
Address: Shop 1, 441-443 King St Newtown New South Wales 2042
Phone: +61 2 9550 2515

#228
Karlangu Aboriginal Art
Category: Art Gallery
Area: Sydney
Address: 129 Pitt St Sydney New South Wales
Phone: +61 2 9252 5430

#229
TAP Gallery
Category: Performing Arts, Art Gallery
Average Price: Modest
Area: Darlinghurst
Address: 278 Palmer Street Darlinghurst New South Wales 2010
Phone: +61 2 9361 0440

#230
Joans Ridge Street Art Gallery
Category: Art Gallery
Area: North Sydney
Address: 53 Ridge St North Sydney New South Wales 2060
Phone: +61 2 9922 5743

#231
Name This Bar
Category: Bar, Music Venues, Art Gallery
Area: Darlinghurst
Address: 197 Oxford St Darlinghurst New South Wales 2010
Phone: +61 2 9356 2123

#232
Rock Lily
Category: Music Venues
Average Price: Modest
Area: Pyrmont
Address: 80 Pyrmont St Pyrmont New South Wales 2009
Phone: +61 800 700 700

#233
Newtown Social Club
Category: Music Venues, Bar
Average Price: Modest
Area: Newtown
Address: 387 King St Newtown New South Wales 2042
Phone: +61 2 9550 3974

#234
Watters Gallery
Category: Art Gallery
Average Price: Exclusive
Area: Darlinghurst
Address: 109 Riley St East Sydney New South Wales 2010
Phone: +61 2 9331 2556

#235
South Sydney Rabbitohs
Category: Professional Sports Team
Area: Redfern
Address: Level 4, 265 Chalmers Street Redfern New South Wales 2016
Phone: +61 2 8306 9900

#236
DOME
Category: Dance Club, Australian, Jazz, Blues
Average Price: Modest
Area: Surry Hills
Address: Cleveland St Surry Hills New South Wales 2010
Phone: +61 2 9699 3460

#237
The Bearded Tit Bar
Category: Music Venues, Beer Bar, Wine Bar
Average Price: Modest
Area: Redfern
Address: 183 Regent St Redfern New South Wales 2016
Phone: +61 2 8283 4082

#238
Comics On The Run
Category: Arts, Entertainment
Area: Balmain
Address: 44 Evans St Balmain
New South Wales 2041
Phone: +61 4 1481 0271

#239
Kaleidoscope Gallery
Category: Art Gallery
Area: Paddington
Address: 30 O'Connor St Sydney
New South Wales
New South Wales 2008
Phone: +61 4 0477 2304

#240
Mark Hanham Gallery
Category: Art Gallery
Area: Surry Hills
Address: 342A Crown St Surry Hills
New South Wales 2010
Phone: +61 2 9358 5553

#241
Artspace Visual Arts
Category: Art Gallery
Area: Woolloomooloo
Address: 5151 Cowper Wharf Rd
Woolloomooloo
New South Wales 2011
Phone: +61 2 9356 0555

#242
Hoyts
Category: Cinema
Area: Haymarket
Address: Level 5, 187 Thomas St
Haymarket
New South Wales
Phone: +61 2 8275 6100

#243
10x8 Gallery
Category: Art Gallery
Area: Chippendale
Address: 28 Broadway Chippendale
New South Wales 2008
Phone: +61 4 1605 3665

#244
Galerie Pompom
Category: Art Gallery
Area: Chippendale
Address: 39 Abercrombie St
Chippendale
New South Wales 2008
Phone: +61 4 3031 8438

#245
Gallery 2010
Category: Art Gallery
Area: Surry Hills
Address: 69 Reservoir St Surry Hills
New South Wales 2010
Phone: +61 8 2182 100

#246
Studio Cee
Category: Art Gallery
Area: Chippendale
Address: 107b Shepherd St
Chippendale
New South Wales 2008
Phone: +61 4 0701 2578

#247
Signarture
Category: Art Gallery, Home Decor
Area: Elizabeth Bay
Address: Birtley Pl Potts Point
New South Wales 2011
Phone: +61 2 8001 6141

#248
Roslyn Oxley9 Gallery
Category: Art Gallery
Area: Paddington
Address: 8 Soudan Lane Off Hampden
St Paddington New South Wales 2021
Phone: +61 2 9331 1919

#249
Sydney Symphony
Category: Arts, Entertainment
Area: The Rocks
Address: Clocktower Sq The Rocks
New South Wales
Phone: +61 2 8215 4600

#250
Gannon House
Category: Art Gallery
Area: The Rocks
Address: 45 Argyle St The Rocks
New South Wales
Phone: +61 2 9251 4474

#251
The Rocks Pop-Up
Category: Art Gallery, Cultural Center
Area: The Rocks
Address: 71 George St The Rocks
New South Wales
Phone: +61 4 0171 3998

#252
Dominik Mersch Gallery
Category: Art Gallery
Area: Darlinghurst
Address: 75 Mclachlan Ave Rushcutters
Bay New South Wales 2011
Phone: +61 4 2330 0802

#253
Australian Theatre
For Young People
Category: Performing Arts, Special
Education
Area: Dawes Point
Address: 5 Hickson Rd Walsh Bay
New South Wales
Phone: +61 2 9270 2400

#254
Chinese Garden of Friendship
Category: Botanical Garden
Area: Sydney
Address: Pier St Darling Harbour
New South Wales
Phone: +61 2 9240 8888

#255
O Nightclub
Category: Dance Club, Music Venues
Area: Potts Point
Address: 39 Darlinghurst Rd Potts Point
New South Wales 2011
Phone: +61 2 9331 6886

#256
Reading Cinemas
Category: Cinema
Area: Haymarket
Address: Market City Shopping Centre,
Level 3, 9-13 Hay St Haymarket
New South Wales
Phone: +61 2 9280 1202

#257
The White Wall
Category: Art Gallery, Coffee, Tea
Area: Rushcutters Bay
Address: 40 Bayswater Rd Rushcutters
Bay New South Wales 2011
Phone: +61 2 8068 5015

#258
Tora Sumi
Category: Tattoo, Art Gallery
Area: Balmain
Address: 381 Darling St Balmain
New South Wales 2041
Phone: +61 2 9818 5045

#259
Public Event Group
Category: Arts, Entertainment
Area: Haymarket
Address: Haymarket
New South Wales 1240
Phone: +61 2 9399 3400

#260
Woodwind Group
Category: Musical Instruments,
Music Venues
Area: Leichhardt
Address: 111 Moore St Leichhardt
New South Wales 2040
Phone: +61 2 9564 1233

#261
Hopes & Wishes Pty
Category: Art Gallery
Area: Millers Point
Address: 12 Kent St Millers Point
New South Wales
Phone: +61 4 3152 1195

#262
MCA ARTBAR
Category: Bar, Arts, Entertainment
Area: The Rocks
Address: Circular Quay The Rocks
New South Wales
Phone: +61 2 9245 2400

#263
Brenda May Gallery
Category: Art Gallery
Area: Waterloo
Address: 2 Danks St Waterloo
New South Wales 2017
Phone: +61 2 9318 1122

#264
Sydney Rock 'N' Roll & Alternative Market
Category: Music Venues
Area: Camperdown
Address: Manning Rd Camperdown
New South Wales 2050
Phone: +61 4 1159 2378

#265
Meyer Gallery
Category: Art Gallery
Area: Darlinghurst
Address: 269 Bourke St Darlinghurst
New South Wales 2010
Phone: +61 2 9380 8014

#266
Metroscreen
Category: Arts, Entertainment
Area: Paddington
Address: Cnr Oatley Rd And Oxford St
Paddington New South Wales 2021
Phone: +61 2 9356 1818

#267
69 John St
Category: Art Gallery
Area: Leichhardt
Address: 69 John St Leichhardt
New South Wales 2040
Phone: +61 2 7901 7072

#268
Billich Gallery
Category: Art Gallery
Area: The Rocks
Address: 100 George St The Rocks
New South Wales
Phone: +61 2 9252 1481

#269
Regional Arts NSW
Category: Arts, Entertainment
Area: Dawes Point
Address: 15 Hickson Rd Walsh Bay
New South Wales
Phone: +44 29 270 2500

#270
Damien Minton Gallery
Category: Art Gallery
Area: Redfern
Address: 583 Elizabeth St Redfern
New South Wales 2016
Phone: +61 2 9699 7551

#271
Somedays
Category: Art Gallery
Area: Surry Hills
Address: 72B Fitzroy St Surry Hills
New South Wales 2010
Phone: +61 2 9331 6637

#272
Sydney Jewish Museum
Category: Museum
Area: Darlinghurst
Address: Burton St 148 Darlinghurst Rd
Darlinghurst New South Wales 2010
Phone: +61 2 9360 7999

#273
Black Eye Gallery
Category: Art Gallery
Area: Darlinghurst
Address: 3/138 Darlinghurst Rd
Darlinghurst
New South Wales 2010
Phone: +61 2 8084 7541

#274
Nicholson Museum
Category: Museum
Area: Camperdown
Address: University of Sydney
Camperdown
New South Wales 2050
Phone: +61 2 9351 2812

#275
Whisper Licensed Cafe & Cocktails
Category: Cocktail Bar, Lounge, Arts, Entertainment
Area: Potts Point
Address: 97 Darlinghurst Rd Potts Point
New South Wales 2011
Phone: +61 4 0419 4586

#276
Biennale of Sydney
Category: Art Gallery
Area: Woolloomooloo
Address: 43- 51 Cowper Wharf Rd
Woolloomooloo
New South Wales 2011
Phone: +61 2 9368 1411

#277
The Weave Arts Centre
Category: Art Gallery
Area: Eveleigh
Address: 231 Wilson St Eveleigh
New South Wales 2020
Phone: +61 2 9519 5766

#278
Elvis Weddings
Category: Arts, Entertainment
Area: Balmain
Address: Balmain
New South Wales 2041
Phone: +61 4 1425 1626

#279
Innovative Event Services
Category: Arts, Entertainment
Area: Potts Point
Address: Potts Point
New South Wales 2011
Phone: +61 2 9356 2146

#280
Defiance Gallery
Category: Art Gallery
Area: Newtown
Address: 47 Enmore Rd Newtown
New South Wales 2042
Phone: +61 2 9557 8483

#281
Samantha Lord
Category: Art Gallery
Area: Surry Hills
Address: Surry Hills
New South Wales 2010
Phone: +61 4 0999 7776

#282
Mary Place Gallery
Category: Art Gallery
Area: Paddington
Address: 12 Mary Pl Paddington
New South Wales 2021
Phone: +61 2 9332 1875

#283
Scenic Studios
Category: Arts, Entertainment
Area: Annandale
Address: Annandale
New South Wales 2038
Phone: +61 2 9660 1125

#284
Sherman Galleries
Category: Art Gallery
Area: Paddington
Address: 16-18 Goodhope St
Paddington
New South Wales 2021
Phone: +61 2 9331 1112

#285
Australian Festival Orchestra
Category: Arts, Entertainment
Area: Paddington
Address: Paddington
New South Wales 2021
Phone: +61 2 9360 2771

#286
**Richard Stuart Theatre
And Production Consultant**
Category: Arts, Entertainment
Area: Leichhardt
Address: Leichhardt
New South Wales 2040
Phone: +61 2 6687 5809

#287
STE Australia Pty
Category: Arts, Entertainment
Area: Leichhardt
Address: 28 Easter St Leichhardt
New South Wales 2040
Phone: +61 2 9564 0106

#288
Steki Taverna
Category: Greek, Music Venues
Area: Newtown
Address: 2 O'Connell St Newtown
New South Wales 2042
Phone: +61 2 9516 2191

#289
Dendy Cinemas Opera Quays
Category: Cinema
Address: 2 E Circular Quay The Rocks
New South Wales
Phone: +61 2 9247 3800

#290
Poole's Rock Wines Pty
Category: Winery
Area: Pyrmont
Address: Level 4, Building B 35
Saunders St Pyrmont
New South Wales 2009
Phone: +61 2 9563 2500

#291
Inner City Clayworkers Gallery
Category: Art Gallery
Area: Glebe
Address: St Johns Rd Glebe
New South Wales 2037
Phone: +61 2 9692 9717

#292
Greg Wilson Gallery
Category: Art Gallery
Area: Chippendale
Address: 107A Shepherd St
Chippendale New South Wales 2008
Phone: +61 2 8399 3708

#293
Iain Howells Art Gallery & Studio
Category: Art Gallery
Area: Balmain
Address: 230 Darling St Balmain
New South Wales 2041
Phone: +61 2 9818 1671

#294
Caramell Dance Entertainment
Category: Arts, Entertainment
Area: Annandale
Address: 78 Pyrmont Bridge Rd
Camperdown
New South Wales 2050
Phone: +61 2 9557 0886

#295
Breathing Colours Gallery
Category: Art Gallery
Area: Balmain
Address: 446 Darling St Balmain
New South Wales 2041
Phone: +61 2 9555 8543

#296
Carriageworks
Category: Venues, Event Space,
Opera, Ballet
Area: Eveleigh
Address: 245 Wilson St Eveleigh
New South Wales 2020
Phone: +61 2 8571 9099

#297
Girls Night Afloat
Category: Arts, Entertainment
Address: Harbourside Jetty
Darling Harbour
New South Wales
Phone: +61 2 9822 5006

#298
**Gavala Aboriginal Art
& Culture Pty**
Category: Art Gallery
Area: Sydney
Address: Shop 131 Harbourside Darling
Harbour New South Wales
Phone: +61 2 9212 7232

#299
**Horus & Deloris
Contemporary Art Space**
Category: Art Gallery
Area: Pyrmont
Address: 102 Pyrmont St Pyrmont
New South Wales 2009
Phone: +61 2 9660 6071

#300
Fairy Fun
Category: Arts, Entertainment
Area: Pyrmont
Address: 2 Wattle Crs Pyrmont
New South Wales 2009
Phone: +61 2 9660 0572

#301
APRA
Category: Arts, Entertainment,
Music, DVDs
Area: Ultimo
Address: 16 Mountain St Ultimo
New South Wales 2007
Phone: +61 2 9935 7900

#302
Gallery Adagio
Category: Art Gallery
Area: Glebe
Address: 91 Glebe Point Rd Glebe
New South Wales 2037
Phone: +61 2 9552 2833

#303
GIG Gallery
Category: Art Gallery
Area: Glebe
Address: 70A Glebe Point Rd Glebe
New South Wales 2037
Phone: +61 2 9660 2785

#304
L3 Central
Category: Art Gallery
Area: Chippendale
Address: 28 Broadway Ultimo
New South Wales 2007
Phone: +61 4 1982 5895

#305
N.S.W. Chess Association
Category: Social Club
Area: Surry Hills
Address: 72 Campbell St Surry Hills
New South Wales 2010
Phone: +61 2 9211 2994

#306
Chess Centre of N.S.W.
Category: Social Club
Area: Surry Hills
Address: 72 Campbell St Surry Hills
New South Wales 2010
Phone: +61 2 9211 2994

#307
Attic Studio
Category: Arts, Entertainment
Area: Glebe
Address: 100 Wigram La Glebe
New South Wales 2037
Phone: +61 2 9518 4615

#308
**Dept of Government
Transport Social Club**
Category: Social Club
Area: Chippendale
Address: 19-25 Regent St Chippendale
New South Wales 2008
Phone: +61 2 9699 8063

#309
Greater Union Organisation Pty
Category: Cinema
Area: Sydney
Address: Head Office Level 20, 227
Elizabeth St NSW New South Wales
Phone: +61 2 9373 6600

#310
Teachers Club
Category: Social Club
Area: Surry Hills
Address: 33 Mary St Surry Hills
New South Wales 2010
Phone: +61 2 9217 2440

#311
Phoenician Club of Aust
Category: Social Club
Area: Chippendale
Address: 173 Broadway St Broadway
New South Wales 2007
Phone: +61 2 9212 5955

#312
Frisbee Club
Category: Social Club
Area: Chippendale
Address: Sydney University Broadway
New South Wales 2007
Phone: +61 2 9351 4960

#313
Theatre Ink
Category: Arts, Entertainment
Area: Millers Point
Address: 7A Agar Steps NSW
New South Wales
Phone: +61 2 9251 5745

#314
Bridge Association of NSW
Category: Social Club
Area: Surry Hills
Address: Level 1 162 Goulburn St East
Sydney New South Wales 2010
Phone: +61 2 9264 8111

#315
Bank Gallery
Category: Art Gallery
Area: Surry Hills
Address: 21 Oxford St Darlinghurst
New South Wales 2010
Phone: +61 2 9261 5692

#316
**Sydney University Women's
Taekwondo**
Category: Social Club
Area: Chippendale
Address: Sydney University Broadway
New South Wales 2007
Phone: +61 2 9351 4960

#317
The Individual Wig
Category: Arts, Entertainment
Area: Surry Hills
Address: 32 Oxford St Darlinghurst
New South Wales 2010
Phone: +61 2 9332 2112

#318
Living Art Gallery
Category: Art Gallery
Area: Chippendale
Address: 1 Meagher St Chippendale
New South Wales 2008
Phone: +61 2 9698 3310

#319
Honey Ant Gallery
Category: Art Gallery
Area: Glebe
Address: 143 St Johns Rd Glebe
New South Wales 2037
Phone: +61 2 8084 2410

#320
**Harrington Street Artists
Co-op Gallery**
Category: Art Gallery
Area: Chippendale
Address: 17 Meagher St Chippendale
New South Wales 2008
Phone: +61 2 9319 7378

#321
Greg Wilson Art Gallery
Category: Art Gallery
Area: Chippendale
Address: 107A Shepherd St
Chippendale
New South Wales 2008
Phone: +61 2 9698 1935

#322
Unicorn Gallery
Category: Art Gallery
Area: Chippendale
Address: 25 Meagher St Chippendale
New South Wales 2008
Phone: +61 2 9699 1029

#323
Peloton Incorporation
Category: Art Gallery
Area: Chippendale
Address: 25 Meagher St Chippendale
New South Wales 2008
Phone: +61 2 9690 2601

#324
Multiple Box
Category: Art Gallery
Area: Darlinghurst
Address: 99 Crown St Waterloo
New South Wales 2017
Phone: +61 2 9690 0213

#325
Gallery 41
Category: Art Gallery
Area: Woolloomooloo
Address: 41 Riley St Woolloomooloo
New South Wales 2011
Phone: +61 4 0822 6827

#326
Encompass
Category: Arts, Entertainment
Area: Darlinghurst
Address: Level 2, 181 Riley St
Darlinghurst New South Wales 2010
Phone: +61 2 8335 7200

#327
Liverpool Street Gallery
Category: Art Gallery
Area: Darlinghurst
Address: 243A Liverpool St East
Sydney New South Wales 2010
Phone: +61 2 8353 7799

#328
Bottland Gallery of Modern Art
Category: Art Gallery
Area: Surry Hills
Address: 249 Riley St Surry Hills
New South Wales 2010
Phone: +61 2 9212 7384

#329
Showcase Gallery
Category: Art Gallery
Area: Darlinghurst
Address: 82 William St Darlinghurst
New South Wales 2010
Phone: +61 4 2629 8884

#330
Kenja Social & Sporting Club
Category: Social Club
Area: Surry Hills
Address: 243 Commonwealth St Surry
Hills New South Wales 2010
Phone: +61 2 9281 7122

#331
First Draft Inc
Category: Art Gallery
Area: Surry Hills
Address: 116 Chalmers St Surry Hills
New South Wales 2010
Phone: +61 2 9698 3665

#332
Galerie d'Art
Category: Art Gallery
Area: Woolloomooloo
Address: 102 Cathedral St
Woolloomooloo
New South Wales 2011
Phone: +61 2 9331 0099

#333
United Galleries
Category: Art Gallery
Area: Darlinghurst
Address: 179-181 Palmer St
Darlinghurst
New South Wales 2010
Phone: +61 2 8915 5300

#334
The Comedy Collective
Category: Comedy Club
Area: Forest Lodge
Address: 115 Wigram Rd Glebe
New South Wales 2037
Phone: +61 2 9552 2999

#335
Darlinghurst Theatre Co.
Category: Performing Arts,
Area: Darlinghurst
Address: 39 Burton St Darlinghurst
New South Wales 2010
Phone: +61 2 9331 3107

#336
Tin Sheds Gallery
Category: Art Gallery
Area: Darlington
Address: 154 City Rd Chippendale
New South Wales 2008
Phone: +61 2 9351 3115

#337
New Guinea Gallery
Category: Art Gallery
Area: Surry Hills
Address: 34 Buckingham St Surry Hills
New South Wales 2010
Phone: +61 2 9310 1118

#338
Line Models
Category: Performing Arts
Area: Surry Hills
Address: 8/285a Crown St Surry Hills
New South Wales 2010
Phone: +61 2 9880 8601

#339
Buckingham House
Category: Social Club
Area: Surry Hills
Address: 45 Buckingham St Surry Hills
New South Wales 2010
Phone: +61 2 9698 8116

#340
Authentic Aboriginal Art
Category: Art Gallery
Area: The Rocks
Address: 45 Argyle St The Rocks
New South Wales
Phone: +61 2 9251 4474

#341
Constable & Hershon Vineyards
Category: Winery
Area: Surry Hills
Address: 432 Elizabeth St Surry Hills
New South Wales 2010
Phone: +61 2 9318 0400

#342
Australian Art Connection
Category: Art Gallery
Area: The Rocks
Address: 12 Playfair St The Rocks
New South Wales
Phone: +61 2 9247 7037

#343
Galleries Direct
Category: Art Gallery
Area: Surry Hills
Address: 129 Devonshire St Surry Hills
New South Wales 2010
Phone: +61 2 9318 7600

#344
Harold Park Paceway
Category: Venues, Event Space,
Social Club
Area: Forest Lodge
Address: Ross St Glebe
New South Wales 2037
Phone: +61 2 9660 3688

#345
NSW Harness Racing Club
Category: Social Club
Area: Forest Lodge
Address: Ross St Glebe
New South Wales 2037
Phone: +61 2 9660 3688

#346
S. H. Ervin Gallery
Category: Art Gallery
Area: Millers Point
Address: Watsons Rd Millers Point
New South Wales
Phone: +61 2 9258 0173

#347
Seductive Art
Gallery By Avi Ohana
Category: Art Gallery
Area: The Rocks
Address: Nurses Wlk The Rocks
New South Wales
Phone: +61 300 882 022

#348
Chalk Horse
Category: Art Gallery
Area: Surry Hills
Address: 8 Lacey St Surry Hills
New South Wales 2010
Phone: +61 2 9211 8999

#349
Ken Duncan Panographs
Category: Art Gallery
Area: The Rocks
Address: 73 George St The Rocks
New South Wales
Phone: +61 2 9241 3460

#350
Theatresports Incorporated
Category: Arts, Entertainment
Area: Surry Hills
Address: Lvl 1, 397 Riley St Surry Hills
New South Wales 2010
Phone: +61 2 9281 7666

#351
Under Water
Category: Art Gallery
Area: Surry Hills
Address: 61 Buckingham St Surry Hills
New South Wales 2010
Phone: +61 2 9699 6610

#352
Glamarama Gallery
Category: Art Gallery
Area: Balmain
Address: 24 Buchanan St Balmain
New South Wales 2041
Phone: +61 300 666 871

#353
Swing Gallery
Category: Art Gallery
Area: Balmain
Address: 24 Buchanan St Balmain
New South Wales 2041
Phone: +61 300 855 520

#354
Perve Gallery
Category: Art Gallery
Area: Balmain
Address: 24 Buchanan St Balmain
New South Wales 2041
Phone: +61 300 666 462

#355
Craft NSW
Category: Art Gallery
Area: The Rocks
Address: 104 George St The Rocks
New South Wales
Phone: +61 2 9241 5825

#356
Arts & Crafts of NSW Society
Category: Art Gallery
Area: The Rocks
Address: 104 George St The Rocks
New South Wales
Phone: +61 2 9241 5825

#357
Feel Good Intro
Category: Social Club
Area: Balmain
Address: 149/20 Buchanan St Balmain
New South Wales 2041
Phone: +61 4 2756 0963

#358
Eastern Suburbs Art Gallery
Category: Art Gallery
Area: Darlinghurst
Address: 1 Flinders St Darlinghurst
New South Wales 2010
Phone: +61 2 9360 6373

#359
Hire A Fortune Teller
Category: Event Planning, Service
Area: The Rocks
Address: 41 George St The Rocks
New South Wales
Phone: +61 2 9247 4982

#360
The Bell Shakespeare Company
Category: Arts, Entertainment
Area: The Rocks
Address: Level 1, 88 George St NSW
New South Wales
Phone: +61 2 9241 2722

#361
Ian Howell's Art Gallery & Studio
Category: Art Gallery
Area: Balmain
Address: 230 Darling St Balmain
New South Wales 2041
Phone: +61 4 1638 8097

#362
Robin Gibson Galleries
Category: Art Gallery
Area: Darlinghurst
Address: 278 Liverpool St Darlinghurst
New South Wales 2010
Phone: +61 2 9331 6692

#363
Gibson Gallery Pty
Category: Art Gallery
Area: Darlinghurst
Address: 278 Liverpool St Darlinghurst
New South Wales 2010
Phone: +61 2 9331 6692

#364
ATYP
Category: Performing Arts,
Area: Dawes Point
Address: 5 Hickson Rd Walsh Bay
New South Wales
Phone: +61 2 9270 2400

#365
Grosvenor Club
Category: Social Club
Area: Darlinghurst
Address: 40 Flinders St Darlinghurst
New South Wales 2010
Phone: +61 2 9331 4256

#366
King Street Gallery
Category: Art Gallery
Area: Darlinghurst
Address: 177 Williams St Darlinghurst
New South Wales 2010
Phone: +61 2 9360 9727

#367
King St Studios Pty
Category: Art Gallery
Area: Darlinghurst
Address: 177 William St Darlinghurst
New South Wales 2010
Phone: +61 2 9360 1655

#368
Gallery 9
Category: Art Gallery
Area: Darlinghurst
Address: 9 Darley St Darlinghurst
New South Wales 2010
Phone: +61 2 9380 9909

#369
Boutwell Draper Gallery
Category: Art Gallery
Area: Redfern
Address: 82 George St Redfern
New South Wales 2016
Phone: +61 2 9310 5662

#370
Big Rig Diner
Category: Social Club
Area: Darlinghurst
Address: 231 Oxford St Darlinghurst
New South Wales 2010
Phone: +61 2 9326 0044

#371
De Norm
Category: Social Club
Area: Darlinghurst
Address: 231 Oxford St Darlinghurst
New South Wales 2010
Phone: +61 2 9326 0044

#372
Old Fitzroy Theatre
Category: Cinema
Area: Woolloomooloo
Address: 129 Dowling St
New South Wales 2011
Phone: +61 4 2803 2838

#373
Sacha Gallery
Category: Art Gallery
Area: Surry Hills
Address: 194 Albion St Surry Hills
New South Wales 2010
Phone: +61 2 9332 3700

#374
Aboriginal Art Gellery The Rocks
Category: Art Gallery
Area: Dawes Point
Address: 15 Hickson Rd The Rocks
New South Wales
Phone: +61 2 9252 0044

#375
Garry Mcewan Gallery
Category: Art Gallery
Area: Darlinghurst
Address: 136A A Darlinghurst Rd
New South Wales 2010
Phone: +61 2 9356 4319

#376
**Charles Hewitt Gallery
& Framing Showroom**
Category: Framing, Art Gallery
Area: Paddington
Address: 335 South Dowling St
Darlinghurst
New South Wales 2010
Phone: +61 2 9331 4988

#377
Sacha Gallery
Category: Art Gallery
Area: Surry Hills
Address: 497 Crown St Surry Hills
New South Wales 2010
Phone: +61 4 1200 0117

#378
Barbra Streisand Fan Club
Category: Social Club
Area: Woolloomooloo
Address: 10 Dowling St
New South Wales 2011
Phone: +61 2 9356 4290

#379
Steven Spielberg Fan Club
Category: Social Club
Area: Woolloomooloo
Address: 10 Dowling St
New South Wales 2011
Phone: +61 2 9356 4290

#380
Robin Williams Fan Club
Category: Social Club
Area: Woolloomooloo
Address: Unit 14/ 10 Dowling St
New South Wales 2011
Phone: +61 2 9356 4290

#381
SBW Stables Theatre
Category: Performing Arts
Area: Darlinghurst
Address: 10 Nimrod St Darlinghurst
New South Wales 2010
Phone: +61 2 9361 3817

#382
Now Actors Management
Category: Arts, Entertainment
Area: Surry Hills
Address: 529A Crown St Surry Hills
New South Wales 2010
Phone: +61 2 9318 2544

#383
Legge Gallery
Area: Redfern
Address: 183 Regent St Redfern
New South Wales 2016
Phone: +61 2 9319 3340

#384
O2 Speakers
Category: Music Venues
Area: Balmain
Address: 101 Mort St Balmain
New South Wales 2041
Phone: +61 2 9818 5199

#385
**Museums & Galleries
Foundations of NSW**
Category: Art Gallery
Area: Woolloomooloo
Address: Cowper Wharf Rd
New South Wales 2011
Phone: +61 2 9358 3433

#386
**Regional Galleries
Association of NSW**
Category: Art Gallery
Area: Woolloomooloo
Address: Cowper Wharf Rd
New South Wales 2011
Phone: +61 2 9358 3433

#387
Maree Mizon Galleries
Category: Art Gallery
Area: Paddington
Address: 76 Glenmore Rd
New South Wales 2021
Phone: +61 2 9358 5050

#388
SMA Entertainment By Design
Category: Performing Arts
Area: Potts Point
Address: Minton House 2-14, Bayswater
Rd Potts Point New South Wales 2011
Phone: +61 300 884 428

#389
**Australian Exhibitions
Touring Agency**
Category: Art Gallery
Area: Woolloomooloo
Address: The Gunnery Cowper Wharf
Rd New South Wales 2011
Phone: +61 2 9358 3418

#390
Dancers Cabaret
Category: Arts, Entertainment
Area: Potts Point
Address: 33 Bayswater Rd Kings Cross
New South Wales 2011
Phone: +61 2 9368 0488

#391
Galerie Des Arts
Category: Art Gallery
Area: Balmain
Address: 38 Montague St Balmain
New South Wales 2041
Phone: +61 2 9818 5279

#392
Alaras N T
Category: Social Club
Area: Surry Hills
Address: 662 Crown St Surry Hills
New South Wales 2010
Phone: +61 2 9319 4052

#393
Australian Naive Art
Category: Art Gallery
Area: Paddington
Address: 43 Greens Rd Paddington
New South Wales 2021
Phone: +61 2 9360 3015

#394
Clune Galleries
Category: Art Gallery
Area: Potts Point
Address: 30 Victoria St Potts Point
New South Wales 2011
Phone: +61 2 9357 3755

#395
Garry Mcewan Gallery
Category: Art Gallery
Area: Potts Point
Address: 115 Macleay St Potts Point
New South Wales 2011
Phone: +61 2 9356 4319

#396
James Dorahy Project Space
Category: Art Gallery
Area: Potts Point
Address: 111 Macleay St Potts Point
New South Wales 2011
Phone: +61 2 9358 2585

#397
The Cross Art Projects
Category: Art Gallery
Area: Potts Point
Address: 8 Llankelly La Kings Cross
New South Wales 2011
Phone: +61 2 9357 2058

#398
Gallery Savah
Category: Art Gallery
Area: Paddington
Address: 20 Glenmore Rd
New South Wales 2021
Phone: +61 2 9360 9979

#399
**Newtown Rugby League
Football Club**
Category: Social Club
Area: Redfern
Address: 249 Chalmers St Redfern
New South Wales 2016
Phone: +61 2 9698 4460

#400
Barry Stern Galleries Pty
Category: Art Gallery
Area: Paddington
Address: 19 Glenmore Rd
New South Wales 2021
Phone: +61 2 9331 4676

#401
Balmain Rowing Club
Category: Social Club
Area: Balmain
Address: Lower White St Balmain
New South Wales 2041
Phone: +61 2 9810 3400

#402
Bloomin' Arty
Category: Art Gallery
Area: Elizabeth Bay
Address: 28 Macleay St Potts Point
New South Wales 2011
Phone: +61 2 8011 4572

#403
Glebe Women's Sports
Category: Social Club
Area: Annandale
Address: 92 Nelson St Annandale
New South Wales 2038
Phone: +61 2 9566 2419

#404
Sara Roney Gallery
Category: Art Gallery
Area: Darlinghurst
Address: 19A Boundary St Rushcutters
Bay New South Wales 2011
Phone: +61 2 9361 0061

#405
Jane Austen Society of Aust
Category: Social Club
Area: Paddington
Address: 26 Macdonald St Paddington
New South Wales 2021
Phone: +61 2 9380 5894

#406
Sydney Bowmen
Category: Social Club
Area: Paddington
Address: 107 Glenmore Rd Paddington
New South Wales 2021
Phone: +61 2 8356 9176

#407
Dennis Baker Galleries
Category: Art Gallery
Area: Paddington
Address: 37 Macdonald St Paddington
New South Wales 2021
Phone: +61 2 9360 1872

#408
Freeland Gallery
Category: Art Gallery
Area: Paddington
Address: 120 Glenmore Rd Paddington
New South Wales 2021
Phone: +61 2 9360 2541

#409
The Marquee Venue
Category: Social Club
Area: Annandale
Address: 128 Pyrmont Bridge Rd
Camperdown New South Wales 2050
Phone: +61 2 9557 0221

#410
Stills Gallery
Category: Art Gallery
Area: Paddington
Address: 36 Gosbell St Paddington
New South Wales 2021
Phone: +61 2 9331 7775

#411
Gallery Loiuse
Category: Art Gallery
Area: Waterloo
Address: 639 Elizabeth St Waterloo
New South Wales 2017
Phone: +61 2 9319 3228

#412
Michael Reid Gallery
Category: Art Gallery
Area: Rushcutters Bay
Address: 44 Roslyn Gardns Elizabeth
Bay New South Wales 2011
Phone: +61 2 8353 3500

#413
Art House Gallery
Category: Art Gallery
Area: Darlinghurst
Address: 66 Mclachlan Ave Rushcutters
Bay New South Wales 2011
Phone: +61 2 9332 1019

#414
Noon Moon Framing Gallery
Category: Framing, Art Gallery
Area: Newtown
Address: 228 King St Newtown
New South Wales 2042
Phone: +61 2 9516 1700

#415
Utopia Art Sydney
Category: Art Gallery
Area: Waterloo
Address: 2 Danks St Waterloo
New South Wales 2017
Phone: +61 2 9699 2900

#416
Aboriginal & Pacific Art
Category: Art Gallery
Area: Waterloo
Address: 2 Danks St Waterloo
New South Wales 2017
Phone: +61 2 9699 2211

#417
Kirman Traders & Hestian Pty
Category: Art Gallery
Area: Paddington
Address: 18 Goodhope St Paddington
New South Wales 2021
Phone: +61 2 9331 1112

#418
Agathon Galleries
Category: Art Gallery
Area: Waterloo
Address: 1D Danks St Waterloo
New South Wales 2017
Phone: +61 2 8399 1888

#419
Bass Tom Sculpture Studio School
Category: Art Gallery
Area: Erskineville
Address: 1A Clara St Erskineville
New South Wales 2043
Phone: +61 2 9565 4851

#420
Artbank
Category: Art Gallery
Area: Waterloo
Address: 198-222 Young St Waterloo
New South Wales 2017
Phone: +61 2 9662 8011

#421
Brian Moore Gallery Pty
Category: Art Gallery
Area: Paddington
Address: 294 Glenmore Rd Paddington
New South Wales 2021
Phone: +61 2 9380 7100

#422
Starrs Productions
Category: Arts, Entertainment
Area: Erskineville
Address: 4 Baldwin St Erskineville
New South Wales 2043
Phone: +61 2 9519 2011

#423
Eddie Glastra Gallery
Category: Art Gallery
Area: Paddington
Address: 44 Gurner St Paddington
New South Wales 2021
Phone: +61 2 9331 6477

#424
Epiphany International Artists
Category: Arts, Entertainment
Area: Annandale
Address: 58 Young St Annandale
New South Wales 2038
Phone: +61 2 9572 7222

#425
Breenspace Pty
Category: Art Gallery
Area: Waterloo
Address: 289 Young St Waterloo
New South Wales 2017
Phone: +61 2 9690 0555

#426
Chase Contemporary & Tribal Art
Category: Art Gallery
Area: Annandale
Address: 2- 4 Annandale St Annandale
New South Wales 2038
Phone: +61 2 9560 4881

#427
Powell Kenny
Category: Arts, Entertainment
Area: Annandale
Address: 132 Albion St Annandale
New South Wales 2038
Phone: +61 2 9560 5335

#428
Christopher & Anna Thorpe Tribal Art
Category: Art Gallery
Area: Paddington
Address: 2 Cascade St Paddington
New South Wales 2021
Phone: +61 2 9331 8302

#429
Darren Knight Gallery
Category: Art Gallery
Area: Waterloo
Address: 840 Elizabeth St Waterloo
New South Wales 2017
Phone: +61 2 9699 5353

#430
Seek Fine Art
Category: Art Gallery
Area: Paddington
Address: Ste3/Grnd Flr 8 Soudan
La Paddington New South Wales 2021
Phone: +61 2 9360 2248

#431
Gallery of Fools
Category: Art Gallery
Area: Paddington
Address: 3 Elizabeth St Paddington
New South Wales 2021
Phone: +61 2 9360 7806

#432
Kaliman Gallery
Category: Art Gallery
Area: Paddington
Address: 56 Sutherland St Paddington
New South Wales 2021
Phone: +61 2 9357 2273

#433
Olsen Carr Art Dealers
Category: Art Gallery
Area: Paddington
Address: 76 Paddington St Paddington
New South Wales 2021
Phone: +61 2 9360 9854

#434
Iain Dawson Gallery
Category: Art Gallery
Area: Paddington
Address: 72A Windsor St Paddington
New South Wales 2021
Phone: +61 2 9358 4337

#435
All Stars Performing Arts
Category: Arts, Entertainment
Area: North Sydney
Address: 181 Blues Point Rd North
Sydney New South Wales 2059
Phone: +61 4 0025 5782

#436
Jensen Gallery
Category: Art Gallery
Area: Paddington
Address: 3-5 Caledonia St Paddington
New South Wales 2021
Phone: +61 2 8964 9461

#437
Aboriginal & Oceanic Arts
Category: Antiques, Art Gallery
Area: Paddington
Address: 64 Elizabeth St Paddington
New South Wales 2021
Phone: +61 2 9328 2512

#438
Sydney Bus Museum
Category: Museum
Area: Leichhardt
Address: 25 Derbyshire Rd Leichhardt
New South Wales 2040
Phone: +61 2 9572 6789

#439
Studio of Artists
Category: Art Gallery
Area: Newtown
Address: 500 King St Newtown
New South Wales 2042
Phone: +61 2 9550 6011

#440
Ceramica Etc
Category: Art Gallery
Area: Newtown
Address: 475 King St Newtown
New South Wales 2042
Phone: +61 2 9550 6057

#441
Megadeck
Category: Arts, Entertainment
Area: Erskineville
Address: 1 Goddard St Erskineville
New South Wales 2043
Phone: +61 2 9550 3459

#442
Windsor Art Gallery
Category: Art Gallery
Area: Paddington
Address: 118B Windsor St Paddington
New South Wales 2021
Phone: +61 2 9328 6013

#443
Sydney Junior Rugby Union
Category: Social Club
Area: North Sydney
Address: 25 Myrtle St Crows Nest
New South Wales 2065
Phone: +61 2 9957 4258

#444
Ardt Gallery
Category: Art Gallery
Area: Leichhardt
Address: 126 Balmain Rd Leichhardt
New South Wales 2040
Phone: +61 2 9569 6538

#445
Marble Museum
Category: Art Gallery
Area: Newtown
Address: 547 King St Newtown
New South Wales 2042
Phone: +61 2 9517 2496

#446
Galleries Primitif
Category: Art Gallery
Area: Paddington
Address: 174 Jersey Rd Woollahra
New South Wales 2025
Phone: +61 2 9363 3115

#447
Associazione Puglia
Category: Social Club
Area: Leichhardt
Address: 65 Renwick St Leichhardt
New South Wales 2040
Phone: +61 2 9569 3082

#448
Pochoir Gallery & Frames Pty
Category: Art Gallery
Area: North Sydney
Address: 77 Berry St North Sydney
New South Wales 2060
Phone: +61 2 9922 2843

#449
Pochoir Gallery
Category: Art Gallery
Area: North Sydney
Address: 77 Berry St North Sydney
New South Wales 2060
Phone: +61 2 9922 2843

#450
Boomerang Aboriginal Art Gallery
Category: Art Gallery
Area: North Sydney
Address: 201 Miller St North Sydney
New South Wales 2060
Phone: +61 2 9959 2238

TOP 500 NIGHTLIFE

The Most Recommended by Locals & Trevelers

(From #1 to #500)

#1
Opera Bar
Category: Lounge
Average Price: Expensive
Area: Sydney
Address: Lower Concourse Level
Sydney
New South Wales
Phone: +61 2 9247 1666

#2
Mojo Music
Category: Bar, Vinyl Records
Average Price: Modest
Area: Sydney
Address: 73 York St Sydney
New South Wales
Phone: +61 2 9262 4999

#3
Since I Left You
Category: Lounge, Wine Bar
Average Price: Modest
Area: Sydney
Address: 338 Kent St Sydney
New South Wales
Phone: +61 2 9262 4986

#4
Grandma's Bar
Category: Cocktail Bar
Average Price: Modest
Area: Sydney
Address: 275 Clarence St Sydney
New South Wales
Phone: +61 2 9264 3004

#5
Rockpool Bar & Grill
Category: Bar, Australian, Australian
Average Price: Exclusive
Area: Sydney
Address: 66 Hunter St Sydney
New South Wales
Phone: +61 2 8078 1900

#6
Goodgod Small Club
Category: Bar, American, Music Venues
Average Price: Inexpensive
Area: Sydney
Address: 55 Liverpool St Sydney
New South Wales
Phone: +61 8 0840 587

#7
Stitch Bar
Category: Burgers, Hot Dogs,
Cocktail Bar
Average Price: Expensive
Area: Sydney
Address: 61 York St Sydney
New South Wales
Phone: +61 2 9279 0380

#8
The SG
Category: Bar
Average Price: Modest
Area: Sydney
Address: 32 York St Sydney
New South Wales
Phone: +61 4 0281 3035

#9
The Bar At The End of The Wharf
Category: Bar
Average Price: Modest
Area: Dawes Point
Address: Hickson Rd Sydney
New South Wales
Phone: +61 2 9250 1761

#10
Blu Bar On 36
Category: Bar
Average Price: Expensive
Area: The Rocks
Address: Level 36, 176 Cumberland
Street Sydney New South Wales
Phone: +61 2 9250 6000

#11
3 Wise Monkeys Pub
Category: Pub, Gastropub
Average Price: Modest
Area: Sydney
Address: 555 George St Sydney
New South Wales
Phone: +61 2 9283 5855

#12
Bambini Trust Cafe
& Wine Room
Category: Café, European, Wine Bar
Average Price: Expensive
Area: Sydney
Address: 185 Elizabeth St Sydney
New South Wales
Phone: +61 2 9283 7098

#13
Rabbit Hole Bar & Dining
Category: Australian, Cocktail Bar
Average Price: Expensive
Area: Sydney
Address: 82 Elizabeth St Sydney
New South Wales
Phone: +61 2 8084 2505

#14
The Rook
Category: Bar, Burgers
Average Price: Modest
Area: Sydney
Address: 56-58 York St Sydney
New South Wales
Phone: +61 2 9262 2505

#15
Uncle Ming's Bar
Category: Bar
Average Price: Modest
Area: Sydney
Address: 55 York Street Sydney
New South Wales
Phone: +61 4 3820 2272

#16
Palmer & Co.
Category: Bar
Average Price: Expensive
Area: Sydney
Address: Abercrombie Ln Sydney
New South Wales
Phone: +61 2 9240 3000

#17
Cantina Bar & Grill
Category: Bar, American
Area: Balmain
Address: 350 Darling Street Sydney
New South Wales 2041
Phone: +61 2 9357 3033

#18
Earl's Juke Joint
Category: Bar
Average Price: Modest
Area: Newtown
Address: 407 King St Sydney
New South Wales 2042
Phone: +61 2 9000 0000

#19
Opera Kitchen
Category: Nightlife, Burgers
Average Price: Modest
Area: Sydney
Address: Bennelong Pt Sydney
New South Wales
Phone: +61 4 5009 9888

#20
Small Bar
Category: Bar
Area: Sydney
Address: 48 Erskine St Sydney
New South Wales
Phone: +61 2 9279 0782

#21
The Basement
Category: Jazz, Blues, Bar,
Music Venues
Average Price: Modest
Area: Sydney
Address: 7 Macquarie Place Sydney
New South Wales
Phone: +61 2 9251 2797

#22
Bar Tapavino
Category: Spanish, Bar
Average Price: Expensive
Area: Sydney
Address: 6 Bulletin Pl Sydney
New South Wales
Phone: +61 2 9247 3221

#23
360 Bar And Restaurant
Category: Bar, European
Average Price: Exclusive
Area: Sydney
Address: Reception Level 4, Sydney
Westfield Centre Sydney
New South Wales
Phone: +61 2 8223 3883

#24
La Rosa
Category: Pizza, Italian, Wine Bar
Average Price: Modest
Area: Sydney
Address: 193 Pitt St Sydney
New South Wales
Phone: +61 2 9223 1674

#25
The Foxhole
Category: Bar, Café
Average Price: Modest
Area: Sydney
Address: 68A Erskine Street Sydney
New South Wales
Phone: +61 2 9279 4969

#26
The Grasshopper Bar
Category: Lounge
Average Price: Expensive
Area: Sydney
Address: 1 Temperance Ln Sydney
New South Wales
Phone: +61 2 9947 9025

#27
The Macquarie Hotel
Category: Pub, Pub Food, Beer Bar,
Jazz, Blues, Brewerie
Area: Surry Hills
Address: 40-44 Wentworth Ave Sydney
New South Wales
Phone: +61 2 8262 8888

#28
The Arthouse Hotel
Category: Bar, Music Venues, Australian
Average Price: Expensive
Area: Sydney
Address: 275 Pitt St Sydney
New South Wales
Phone: +61 2 9284 1200

#29
Pool Club
Category: Bar
Average Price: Expensive
Area: Sydney
Address: 320 George St Sydney
New South Wales
Phone: +61 2 9254 8000

#30
The Sugarmill
Category: Bar
Average Price: Modest
Area: Potts Point
Address: 37 Darlinghurst Rd Sydney
New South Wales 2011
Phone: +61 2 9368 7333

#31
Zeta Bar
Category: Hotel, Cocktail Bar
Average Price: Expensive
Area: Sydney
Address: 488 George St Sydney
New South Wales
Phone: +61 2 9265 6070

#32
Jacksons On George
Category: Venues, Event Space, Pub
Average Price: Modest
Area: Sydney
Address: 176 George St Sydney
New South Wales
Phone: +61 2 9247 2727

#33
Mizuya
Category: Japanese, Karaoke
Average Price: Modest
Area: Sydney
Address: 614 George St Sydney
New South Wales
Phone: +61 2 9266 0866

#34
The Cuban Place
Category: Cuban, Music Venues, Bar
Average Price: Expensive
Area: Sydney
Address: 125 York St Sydney
New South Wales
Phone: +61 2 9264 4224

#35
The Loft
Category: Lounge
Average Price: Expensive
Area: Sydney
Address: 3 Lime St, King St Wharf
Sydney New South Wales
Phone: +61 2 9299 4770

#36
Ryans Bar
Category: Bar
Average Price: Modest
Area: Sydney
Address: Level 4, 264-278 George St
Square Sydney New South Wales
Phone: +61 2 9252 4369

#37
Bavarian Bier Cafe
Category: German, Beer Bar
Average Price: Modest
Area: Sydney
Address: 24 York St Sydney
New South Wales
Phone: +61 2 8297 4111

#38
Low 302
Category: Tapas, Lounge
Average Price: Modest
Area: Darlinghurst
Address: 302 Crown St, Sydney
New South Wales 2010
Phone: +61 2 9368 1548

#39
GPO Sydney
Category: Venues, Event Space,
Restaurant, Bar
Average Price: Expensive
Area: Sydney
Address: 1 Martin Pl Sydney
New South Wales
Phone: +61 2 9229 7700

#40
Fortune of War
Category: Pub
Average Price: Modest
Area: The Rocks
Address: 137 George St Sydney
New South Wales
Phone: +61 2 9247 2714

#41
Bungalow 8
Category: Bar, Austrian, Dance Club
Average Price: Modest
Area: Sydney
Address: 3 Lime St Sydney
New South Wales
Phone: +61 2 9299 4660

#42
Fix St James
Category: Wine Bar, Italian, Australian
Average Price: Expensive
Area: Sydney
Address: 111 Elizabeth St Sydney
New South Wales
Phone: +61 2 9232 2767

#43
Orient Hotel Restaurant
Category: Venues, Event Space,
Restaurant, Pub
Average Price: Modest
Area: The Rocks
Address: 89 George St Sydney
New South Wales
Phone: +61 2 9251 5631

#44
Shirt Bar
Category: Bar
Average Price: Modest
Area: Sydney
Address: 7 Sussex Ln Sydney
New South Wales
Phone: +61 2 8068 8222

#45
The Ship Inn
Category: Pub, Restaurant
Average Price: Modest
Area: Sydney
Address: Corner Alfred & Pitt Streets
Sydney New South Wales
Phone: +61 2 9241 2433

#46
Ash St Cellar
Category: Wine Bar
Average Price: Modest
Area: Sydney
Address: 1 Ash St Sydney
New South Wales
Phone: +61 2 9240 3000

#47
Marble Bar
Category: Lounge, Cocktail Bar
Average Price: Expensive
Area: Sydney
Address: 488 George St Sydney
New South Wales
Phone: +61 2 9266 2000

#48
The Morrison Bar & Oyster Room
Category: Bar, Seafood
Average Price: Modest
Area: Sydney
Address: 225 George St Sydney
New South Wales
Phone: +61 2 9247 6744

#49
Devine Food & Wine
Category: Wine Bar, Italian, European
Average Price: Expensive
Area: Sydney
Address: 32 Market Street Sydney
New South Wales
Phone: +61 2 9262 6906

#50
Cruise Bar
Category: Lounge, Australian,
Cocktail Bar
Average Price: Modest
Area: The Rocks
Address: Level 1-3, Overseas
Passenger Terminal Sydney
New South Wales
Phone: +61 2 9251 1188

#51
Tank Stream Bar
Category: Wine Bar
Average Price: Modest
Area: Sydney
Address: 1 Tankstream Way Sydney
New South Wales
Phone: +61 2 9240 3100

#52
The Passage
Category: European, Tapas, Bar
Average Price: Modest
Area: Darlinghurst
Address: 231A Victoria St Sydney
New South Wales 2010
Phone: +61 2 9358 6116

#53
Hemmesphere
Category: Lounge, Cocktail Bar
Average Price: Exclusive
Area: Sydney
Address: Level 4, 252 George St
Sydney New South Wales
Phone: +61 2 9240 3000

#54
Pure Platinum
Category: Adult Entertainment,
Restaurant
Area: Sydney
Address: 252 Pitt St Sydney
New South Wales
Phone: +61 2 9267 4454

#55
P.J.O'Brien's Irish Pub
Category: Pub, Sports Bar,
Music Venues
Average Price: Modest
Area: Sydney
Address: 57 King St Sydney
New South Wales
Phone: +61 2 9290 1811

#56
The Grand Hotel
Category: Venues, Event Space, Hotel
Average Price: Modest
Area: Sydney
Address: 30 Hunter St Sydney
New South Wales
Phone: +61 2 9232 3755

#57
1912 Dining Bar
Category: Japanese, Jazz, Blues,
Asian Fusion
Average Price: Modest
Area: Haymarket
Address: 27-33 Goulburn St Sydney
New South Wales
Phone: +61 2 8970 5813

#58
Cargo Bar / Lounge
Category: Lounge, Restaurant,
Social Club
Average Price: Expensive
Area: Sydney
Address: Lime Street 21 Sydney
New South Wales
Phone: +61 2 9262 1777

#59
The Spice Cellar
Category: Dance Club, Tapas, Wine Bar
Average Price: Modest
Area: Sydney
Address: 58 Elizabeth St Sydney
New South Wales
Phone: +61 2 9223 5585

#60
Angel Hotel
Category: Venues, Event Space,
Hotel, Pub
Average Price: Modest
Area: Sydney
Address: 125 Pitt St Sydney
New South Wales 2001
Phone: +61 2 9233 3131

#61
Cargo Bar & Lounge
Category: Dance Club, Bar
Average Price: Modest
Area: Sydney
Address: 52-60 The Promenade Sydney
New South Wales
Phone: +61 2 9262 1777

#62
Stacks Taverna
Category: Mediterranean, Bar, Greek
Average Price: Modest
Area: Sydney
Address: 1-25 Harbour St Sydney
New South Wales
Phone: 1300 989 989

#63
Jet Bar Cafe
Category: Café, Bar
Average Price: Modest
Area: Sydney
Address: Shop 55, 455 George Street
Sydney New South Wales
Phone: +61 2 9283 5004

#64
Sofitel Wentworth Sydney Lounge
Category: Lounge, Café
Average Price: Modest
Area: Sydney
Address: 101 Phillip St Sydney
New South Wales
Phone: +61 2 9228 9188

#65
TOKIO Hotel
Category: Lounge
Average Price: Modest
Area: Sydney
Address: 1/101 Wheat Road Sydney
New South Wales
Phone: +61 2 9266 0600

#66
Chinese Laundry
Category: Dance Club
Average Price: Expensive
Area: Sydney
Address: 111 Sussex St, Sydney
Sydney New South Wales
Phone: +61 2 8295 9999

#67
Hotel Coronation
Category: Hotel, Pub
Average Price: Modest
Area: Sydney
Address: 5-7 Park St Sydney
New South Wales
Phone: +61 2 9266 3100

#68
Morrison Bar & Oyster Room
Category: Pub
Average Price: Modest
Area: Sydney
Address: 225 George St Sydney
New South Wales
Phone: +61 2 9247 6744

#69
Manning Bar
Category: Music Venues, Pub
Average Price: Inexpensive
Area: Camperdown
Address: Manning Road Sydney
New South Wales 2006
Phone: +61 2 9563 6000

#70
Shout Tune Bar
Category: Karaoke
Average Price: Modest
Area: Sydney
Address: Levels 1 And 2, 95 Bathurst St
Sydney New South Wales
Phone: +61 2 9283 8080

#71
Globe Bar & Brasserie
Category: Brasseries, Bar, Tea Room
Average Price: Expensive
Area: Millers Point
Address: 115 Kent St Sydney
New South Wales
Phone: +61 2 8248 5252

#72
The Hudson
Category: Bar, Australian
Area: Sydney
Address: 49 Lime St Sydney
New South Wales
Phone: +61 2 9279 3379

#73
80 Proof
Category: Bar, Australian
Area: Sydney
Address: 561 George St Sydney
New South Wales
Phone: +61 2 9262 7210

#74
Balcony Bar
Category: Wine Bar
Area: Sydney
Address: 46 Erskine Street Sydney
New South Wales
Phone: +61 2 9299 8821

#75
Laughing Buddha Bar
Category: Lounge
Area: Sydney
Address: Shop 9.33 Sydney
New South Wales
Phone: +61 2 9264 6954

#76
Just Pure Bistro, JPB
Category: Bar, Bistros
Average Price: Expensive
Area: Sydney
Address: 68 Market St Sydney
New South Wales
Phone: +61 2 9238 8888

#77
Tokkuri Saki & Wine Bar
Category: Japanese, Wine Bar
Area: Sydney
Address: 273 George St Sydney
New South Wales
Phone: +61 2 9252 6345

#78
Pontoon Bar
Category: Lounge
Average Price: Modest
Address: Cockle Bay Wharf Sydney
New South Wales
Phone: +61 2 9267 7099

#79
Bello Cafe
Category: Restaurant, Pub
Area: Sydney
Address: 22 Loftus St Sydney
New South Wales
Phone: +61 2 9251 0105

#80
The Sydney Cove Oyster Bar
Category: Restaurant, Bar
Area: Sydney
Address: East Circular Quay 1 Sydney
New South Wales
Phone: +61 9 2472 937

#81
Wallaby Bar
Category: Dance Club
Area: Sydney
Address: 201 Sussex St Sydney
New South Wales
Phone: +61 2 9267 4118

#82
Wine Odyssey Australia
Category: Bar, Australian
Area: The Rocks
Address: Argyle Street 39 Sydney
New South Wales
Phone: 1300 136 498

#83
The Bar
Category: Bar
Area: Sydney
Address: 93 Macquarie St Sydney
New South Wales
Phone: +61 2 9252 4600

#84
Eye Bar
Category: Bar
Area: Potts Point
Address: 68 Darlinghurst Rd Sydney
New South Wales 2011
Phone: +61 2 9357 4665

#85
Scary Canary
Category: Bar
Average Price: Modest
Area: Sydney
Address: 469 Kent St Sydney
New South Wales
Phone: +61 2 9267 7087

#86
Nick's Bar & Grill
Category: Steakhouse, Seafood
Average Price: Expensive
Area: Sydney
Address: The Promenade Sydney
New South Wales
Phone: 1300 989 989

#87
Easy Tiger
Category: Cocktail Bar
Average Price: Modest
Area: Paddington
Address: 106 Oxford St Sydney
New South Wales 2021
Phone: +61 2 9360 7994

#88
Mio Bar
Category: Bar, Café
Area: Sydney
Address: 35 Clarence Street Sydney
New South Wales
Phone: +61 2 9279 0548

#89
Papa Gedes Bar
Category: Cocktail Bar, Wine Bar
Average Price: Modest
Area: Sydney
Address: Rear 348 Kent St Sydney
New South Wales
Phone: +61 2 9299 5671

#90
Concourse Bar
Category: Bar
Area: Sydney
Address: Wynyard Railway Station,
33 York St Sydney New South Wales
Phone: +61 2 9279 0544

#91
Bacco Wine Bar Pasticceria
Category: Wine Bar, Café
Average Price: Modest
Area: Sydney
Address: 2 Chifley Sq Sydney
New South Wales
Phone: +61 2 9223 9552

#92
Cheers Bar
Category: Sports Bar
Average Price: Modest
Area: Sydney
Address: 561 George St Sydney
New South Wales
Phone: +61 2 9261 8313

#93
The Fox Hole
Category: Bar, Café
Average Price: Inexpensive
Area: Sydney
Address: 68A Erskine St Sydney
New South Wales
Phone: +61 2 9279 4369

#94
The Office Hotel
Category:
Average Price: Modest
Area: Sydney
Address: Cnr Kent And Erskine Streets
Sydney New South Wales
Phone: +61 2 9279 3133

#95
GPO Cheese & Wine Room
Category: Wine Bar, Cheese Shop
Average Price: Expensive
Area: Sydney
Address: 1 Martin Pl Sydney
New South Wales
Phone: +61 2 9229 7701

#96
Home Bar
Category: Dance Club
Area: Sydney
Address: 101 Wheat Road, Darling
Harbour Sydney New South Wales
Phone: +61 2 9266 0600

#97
V Bar
Category: Lounge
Area: Sydney
Address: 111 Liverpool St Sydney
New South Wales
Phone: +61 2 9264 9188

#98
Martin Place Bar
Category: Bar
Average Price: Modest
Area: Sydney
Address: 51 Martin Pl Sydney
New South Wales
Phone: +61 2 9231 5575

#99
La Cita
Category: Latin American, Dance Club
Area: Sydney
Address: 9 Lime St Sydney
New South Wales
Phone: +61 2 9299 9100

#100
Customs House Bar
Category: Pub
Average Price: Expensive
Area: Sydney
Address: Macquarie Pl Sydney
New South Wales
Phone: +61 2 9259 7317

#101
Bar Century
Category: Pub, Hostels
Average Price: Inexpensive
Area: Sydney
Address: 640 George St Sydney
New South Wales
Phone: +61 2 9261 8333

#102
Four Seasons Hotel Lounge
Category: Lounge
Average Price: Expensive
Area: Sydney
Address: 199 George St Sydney
New South Wales
Phone: +61 2 9250 3100

#103
Cafe Chicane
Category: Café, Bar
Average Price: Expensive
Area: Sydney
Address: Shp2/ 10 Bond St Sydney
New South Wales
Phone: +61 2 9232 4456

#104
Capital Grill
Category: Bar, Café, European
Area: Sydney
Address: 1 Macquarie Place Sydney
Sydney New South Wales
Phone: +61 2 9247 4445

#105
Verandah Main Bar & BBQ
Category: Bar, Gastropub
Average Price: Modest
Area: Sydney
Address: 55 - 65 Elizabeth St Sydney
New South Wales
Phone: +61 2 9239 5888

#106
Mr Tipply's
Category: Cocktail Bar
Average Price: Expensive
Area: Sydney
Address: 347 Kent St Sydney
New South Wales
Phone: +61 2 9299 4877

#107
Pailou Bar
Category: Bar
Area: Haymarket
Address: 401 Sussex St Sydney
New South Wales
Phone: +61 2 9281 7227

#108
Gilt Lounge
Category: Cocktail Bar
Average Price: Expensive
Area: Sydney
Address: 49 Market St Sydney
New South Wales
Phone: +61 2 8262 0000

#109
York 75
Category: Sports Bar
Area: Sydney
Address: Corner of York & King St
Sydney New South Wales
Phone: +61 2 8297 7020

#110
Chequers Health
Category: Adult Entertainment
Average Price: Modest
Area: Sydney
Address: 79 Goulburn St Sydney
New South Wales
Phone: +61 2 9212 5152

#111
Bavarian Bier Cafe
Category: German, Beer Bar
Area: Sydney
Address: 16 O'Connell St Sydney
New South Wales
Phone: +61 2 9221 0100

#112
Duck And Swan Hotel
Category: Pub
Average Price: Modest
Area: Chippendale
Address: Rose Street 74 Sydney
New South Wales 2007
Phone: +61 2 9319 4778

#113
The Boston
Category: Bar
Address: Gateway, 1 Macquarie Pl
Sydney New South Wales
Phone: +61 2 9241 5858

#114
Fred's Bar
Category: Wine Bar
Average Price: Modest
Area: Sydney
Address: 1 Alfred St Sydney
New South Wales
Phone: +61 2 9251 0384

#115
Minus 5
Category: Bar
Average Price: Modest
Area: Sydney
Address: Circular Quay Sydney
New South Wales
Phone: +61 2 9251 0311

#116
The Vault Hotel
Category: Restaurant, Wine Bar
Address: 122 Pitt St Sydney
New South Wales
Phone: +61 2 9235 3999

#117
The Royal George
Category: Bar, Pub Food
Average Price: Modest
Area: Sydney
Address: 330 George St Sydney
New South Wales
Phone: +61 2 9254 8002

#118
The Spanish Club
Category: Music Venues, Spanish
Area: Sydney
Address: 88 Liverpool St Sydney
New South Wales
Phone: +61 2 9267 8440

#119
Cityheroes Pool & Billiard
Category: Pool Hall
Area: Sydney
Address: 505 George St Sydney
New South Wales
Phone: +61 2 8034 3201

#120
City Tattersalls Club
Category: Social Club, Bar
Area: Sydney
Address: 198 Pitt St Sydney
New South Wales
Phone: +61 2 9267 9421

#121
Strike King Street Wharf
Category: Bar, Bowling, Karaoke
Average Price: Modest
Address: 22 The Promenade Sydney
New South Wales
Phone: 1300 787 453

#122
Little Rumour
Category: Bar, Burgers, Pizza
Average Price: Modest
Area: Sydney
Address: 4 Castlereagh St Sydney
New South Wales
Phone: +61 2 9232

#123
Club Grand HIT
Category: Dance Club, Lounge
Average Price: Exclusive
Address: 155 Castlereigh St Sydney
New South Wales
Phone: +61 2 9283 5090

#124
Redoak Boutique Beer Cafe
Category: Pub, Australian, Beer Bar
Average Price: Modest
Area: Sydney
Address: 201 Clarence St Sydney
New South Wales
Phone: +61 2 9262 3303

#125
Assembly
Category: Bar
Average Price: Modest
Area: Sydney
Address: 488 Kent St Sydney
New South Wales
Phone: +61 2 9283 8808

#126
World Square Pub
Category: Pub
Area: Sydney
Address: 680 George Street Sydney
New South Wales
Phone: +61 2 8272 2400

#127
Pavillion Holdings
Category: Dance Club
Area: Sydney
Address: 123 Clarence St Sydney
New South Wales
Phone: +61 2 9299 5910

#128
P.J. Gallaghers Irish Pub
Category: Pub
Average Price: Modest
Area: Sydney
Address: 66 King St Sydney
New South Wales
Phone: +61 2 9626 3277

#129
Opia Cafe, Bar & Pizzeria
Category: Bar, Italian, Café
Area: Sydney
Address: 115 Clarence St Sydney
New South Wales
Phone: +61 2 9299 9119

#130
Fuku Sake & Wine Bar
Category: Japanese, Wine Bar
Area: Sydney
Address: 644 George St Sydney
New South Wales
Phone: +61 2 9261 8977

#131
Suriya Lounge Bar
Category: Bar
Area: Sydney
Address: 20 Sussex Street Sydney
New South Wales
Phone: +61 2 9262 6988

#132
The Bull & Bear
Category: Bar
Average Price: Expensive
Address: 16 Phillip Ln Sydney
New South Wales
Phone: +61 2 9241 1911

#133
Strand Hotel
Category: Pub
Area: Darlinghurst
Address: 99 William St Sydney
New South Wales 2010
Phone: +61 2 9360 6910

#134
Scruffy Murphy's Hotel
Category: Hotel, Dance Club
Average Price: Inexpensive
Area: Haymarket
Address: 43-49 Goulburn St Sydney
New South Wales
Phone: +61 2 9211 2002

#135
Roys Famous
Category: Bar, Café
Area: Potts Point
Address: Potts Point Sydney
New South Wales 2011
Phone: +61 2 9357 3579

#136
Star Bar And Grill
Category: Bar
Average Price: Modest
Address: 600 George St Sydney
New South Wales
Phone: +61 2 9267 7827

#137
Noble Canteen & Cocktails
Category: Cocktail Bar, Thai
Area: Sydney
Address: 50 King St Sydney
New South Wales
Phone: +61 2 9299 2929

#138
Agincourt Hotel
Category: Dance Club, Bar
Average Price: Inexpensive
Area: Ultimo
Address: 871 George St Sydney
New South Wales
Phone: +61 2 9281 4566

#139
Abode
Category: Cocktail Bar, Sports Bar
Average Price: Modest
Area: Sydney
Address: 150 Day St Sydney
New South Wales
Phone: +61 2 9260 2945

#140
Crystal Bar
Category: Cocktail Bar
Average Price: Expensive
Area: Sydney
Address: 1 Martin Pl Sydney
New South Wales
Phone: +61 2 9229 7799

#141
Sanctuary Hotel
Category: Venues, Event Space,
Pub, European
Average Price: Modest
Area: Sydney
Address: 545 Kent Street Sydney
New South Wales
Phone: +61 2 9264 1119

#142
121BC
Category: Bar
Average Price: Expensive
Area: Surry Hills
Address: 4/ 50 Holt St Surry Hills
New South Wales 2010
Phone: +61 2 9699 1582

#143
St Andrew's Cathedral
Category: Landmark/Historical,
Music Venues, Church
Average Price: Inexpensive
Area: Sydney
Address: Corner of Bathurst And
George Streets Sydney
New South Wales
Phone: +61 2 9265 1661

#144
Slip Inn
Category: Hotel, Bar
Average Price: Modest
Area: Sydney
Address: 111 Sussex St Sydney
New South Wales
Phone: +61 2 8295 9999

#145
Bar Eleven
Category: Bar
Average Price: Modest
Area: Sydney
Address: 161 Sussex St Sydney
New South Wales
Phone: +61 2 9290 4712

#146
King St Brewhouse
Category: Australian, Brewerie, Beer
Average Price: Modest
Area: Sydney
Address: 22 The Promenade Sydney
New South Wales
Phone: +61 2 8270 7901

#147
30 Knots
Category: Pub Food, Wine Bar
Area: Sydney
Address: Level 1, 30 Hunter St Sydney
New South Wales
Phone: +61 2 9232 3755

#148
Nine Bar
Category:
Average Price: Inexpensive Cocktail Bar
Area: Sydney
Address: 352 Sussex St Sydney
New South Wales
Phone: +61 2 8268 9070

#149
Players
Category: Sports Bar, Pub Food, Beer
Area: Surry Hills
Address: 589 Crown St Sydney
New South Wales 2010
Phone: +61 2 9699 3460

#150
Coach Bar
Category: Bar, Cabaret, Indian
Area: Sydney
Address: 1 Martin Place Sydney
New South Wales
Phone: +61 2 9229 7700

#151
Glasshouse UTS
Category: Bar
Area: Chippendale
Address: 15 Broadway Sydney
New South Wales 2007
Phone: +61 2 9514 1146

#152
Upstairs Beresford
Category: Bar
Area: Surry Hills
Address: 354 Bourke St Sydney
New South Wales 2010
Phone: +61 2 8313 5000

#153
Saké
Category: Japanese, Bar
Average Price: Expensive
Area: The Rocks
Address: 12 Argyle St Sydney
New South Wales
Phone: +61 2 9259 5656

#154
Parke Davis
Category: Cocktail Bar
Area: Sydney
Address: 125 York St Sydney
New South Wales
Phone: +61 2 9264 4224

#155
Hot Sydney Asain Escort
Category: Adult Entertainment
Area: Sydney
Address: 91 Liverpool St Sydney
New South Wales
Phone: +61 4 0512 3533

#156
GPO Middle Bar
Category: Sports Bar
Area: Sydney
Address: 1 Martin Pl Sydney
New South Wales
Phone: +61 2 9229 7700

#157
Vui Va Say
Category: Vietnamese, Cocktail Bar
Area: Newtown
Address: 127 King St Sydney
New South Wales
Phone: +61 9 5172 446

#158
The Den
Category: Cocktail Bar, Lounge
Area: Sydney
Address: 330 George St Sydney
New South Wales
Phone: +61 2 9254 8100

#159
Verandah Restaurant & Wine Bar
Category: European, Wine Bar
Area: Sydney
Address: 55 - 65 Elizabeth Street
Sydney New South Wales
Phone: +61 2 9239 5888

#160
Gin Garden
Category: Bar
Area: Sydney
Address: 252 George St Sydney
New South Wales
Phone: +61 2 9240 3100

#161
The Lane
Category: Wine Bar, Café
Area: Sydney
Address: Cnr Curtin Pl & Hamilton St
Sydney New South Wales
Phone: +61 2 9233 3242

#162
Club DJ
Category: Djs, Dance Club
Area: Rushcutters Bay
Address: 40 Bayswater Rd Sydney
New South Wales 2011
Phone: +61 4 1127 7576

#163
Changeroom, Ivy
Category: Lounge
Area: Sydney
Address: 320 George St Sydney
New South Wales
Phone: +61 2 9254 8000

#164
Fideli's Bar & Restaurant
Category: Jazz, Blues, Food, Lounge
Area: Sydney
Address: 77 York St Sydney
New South Wales
Phone: +61 2 9262 3140

#165
Comedy Court Australia
Category: Comedy Club
Area: Sydney
Address: 600 George St Sydney
New South Wales
Phone: +61 2 9547 2578

#166
Square Bar
Category: Pub
Area: Sydney
Address: 389 Pitt St Sydney
New South Wales
Phone: +61 2 8268 1888

#167
One22
Category: Dance Club
Area: Sydney
Address: 122 Pitt St Sydney
New South Wales
Phone: +61 4 3218 8509

#168
Eden Bar & Restaurant
Category: Wine Bar, Australian,
Australian
Area: Sydney
Address: 19-35 Martin Pl Sydney
New South Wales
Phone: +61 2 9223 4333

#169
Morrison Bar & Oyster Room
Category: Pub
Area: Sydney
Address: 225 George St Sydney
New South Wales
Phone: +61 2 9247 6744

#170
M9 Laser Skirmish
Category: Bar, Laser Tag, Venues,
Event Space
Area: Sydney
Address: 2-10 Darling Dr Sydney
New South Wales
Phone: +61 2 9233 6678

#171
Australian Music Centre
Category: Music Venues
Area: The Rocks
Address: 16 Mountain St Sydney
New South Wales 2007
Phone: +61 2 9935 7805

#172
Le Pub Balmain
Category: Bar
Area: Balmain
Address: 255 Darling Street Sydney
New South Wales 2041
Phone: +61 2 9555 5711

#173
Easy Tiger
Category: Bar
Area: Paddington
Address: 106 Oxford St Sydney
New South Wales 2021
Phone: +61 2 9360 7994

#174
The Tilbury Hotel
Category: Pub, Australian
Average Price: Expensive
Area: Woolloomooloo
Address: 12-18 Nicholson St Sydney
New South Wales 2011
Phone: +61 2 9368 1955

#175
The Sussex Hotel
Category: Pub
Average Price: Inexpensive
Area: Sydney
Address: 20 Sussex St Sydney
New South Wales
Phone: +61 2 9262 6988

#176
Big Echo Karaoke Box
Category: Karaoke, Bar
Average Price: Modest
Area: Sydney
Address: 104 Bathurst St Sydney
New South Wales
Phone: +61 2 9283 2666

#177
Mr B's Hotel
Category: Chinese, Pub, Asian Fusion
Average Price: Modest
Area: Haymarket
Address: 396 Pitt St, Sydney
New South Wales
Phone: +61 2 8080 7777

#178
The Little Guy
Category: Bar
Average Price: Modest
Area: Glebe
Address: 87 Glebe Point Rd Glebe
New South Wales 2037
Phone: +61 2 8084 0758

#179
Different Drummer
Category: Lounge, Spanish
Average Price: Expensive
Area: Glebe
Address: 185 Glebe Point Rd Glebe
New South Wales 2037
Phone: +61 2 9552 3406

#180
Darlie Laundromatic
Category: Café, Lounge, Gastropub
Average Price: Modest
Area: Darlinghurst
Address: 304A Palmer St Darlinghurst
New South Wales 2010
Phone: +61 2 8095 0129

#181
Courthouse Hotel
Category: Hotel, Pub, Burgers
Average Price: Modest
Area: Newtown
Address: 202 Street Newtown
New South Wales 2042
Phone: +61 2 9519 8273

#182
Asian Babes Escort
Category: Adult Entertainment
Area: Haymarket
Address: 420 Pitt St Sydney
New South Wales
Phone: +61 4 2069 3620

#183
Mary's
Category: Bar, Burgers, American
Average Price: Modest
Area: Newtown
Address: 6 Mary St Newtown
New South Wales 2042
Phone: +61 2 4995 9550

#184
The Vanguard
Category: Jazz, Blues, Music Venues
Average Price: Expensive
Area: Newtown
Address: 42 King St Newtown
New South Wales 2042
Phone: +61 2 9557 9409

#185
Love, Tilly Devine
Category: Wine Bar
Average Price: Expensive
Area: Darlinghurst
Address: 91 Crown Lane Darlinghurst
New South Wales 2010
Phone: +61 2 9326 9297

#186
Eau De Vie
Category: Bar
Average Price: Expensive
Area: Darlinghurst
Address: 229 Darlinghurst Road
Darlinghurst
New South Wales 2010
Phone: +61 4 2226 3226

#187
Young Henrys
Category: Brewerie, Beer Bar
Average Price: Modest
Area: Newtown
Address: 76 Wilford St Newtown
New South Wales 2042
Phone: +61 2 9519 0048

#188
The Wild Rover
Category: Cocktail Bar,
Wine Bar, Beer Bar
Average Price: Modest
Area: Surry Hills
Address: 75 Campbell St Surry Hills
New South Wales 2010
Phone: +61 2 9280 2235

#189
Nomad
Category: Wine Bar, Australian
Average Price: Expensive
Area: Surry Hills
Address: 16 Foster St Surry Hills
New South Wales 2010
Phone: +61 9 2803 395

#190
Harbourside Cellars
Category: Bar
Area: Sydney
Address: 10 Darling Dr Sydney
New South Wales
Phone: +61 2 9281 6155

#191
Sepia Wine Bar
Category: Wine Bar
Area: Sydney
Address: 201 Sussex St Sydney
New South Wales
Phone: +61 2 9283 1990

#192
XOXO Saturdays
Category: Dance Club
Area: Sydney
Address: 200 Sussex St Sydney
New South Wales
Phone: +61 4 0180 0630

#193
Sydney Adult Book Exchange
Category: Adult Entertainment
Area: Sydney
Address: 16 Goulburn St Sydney
New South Wales
Phone: +61 2 9267 1965

#194
Red Door Agency
Category: Adult Entertainment
Area: Sydney
Address: 44 Market St Sydney
New South Wales
Phone: +61 2 9799 2882

#195
D One Entertainment
Category: Art Gallery, Comedy Club
Area: Sydney
Address: 600 George St Sydney
New South Wales
Phone: +61 2 9547 2578

#196
Sydney Dating
Category: Adult Entertainment
Area: Sydney
Address: 89 York St Sydney
New South Wales
Phone: +61 2 9279 0055

#197
City Touch
Category: Adult Entertainment
Area: Sydney
Address: 70 Erskine St Sydney
New South Wales
Phone: +61 2 9279 2885

#198
Sirs For Massage
Category: Adult Entertainment
Area: Sydney
Address: 80 Erskine St Sydney
New South Wales
Phone: +61 2 9262 1829

#199
Sirs The Corporate Touch
Category: Adult Entertainment
Area: Sydney
Address: 80 Erskine St Sydney
New South Wales 2001
Phone: +61 2 9262 1624

#200
Sirs
Category: Adult Entertainment
Area: Sydney
Address: 80 Erskine St Sydney
New South Wales 2001
Phone: +61 2 9262 1829

#201
Zanadu Massage And Relaxation
Category: Adult Entertainment
Area: Sydney
Address: 248 Pitt St Sydney
New South Wales
Phone: +61 2 9283 5888

#202
Joyfinder
Category: Adult Entertainment
Area: Sydney
Address: 49-51 York St Sydney
New South Wales
Phone: +61 2 8324 7485

#203
Park St Adult Book Exchange
Category: Adult Entertainment
Area: Sydney
Address: 44 Park St Sydney
New South Wales
Phone: +61 2 9267 6812

#204
Australian Chamber Orchestra
Category: Music Venues
Area: Sydney
Address: 2 East Circular Quay Sydney
New South Wales
Phone: +61 2 8274 3800

#205
Evocative Management Australia
Category: Music Venues
Area: Sydney
Address: Sydney
New South Wales
Phone: 1300 642 285

#206
Transexual Trisha
Category: Adult Entertainment
Area: Sydney
Address: Castlereagh St Sydney
New South Wales
Phone: +61 4 2535 9665

#207
Bar Fredo
Category: Bar
Area: Sydney
Address: 19-29 Martin Pl Sydney
New South Wales
Phone: +61 2 9233 3740

#208
Mojo Escorts
Category: Adult Entertainment
Area: Sydney
Address: 7 Bridge St Sydney
New South Wales
Phone: +61 2 9251 7444

#209
Madesco Escorts
Category: Adult Entertainment
Area: Sydney
Address: 2 Chifley Sydney
New South Wales
Phone: 1300 558 766

#210
Lucky Tsotsi Shebeen & Bar
Category: Bar, African
Average Price: Modest
Area: Darlinghurst
Address: 245 Oxford St Darlinghurst
New South Wales 2010
Phone: +61 2 8354 1306

#211
Shirts Off
Category: Adult Entertainment
Area: Sydney
Address: Bridge St Sydney
New South Wales
Phone: +61 2 8668 4153

#212
Hickson's Food And Wine
Category: Wine Bar, Tapas
Area: Dawes Point
Address: 17 Hickson Rd Sydney
New South Wales
Phone: +61 2 9241 2031

#213
El Loco
Category: Mexican, Pub
Average Price: Modest
Area: Surry Hills
Address: 64 Foveaux St Surry Hills
New South Wales 2010
Phone: +61 2 9211 4945

#214
Arcadia Liquors
Category: Bar
Average Price: Modest
Area: Redfern
Address: 7 Cope St Redfern
New South Wales 2016
Phone: +61 4 1165 2987

#215
Kuleto's Cocktail Bar
Category: Cocktail Bar
Average Price: Modest
Area: Newtown
Address: 157 King St Newtown
New South Wales 2042
Phone: +61 2 9519 6369

#216
Glenmore Hotel
Category: Hotel, Pub
Average Price: Modest
Area: The Rocks
Address: 96 Cumberland St The Rocks
New South Wales
Phone: +61 2 9247 4794

#217
The Hero of Waterloo Hotel
Category: Pub, Pub Food
Average Price: Modest
Area: Millers Point
Address: 81 Lower Fort St Millers Point
New South Wales
Phone: +61 2 9252 4553

#218
Shakespeare Hotel
Category: Pub, Hotel
Average Price: Inexpensive
Area: Surry Hills
Address: 200 Devonshire St Surry Hills
New South Wales 2010
Phone: +61 2 9319 6883

#219
Hive Bar
Category: Wine Bar, Dance Club, Pub
Average Price: Modest
Area: Erskineville
Address: 93 Erskineville Road
Erskineville
New South Wales 2043
Phone: +61 2 9519 9911

#220
The Wine Library
Category: Tapas, Wine Bar
Average Price: Modest
Area: Paddington
Address: 18 Oxford St Woollahra
New South Wales 2025
Phone: +61 2 9360 5686

#221
The Victoria Room
Category: Mediterranean, Tea Room,
Cocktail Bar
Average Price: Expensive
Area: Darlinghurst
Address: 235 Victoria St Darlinghurst
New South Wales 2010
Phone: +61 2 9357 4488

#222
Corridor
Category: Lounge, Tapas
Average Price: Modest
Area: Newtown
Address: 153A King St Newtown
New South Wales 2042
Phone: +61 4 2287 3879

#223
Newtown Hotel
Category: Pub, Greek
Average Price: Modest
Area: Newtown
Address: 174 King St Newtown
New South Wales 2042
Phone: +61 2 9557 6399

#224
Harts Pub
Category: Pub
Average Price: Modest
Area: The Rocks
Address: 176 Cumberland St The Rocks
New South Wales
Phone: +61 2 9251 6030

#225
Mr Falcon's
Category: Bar
Average Price: Modest
Area: Glebe
Address: 92 Glebe Point Rd Glebe
New South Wales 2037
Phone: +61 9 9029 6626

#226
The Goldfish
Category: Lounge, Dance Club
Average Price: Modest
Area: Potts Point
Address: 111 Darlinghurst Rd Potts
Point New South Wales 2011
Phone: +61 2 8354 6630

#227
The Local Taphouse
Category: Pub, Australian, Beer Bar
Average Price: Modest
Area: Darlinghurst
Address: 122 Flinders St Darlinghurst
New South Wales 2010
Phone: +61 2 9360 0088

#228
The World Bar
Category: Bar, Dance Club,
Music Venues
Average Price: Modest
Area: Potts Point
Address: 24 Bayswater Rd Potts Point
New South Wales 2011
Phone: +61 2 9357 7700

#229
Fico Wine Bar
Category: Wine Bar
Average Price: Modest
Area: Surry Hills
Address: 544 Bourke St Surry Hills
New South Wales 2010
Phone: +61 2 9699 2133

#230
The Friend In Hand
Category: Pub, Pub Food
Average Price: Modest
Area: Glebe
Address: 58 Cowper St Glebe
New South Wales 2037
Phone: +61 2 9660 2326

#231
The Soda Factory
Category: Bar, American
Average Price: Modest
Area: Surry Hills
Address: 16 Wentworth Ave Surry Hills
New South Wales 2010
Phone: +61 2 8096 9120

#232
The Winery
Category: Wine Bar, Tapas
Average Price: Expensive
Area: Surry Hills
Address: 285A Crown Street Surry Hills
New South Wales 2010
Phone: +61 2 9331 0833

#233
Loft UTS
Category: Bar
Average Price: Inexpensive
Area: Ultimo
Address: 15 Broadway Road Ultimo
New South Wales 2007
Phone: +61 2 9514 2345

#234
Treehouse
Category: European, Lounge
Average Price: Modest
Area: North Sydney
Address: 60 Miller St North Sydney
New South Wales 2055
Phone: +61 2 8458 8980

#235
Toko
Category: Japanese, Cocktail Bar
Average Price: Expensive
Area: Surry Hills
Address: 490 Crown St Surry Hills
New South Wales 2010
Phone: +61 2 9357 6100

#236
Oxford Art Factory
Category: Dance Club, Art Gallery,
Music Venues
Average Price: Modest
Area: Surry Hills
Address: 36-42 Oxford St Darlinghurst
New South Wales 2010
Phone: +61 2 9332 3711

#237
Clock Hotel
Category: Lounge, Gastropub, Pub
Average Price: Modest
Area: Surry Hills
Address: 470 Crown St Surry Hills
New South Wales 2010
Phone: +61 2 9331 5333

#238
Side Bar
Category: Bar
Average Price: Inexpensive
Area: Haymarket
Address: 509 Pitt Street Sydney
New South Wales
Phone: +61 2 9288 7888

#239
Zanzibar Newtown
Category: Hotel, Pub, Tapas
Average Price: Modest
Area: Newtown
Address: 323 King St Newtown
New South Wales 2042
Phone: +61 2 9519 1511

#240
Bank Hotel
Category: Hotel, Pub
Average Price: Modest
Area: Newtown
Address: 324 King St Newtown
New South Wales 2042
Phone: +61 2 8568 1988

#241
Australian Youth Hotel
Category: Hotel, Pub, Gastropub
Average Price: Modest
Area: Glebe
Address: 63 Bay St Glebe
New South Wales 2037
Phone: +61 2 9692 0414

#242
Hinky Dinks
Category: Cocktail Bar
Average Price: Modest
Area: Darlinghurst
Address: 185 Darlinghurst Rd
Darlinghurst
New South Wales 2010
Phone: +61 2 8084 6379

#243
The Roosevelt
Category: Bar
Average Price: Expensive
Area: Potts Point
Address: 32 Orwell Street Potts Point
New South Wales 2011
Phone: +61 4 2320 3119

#244
Bishop Sessa
Category: Australian, Wine Bar,
Gastropub
Average Price: Exclusive
Area: Surry Hills
Address: 527 Crown Street Surry Hills
New South Wales 2010
Phone: +61 2 8065 7223

#245
Ventuno
Category: Wine Bar, Italian
Average Price: Modest
Area: Millers Point
Address: 21 Hickson Rd Millers Point
New South Wales
Phone: +61 2 9247 4444

#246
Riley St Garage
Category: Wine Bar, Seafood, Australian
Average Price: Exclusive
Area: Woolloomooloo
Address: 55 Riley St Woolloomooloo
New South Wales 2011
Phone: +61 2 9326 9055

#247
Verona Cinema & Bar
Category: Cinema, Bar
Average Price: Modest
Area: Paddington
Address: 17 Oxford St Paddington
New South Wales 2021
Phone: +61 2 9360 6099

#248
Chez Dee
Category: Cocktail Bar,
Breakfast & Brunch, Delicatessen
Average Price: Expensive
Area: Potts Point
Address: 62 Kellett St Potts Point
New South Wales 2011
Phone: +61 2 8354 1544

#249
Lo-Fi
Category: Lounge, Music Venues
Average Price: Modest
Area: Darlinghurst
Address: 383 Bourke St Darlinghurst
New South Wales 2010
Phone: +61 2 9331 6200

#250
Gardels Bar
Category: Lounge, Argentine
Area: Surry Hills
Address: 358 Cleveland Street
New South Wales 2010
Phone: +61 2 8399 1440

#251
Button Bar
Category: Wine Bar, Cocktail Bar
Average Price: Modest
Area: Surry Hills
Address: 65 Foveaux St Surry Hills
New South Wales 2010
Phone: +61 2 9212 1757

#252
Ching-A-Lings
Category: Bar
Average Price: Modest
Area: Darlinghurst
Address: Lvl 1/ 133 Oxford St
New South Wales 2010
Phone: +61 2 9360 3333

#253
Freda's
Category: Bar, Australian
Average Price: Modest
Area: Chippendale
Address: 109 Regent Street
New South Wales 2008
Phone: +61 8 9717 336

#254
Metro Theatre
Category: Music Venues
Average Price: Modest
Area: Sydney
Address: 624 George St Sydney
New South Wales
Phone: +61 2 9550 3666

#255
Sticky Bar
Category: Lounge
Average Price: Modest
Area: Darlinghurst
Address: 182 Campbell Surry Hills
New South Wales 2010
Phone: +61 4 1609 6916

#256
The Devonshire
Category: Australian, Bar
Average Price: Expensive
Area: Surry Hills
Address: 204 Devonshire St Surry Hills
New South Wales 2010
Phone: +61 2 9698 9427

#257
Paddington Inn Hotel
Category: Hotel, Bar
Average Price: Modest
Area: Paddington
Address: 338 Oxford St Paddington
New South Wales 2021
Phone: +61 2 9380 5913

#258
Bay 88
Category: Café, Food, Wine Bar
Average Price: Modest
Area: Rushcutters Bay
Address: 86 - 88 Bayswater Road
Bay New South Wales 2011
Phone: +61 2 8021 7389

#259
The Argyle
Category: Bar, Austrian
Average Price: Modest
Area: The Rocks
Address: 18 Argyle St The Rocks
New South Wales
Phone: +61 2 9247 5500

#260
Flinders Hotel
Category: Pub
Average Price: Modest
Area: Darlinghurst
Address: 63 Flinders St Darlinghurst
New South Wales 2010
Phone: +61 2 9356 3622

#261
Bar H
Category: Bar, European
Average Price: Expensive
Area: Surry Hills
Address: 80 Campbell St Surry Hills
New South Wales 2010
Phone: +61 2 9280 1980

#262
The Australian Heritage Hotel
Category: Hotel, Pub
Average Price: Modest
Area: The Rocks
Address: 100 Cumberland St The Rocks
New South Wales
Phone: +61 2 9247 2229

#263
The Rose Hotel
Category: Pub, Pizza, Gluten-Free
Average Price: Inexpensive
Area: Chippendale
Address: 54 Cleveland St Chippendale
New South Wales 2008
Phone: +61 2 9318 1133

#264
Jazushi
Category: Japanese, Sushi Bar,
Jazz, Blues
Average Price: Expensive
Area: Surry Hills
Address: 145 Devonshire St Surry Hills
New South Wales 2010
Phone: +61 2 9699 8977

#265
Excelsior Hotel
Category: Pub
Average Price: Inexpensive
Area: Surry Hills
Address: 64 Foveaux St Surry Hills
New South Wales 2010
Phone: +61 2 9211 4945

#266
Helm Bar
Category: Bar, Pizza
Average Price: Modest
Area: Sydney
Address: 7 Wheat Road Darling Harbour
New South Wales
Phone: +61 2 9290 1571

#267
Hotel Sweeney's
Category: Thai, Beer Gardens, Pub
Average Price: Inexpensive
Area: Sydney
Address: 236 Clarence St Sydney
New South Wales
Phone: +61 2 9267 1116

#268
liza
Category: Japanese, Bar
Area: Newtown
Address: 184 King Street Newtown
New South Wales 2042
Phone: +61 2 8095 9260

#269
The Hazy Rose
Category: Bar
Average Price: Modest
Area: Darlinghurst
Address: 83 Stanley St Darlinghurst
New South Wales 2010
Phone: +61 2 9357 5036

#270
The Nag's Head Hotel
Category: Restaurant, Pub
Average Price: Inexpensive
Area: Glebe
Address: 162 St Johns Rd Glebe
New South Wales 2037
Phone: +61 2 9660 1591

#271
Vasco
Category: Italian, Cocktail Bar
Average Price: Modest
Area: Redfern
Address: 421 Cleveland St Surry Hills
New South Wales 2016
Phone: +61 2 9318 2993

#272
Roxbury Hotel
Category: Pub, Comedy Club
Average Price: Modest
Area: Glebe
Address: 182 St. Johns Rd Glebe
New South Wales 2037
Phone: +61 2 9692 0822

#273
Barrio Chino
Category: Bar, Mexican
Average Price: Modest
Area: Potts Point
Address: 28-30 Bayswater Rd Potts
Point New South Wales 2011
Phone: +61 2 8021 9750

#274
Royal Albert Hotel
Category: Pub, Pub Food, Gastropub
Average Price: Inexpensive
Area: Surry Hills
Address: 140 Commonwealth Street
Surry Hills New South Wales 2010
Phone: +61 2 9281 2522

#275
Mr. Fox
Category: Bar, Café
Average Price: Expensive
Area: Surry Hills
Address: 557 Crown St Surry Hills
New South Wales 2010
Phone: +61 4 1469 1811

#276
Sappho Books Cafe & Wine Bar
Category: Wine Bar, Café, Bookstore
Average Price: Modest
Area: Glebe
Address: 51 Glebe Point Rd Glebe
New South Wales 2037
Phone: +61 2 9552 4498

#277
The Lodge Wine Bar
Category: Wine Bar
Area: Balmain
Address: 3/415 Darling St Balmain
New South Wales 2041
Phone: +61 4 1034 9810

#278
Beach Haus
Category: Dance Club
Area: Potts Point
Address: 5 Roslyn Street Sydney
New South Wales 2011
Phone: +61 2 8065 1812

#279
Formaggi Ocello
Category: Wine Bar, Café, Delicatessen
Average Price: Inexpensive
Area: Surry Hills
Address: Shop 16, 425 Bourke St Surry
Hills New South Wales 2010
Phone: +61 2 9357 7878

#280
Heritage Belgian Beer Café
Category: Belgian, Beer Bar
Average Price: Modest
Area: The Rocks
Address: 135 Harrington St The Rocks
New South Wales
Phone: +61 2 8488 2460

#281
Hard Rock Cafe Sydney
Category: Bar, Café
Average Price: Modest
Area: Sydney
Address: 2-10 Darling Drv Darling
Harbour
New South Wales
Phone: +61 2 9280 0077

#282
Blacksheep
Category: Tapas, Bar
Average Price: Expensive
Area: Newtown
Address: 256 King St Newtown
New South Wales 2042
Phone: +61 2 8033 3455

#283
Eathouse Diner
Category: European, Wine Bar
Average Price: Expensive
Area: Redfern
Address: 306 Chalmers St Redfern
New South Wales 2016
Phone: +61 2 8084 9479

#284
Harold Park Hotel
Category: Pub
Average Price: Inexpensive
Area: Forest Lodge
Address: 70A Ross Street Glebe
New South Wales 2037
Phone: +61 2 9660 4745

#285
Well Connected Internet Cafe
Category: Wine Bar, Café, Internet Café
Average Price: Modest
Area: Glebe
Address: 35 Glebe Point Rd Glebe
New South Wales 2037
Phone: +61 2 9566 2655

#286
Forresters Hotel
Category: Beer Bar, Pizza
Average Price: Modest
Area: Surry Hills
Address: 336 Riley St Surry Hills
New South Wales 2010
Phone: +61 2 9212 3035

#287
Cherry
Category: Bar
Average Price: Exclusive
Area: Pyrmont
Address: The Star Casino, 80 Pyrmont
St Pyrmont New South Wales 2009
Phone: +61 2 9777 9000

#288
Hello Sailor
Category: Bar, Seafood
Average Price: Modest
Area: Darlinghurst
Address: 96 Oxford St, Entry Through
Foley St Darlinghurst
New South Wales 2010
Phone: +61 2 9332 2442

#289
The Colombian Hotel
Category: Dance Club, Gay Bar, Pub
Average Price: Modest
Area: Darlinghurst
Address: 117 Oxford St Darlinghurst
New South Wales 2010
Phone: +61 2 9360 2151

#290
East Sydney Hotel
Category: Pub, Pub Food
Average Price: Inexpensive
Area: Woolloomooloo
Address: 113 Cathedral St
New South Wales 2011
Phone: +61 2 9359 1975

#291
Pacific Penthouse
Category: Pub Food, Cocktail Bar,
Beer Gardens
Average Price: Modest
Area: Glebe
Address: Bridge Rd & Glebe Point Rd
New South Wales 2037
Phone: +61 2 9660 1417

#292
Royal Sovereign Hotel
Aka Darlo Bar
Category: Hotel, Bar
Average Price: Modest
Area: Darlinghurst
Address: Darlinghurst Rd Darlinghurst
New South Wales 2010
Phone: +61 2 9331 3672

#293
The Piano Room
Category: Dance Club
Area: Potts Point
Address: 1 Bayswater Rd Kings Cross
New South Wales 2011
Phone: +61 2 8324 4500

#294
Bar Racuda
Category: Cocktail Bar
Average Price: Modest
Area: Newtown
Address: 105 Enmore Rd Enmore
New South Wales 2042
Phone: +61 2 9519 1121

#295
The Midnight Special
Category: Wine Bar
Average Price: Modest
Area: Newtown
Address: 44 Enmore Rd Newtown
New South Wales 2042
Phone: +61 2 9999 9999

#296
Bar Rialto
Category: Pizza, Italian, Cocktail Bar
Area: Surry Hills
Address: 559 Crown St Surry Hills
New South Wales 2010
Phone: +61 2 9310 2266

#297
Duck Inn
Category: Pub
Average Price: Modest
Area: Chippendale
Address: 74 Rose St Chippendale
New South Wales 2008
Phone: +61 2 9319 4415

#298
Farmhouse Kings Cross
Category: Bar, Australian
Area: Rushcutters Bay
Address: 4/40 Bayswater Road
New South Wales 2011
Phone: +61 4 8841 3791

#299
The Dolphin Hotel
Category: Pub, Sports Bar
Average Price: Modest
Area: Surry Hills
Address: 412 Crown St Surry Hills
New South Wales 2010
Phone: +61 2 9331 4800

#300
Bar 100
Category: Bar
Average Price: Modest
Area: The Rocks
Address: 100 George St The Rocks
New South Wales
Phone: +61 2 8070 9311

#301
The White Horse
Category: Gastropub, French, Wine Bar
Average Price: Modest
Area: Surry Hills
Address: 381-385 Crown St Surry Hills
New South Wales 2010
Phone: +61 2 8333 9900

#302
The Yardhouse
Category: Nightlife
Area: Haymarket
Address: 730-742 George Street
New South Wales
Phone: +61 2 9212 2111

#303
Name This Bar
Category: Bar, Music Venues, Art
Gallery
Area: Darlinghurst
Address: 197 Oxford St Darlinghurst
New South Wales 2010
Phone: +61 2 9356 2123

#304
Li'l Darlin
Category: Tapas, Cocktail Bar
Average Price: Inexpensive
Area: Surry Hills
Address: 420 Elizabeth St Surry Hills
New South Wales 2010
Phone: +61 2 9698 5488

#305
Ms. G's
Category: Bar, Asian Fusion,
Vietnamese
Average Price: Expensive
Area: Potts Point
Address: 155 Victoria St Potts Point
New South Wales 2011
Phone: +61 2 9240 3000

#306
Hustle & Flow Bar
Category: Bar, Music Venues
Average Price: Modest
Area: Redfern
Address: 105 Regent St Redfern
New South Wales 2016
Phone: +61 2 9310 5593

#307
Dove & Olive
Category: Beer, Wine, Spirits,
Australian, Cocktail Bar
Average Price: Modest
Area: Surry Hills
Address: 156 Devonshire St Surry Hills
New South Wales 2010
Phone: +61 2 9699 6001

#308
Kauri Foreshore Hotel
Category: Pub
Average Price: Inexpensive
Area: Glebe
Address: 2 Bridge St Glebe
New South Wales 2037
Phone: +61 2 9660 0112

#309
The Red Door
Category: Bar, Australian
Average Price: Modest
Area: Surry Hills
Address: 65-67 Foveaux St Surry Hills
New South Wales 2010
Phone: +61 2 9211 0664

#310
Li'l Darlin
Category: Bar
Average Price: Modest
Area: Darlinghurst
Address: 235 Victoria St Darlinghurst
New South Wales 2010
Phone: +61 2 8084 6100

#311
Palms Nightclub
Category: Gay Bar
Average Price: Modest
Area: Darlinghurst
Address: 124 Oxford Street
New South Wales 2010
Phone: +61 2 9357 4166

#312
The Wanderer
Category: Cocktail Bar, American
Average Price: Modest
Area: Surry Hills
Address: 501 Elizabeth St Surry Hills
New South Wales 2010
Phone: +61 4 5034 5725

#313
Cafe Lounge
Category: Café, Music Venues, Bar
Average Price: Modest
Area: Darlinghurst
Address: 277 Goulburn St Surry Hills
New South Wales 2010
Phone: +61 2 9016 3951

#314
Mad Pizza E Bar
Category: Bar, Pizza
Average Price: Modest
Area: Darlinghurst
Address: 312 Victoria St
New South Wales 2010
Phone: +61 2 9020 7186

#315
Emmilou
Category: Lounge
Average Price: Modest
Area: Surry Hills
Address: 413 Bourke St Surry Hills
New South Wales 2010
Phone: +61 2 9360 6991

#316
Porterhouse Irish Pub
Category: Pub, Irish
Average Price: Modest
Area: Surry Hills
Address: 233 Riley St Surry Hills
New South Wales 2010
Phone: +61 2 9211 4454

#317
Hot Damn! - Qbar
Category: Bar
Average Price: Inexpensive
Area: Darlinghurst
Address: 34 Oxford St Darlinghurst
New South Wales 2010
Phone: +61 2 9331 2956

#318
Chamberlain Hotel
Category: Pub
Average Price: Inexpensive
Area: Haymarket
Address: 428 Pitt Street Sydney
New South Wales
Phone: +61 2 9288 0888

#319
Albion Place Hotel
Category: Pub
Average Price: Modest
Area: Sydney
Address: 531 George St Sydney
New South Wales
Phone: +61 9 9930 760

#320
Quay Bar
Category: Bar, Café
Average Price: Inexpensive
Area: Sydney
Address: Customs House, 31 Alfred
Street Circular Quay New South Wales
Phone: +61 2 9247 4898

#321
Mille Vini
Category: Tapas, Italian, Wine Bar,
Australian
Average Price: Modest
Area: Surry Hills
Address: 397 Crown Street, Sydney
Surry Hills New South Wales 2010
Phone: +61 9 3573 3660

#322
Phillip's Foote
Category: Pub
Average Price: Expensive
Area: The Rocks
Address: 101 George St The Rocks
New South Wales
Phone: +61 2 9241 1485

#323
Kit And Kaboodle
Category: Bar
Average Price: Expensive
Area: Potts Point
Address: 33 Darlinghurst Road Potts
Point New South Wales 2011
Phone: +61 2 9368 0300

#324
O'Malleys Hotel
Category: Pub
Average Price: Inexpensive
Area: Potts Point
Address: 228 William St Woolloomooloo
New South Wales 2011
Phone: +61 2 9357 2211

#325
King Street Brewhouse
Category: Sports Bar, Restaurant
Average Price: Modest
Area: Sydney
Address: 22 The Promenade Sydney
New South Wales
Phone: +61 2 8270 7901

#326
Timbah
Category: Wine Bar
Average Price: Expensive
Area: Glebe
Address: U1/375 Glebe Point Road
Glebe New South Wales 2037
Phone: +61 2 9571 7005

#327
The Imperial Hotel
Category: Dance Club, Gay Bar, Pub
Average Price: Modest
Area: Erskineville
Address: 35 Erskineville Rd Erskineville
New South Wales 2043
Phone: +61 2 9519 9899

#328
Trinity Bar & Restaurant
Category: Pub, Australian
Average Price: Modest
Area: Surry Hills
Address: 505 Crown St Surry Hills
New South Wales 2010
Phone: +61 2 9319 6802

#329
The Cricketers Arms Hotel
Category: Bar
Average Price: Modest
Area: Surry Hills
Address: 106 Fitzroy St Surry Hills
New South Wales 2010
Phone: +61 2 9331 3301

#330
Firehouse Hotel
Category: Bar, Pub Food
Average Price: Modest
Area: North Sydney
Address: 86 Walker St North Sydney
New South Wales 2060
Phone: +61 2 8904 9696

#331
Juju
Category: Japanese, Karaoke
Average Price: Modest
Area: Potts Point
Address: Shop 301 82-94 Darlinghurst
Road Potts Point New South Wales 2011
Phone: +61 2 9357 7100

#332
Royal Hotel Paddington
Category: Restaurant, Pub, Hotel
Average Price: Modest
Area: Paddington
Address: 237 Glenmore Rd Paddington
New South Wales 2021
Phone: +61 2 9331 2604

#333
Tappo
Category: Italian, Wine Bar
Area: Pyrmont
Address: 2-14 Bunn St Pyrmont
New South Wales 2009
Phone: +61 9 5521 509

#334
Durty Nelly's Bar
Category: Bar, Australian
Area: Paddington
Address: 9 Glenmore Rd Paddington
New South Wales 2021
Phone: +61 2 9360 4467

#335
The Standard
Category: Bar, Music Venues
Area: Darlinghurst
Address: 383 Bourke Street
New South Wales 2010
Phone: +61 2 9552 6333

#336
Toxteth Hotel
Category: Pub
Average Price: Modest
Area: Glebe
Address: 345 Glebe Point Road Glebe
New South Wales 2037
Phone: +61 2 9660 2370

#337
PLAY BAR
Category: Bar
Average Price: Modest
Area: Surry Hills
Address: 72 Campbell St Surry Hills
New South Wales 2010
Phone: +61 2 9280 0885

#338
Toku Toku
Category: Japanese, Tapas, Wine Bar
Average Price: Expensive
Area: Glebe
Address: 36 Glebe Point Rd Glebe
New South Wales 2037
Phone: +61 2 9660 9636

#339
Ding Dong Dang
Category: Karaoke, Bar
Average Price: Exclusive
Area: Surry Hills
Address: 7 Randle Street Surry Hills
New South Wales 2010
Phone: +61 2 9281 9000

#340
Hotel Hollywood
Category: Pub
Average Price: Inexpensive
Area: Surry Hills
Address: 2 Foster St Surry Hills
New South Wales 2010
Phone: +61 2 9281 2765

#341
Dynasty Karaoke Club
Category: Karaoke
Average Price: Modest
Area: Haymarket
Address: 63 Dixon St. Haymarket
New South Wales
Phone: +61 2 9281 9006

#342
Marlborough Hotel
Category: Venues, Event Space,
Pub, Cocktail Bar
Average Price: Modest
Area: Newtown
Address: 145 King St Newtown
New South Wales 2042
Phone: +61 2 9519 1222

#343
The Royal
Category: Pub, Food
Area: Darlington
Address: 370 Abercrombie St
New South Wales 2008
Phone: +61 2 9698 8557

#344
Gaslight Inn
Category:
Average Price: Modest
Area: Darlinghurst
Address: 278 Crown St Darlinghurst
New South Wales 2010
Phone: +61 2 9360 6746

#345
Yulli's
Category: Wine Bar, Vegetarian, Tapas
Average Price: Modest
Area: Surry Hills
Address: 417 Crown St Surry Hills
New South Wales 2010
Phone: +61 2 9319 6609

#346
Jekyll & Hyde
Category: Wine Bar, Breakfast & Brunch
Average Price: Modest
Area: Darlinghurst
Address: 332 Victoria Rd Darlinghurst
New South Wales 2010
Phone: +61 2 9360 5568

#347
The Lansdowne
Category: Pub, Music Venues,
Pub Food
Average Price: Inexpensive
Area: Chippendale
Address: 2 - 6 City Rd Chippendale
New South Wales 2008
Phone: +61 2 8218 2333

#348
Star Karaoke
Category: Karaoke
Area: Pyrmont
Address: 80 Pyrmont St Pyrmont
New South Wales 2009
Phone: 1800 700 700

#349
Pumphouse Restaurant & Bar
Category: Pub, Australian
Area: Haymarket
Address: 17 Little Pier St Darling
Harbour New South Wales
Phone: +61 2 8217 4100

#350
Botany View Hotel
Category: Pub
Average Price: Modest
Area: Newtown
Address: 597 King St Newtown
New South Wales 2042
Phone: +61 2 9519 4501

#351
Stonewall Hotel
Category: Gay Bar
Average Price: Inexpensive
Area: Darlinghurst
Address: 175 Oxford St Darlinghurst
New South Wales 2010
Phone: +61 2 9360 1963

#352
Light Brigade Hotel
Category: Sports Bar
Average Price: Modest
Area: Paddington
Address: 2A Oxford St Woollahra
New South Wales 2025
Phone: +61 2 9357 0888

#353
East Village Hotel
Category: Pub
Average Price: Modest
Area: Darlinghurst
Address: 234 Palmer St Darlinghurst
New South Wales 2010
Phone: +61 2 9331 5457

#354
Seymour Centre
Category: Performing Arts,
Music Venues
Average Price: Modest
Area: Darlington
Address: Corner of City Rd And
Cleveland St Chippendale
New South Wales 2008
Phone: +61 2 9351 7944

#355
GT's Hotel
Category: Comedy Club,
Music Venues, Pub
Average Price: Modest
Area: Surry Hills
Address: 64 Devonshire St Surry Hills
New South Wales 2010
Phone: +61 2 9211 1687

#356
The Bourbon
Category: Bar, American, Jazz, Blues
Average Price: Modest
Area: Potts Point
Address: 22 Darlinghurst Rd Potts Point
New South Wales 2011
Phone: +61 2 9035 8888

#357
Tandoori Palace
Category: Indian, Karaoke
Area: Darlinghurst
Address: 86 Oxford St Darlinghurst
New South Wales 2010
Phone: +61 2 9331 7072

#358
Woolloomooloo Bay Hotel
Category: Pub, Sports Bar
Average Price: Modest
Area: Woolloomooloo
Address: 2 Bourke St
New South Wales 2011
Phone: +61 2 9357 1177

#359
Old Fitzroy Hotel
Category: Bar, Thai
Average Price: Inexpensive
Area: Woolloomooloo
Address: 129 Dowling St
New South Wales 2011
Phone: +61 2 9356 3848

#360
Rose of Australia Hotel
Category: Pub, Restaurant, Beer,
Wine, Spirits
Average Price: Expensive
Area: Erskineville
Address: 1 Swanson St Erskineville
New South Wales 2043
Phone: +61 2 9565 1441

#361
**Wine Odyssey Wine Bar
& Restaurant**
Category: Wine Bar
Area: The Rocks
Address: 39 Argyle St The Rocks
New South Wales
Phone: +61 2 8114 0256

#362
Wentworth Park Greyhounds
Category: Nightlife, Active Life
Average Price: Expensive
Area: Glebe
Address: Wentworth Park Rd Glebe
New South Wales 2037
Phone: +61 2 8587 1202

#363
99
Category: Lounge
Area: Glebe
Address: 99 Glebe Point Rd Glebe
New South Wales 2037
Phone: +61 4 1120 9930

#364
Vini
Category: Wine Bar, Tapas, Italian
Average Price: Expensive
Area: Surry Hills
Address: 118 Devonshire St Surry Hills
New South Wales 2010
Phone: +61 2 9698 5131

#365
Spectrum
Category: Music Venues, Dance Club
Area: Surry Hills
Address: 34-44 Oxford Street
Darlinghurst
New South Wales 2010
Phone: +61 2 9360 1375

#366
Bar Sport
Category: Café, Sports Bar
Average Price: Inexpensive
Area: Leichhardt
Address: 2A Norton Street Leichhardt
New South Wales 2040
Phone: +61 2 9569 2397

#367
Paddington Woollahra RSL Club
Category: Sports Bar
Average Price: Inexpensive
Area: Paddington
Address: 220-232 Oxford St Paddington
New South Wales 2021
Phone: +61 2 9331 1203

#368
The Royal Oak
Category: Gastropub, Pub
Average Price: Modest
Area: Balmain
Address: 36 College St Balmain
New South Wales 2041
Phone: +61 2 9810 2311

#369
Zinc Cafe
Category: Wine Bar, Café, Coffee, Tea
Average Price: Expensive
Area: Potts Point
Address: 77 Macleay Street Potts Point
New South Wales 2011
Phone: +61 2 9358 6777

#370
Excelsior Hotel Glebe
Category: Pub
Average Price: Modest
Area: Glebe
Address: 101 Bridge Rd Glebe
New South Wales 2037
Phone: +61 2 9552 9700

#371
Yebisu Izakaya
Category: Japanese, Bar, Sushi Bar
Average Price: Modest
Area: Sydney
Address: 501 George St Sydney
New South Wales
Phone: +61 2 9266 0301

#372
Nortons On Norton
Category: Pub
Average Price: Modest
Area: Leichhardt
Address: 1 Norton St Leichhardt
New South Wales 2040
Phone: +61 2 9560 3322

#373
The Chip Off The Old Block
Category: Bar
Average Price: Modest
Area: Chippendale
Address: 3 Little Queen St Chippendale
New South Wales 2008
Phone: +61 2 9318 0815

#374
Onyx Lounge
Category: Cocktail Bar, Wine Bar, Tapas
Average Price: Inexpensive
Area: Newtown
Address: 324 King St Newtown
New South Wales 2042
Phone: +61 4 5154 1712

#375
Rupert And Rudy's
Category: Cocktail Bar, American
Area: Darlinghurst
Address: 78 Stanley St Darlinghurst
New South Wales 2010
Phone: +61 2 7901 0396

#376
Name This Bar
Category: Lounge
Area: Darlinghurst
Address: 197 Oxford St Darlinghurst
New South Wales 2010
Phone: +61 2 9356 2123

#377
The Observer Hotel
Category: Bar
Area: The Rocks
Address: 69 George St The Rocks
New South Wales
Phone: +61 2 9252 4169

#378
Velluto Private Dining Room & Events
Category: Lounge, Venues,
Event Space
Average Price: Expensive
Area: Elizabeth Bay
Address: 50 Macleay St Potts Point
New South Wales 2011
Phone: +61 2 9357 1100

#379
Jonkanoo A Caribbean Joint
Category: Caribbean, Bar
Area: Surry Hills
Address: 583 Crown St Surry Hills
New South Wales 2010
Phone: +61 4 1592 2240

#380
Steki Taverna
Category: Greek, Music Venues
Area: Newtown
Address: 2 O'Connell St Newtown
New South Wales 2042
Phone: +61 2 9516 2191

#381
Elephant Bar
Category:
Area: Paddington
Address: 237 Glenmore Rd Paddington
New South Wales 2021
Phone: +61 2 9331 2604

#382
Burdekin Hotel
Category: Pub
Average Price: Modest
Area: Darlinghurst
Address: 2 Oxford St Darlinghurst
New South Wales 2010
Phone: +61 2 9331 3066

#383
Cornerstone Bar & Food
Category: Bar, Australian
Area: Eveleigh
Address: 245 Wilson St Eveleigh
New South Wales 2020
Phone: +61 2 8571 9004

#384
Buzzbar Cafe
Category: Bar, Mediterranean
Area: Newtown
Address: 349 King Street Newtown
New South Wales 2042
Phone: +61 2 9557 9191

#385
Eastbank Cafe Bar Pizzeria
Category: Bar, Café, Pizza
Average Price: Exclusive
Address: 61-69 Macquarie St Circular
Quay New South Wales
Phone: +61 2 9241 6722

#386
Bedlam Bar
Category: Bar, Pub Food
Area: Glebe
Address: 2-12 Glebe Point Rd Glebe
New South Wales 2037
Phone: +61 2 9660 6999

#387
Lord Roberts Hotel
Category: Pub
Area: Darlinghurst
Address: 64 Stanley St East Sydney
New South Wales 2010
Phone: +61 2 9331 1326

#388
Sapphire Lounge
Category: Dance Club, Lounge
Area: Potts Point
Address: 2 Kellett St Kings Cross
New South Wales 2011
Phone: +61 2 9331 0058

#389
Brooklyn Social
Category: Cocktail Bar, Burgers
Area: Surry Hills
Address: 17 Randle St Surry Hills
New South Wales 2010
Phone: +61 4 5197 2057

#390
Off Broadway Hotel
Category: Pub
Area: Chippendale
Address: Bay Street Broadway
New South Wales 2007
Phone: +61 2 9212 5560

#391
Triple Ace Bar
Category: Hotel, Pub
Average Price: Inexpensive
Area: Haymarket
Address: Cnr Campbell & Elizabeth Sts
Surry Hills New South Wales 2010
Phone: +61 2 9211 6888

#392
Zebra Lounge
Category: Bar, Café
Average Price: Expensive
Area: Pyrmont
Address: 1 Harris St Pyrmont
New South Wales 2009
Phone: +61 2 9571 5503

#393
Lord Wolseley Hotel
Category: Pub, Hotel, Restaurant
Average Price: Inexpensive
Area: Ultimo
Address: 265 Bulwara Rd Ultimo
New South Wales 2007
Phone: +61 2 9660 1736

#394
Mercantile Hotel
Category: Bar
Average Price: Modest
Area: The Rocks
Address: 25 George St The Rocks
New South Wales
Phone: +61 2 9247 3570

#395
Leichhardt Hotel
Category: Venues, Event Space, Bar
Average Price: Inexpensive
Area: Leichhardt
Address: 95 Norton St Leichhardt
New South Wales 2040
Phone: +61 2 9518 3476

#396
Imperial Hotel Pty
Category: Pub, Gastropub
Average Price: Modest
Area: Paddington
Address: 252 Oxford St Paddington
New South Wales 2021
Phone: +61 2 9331 2023

#397
Rose, Shamrock & Thistle Hotel
Category: Bar
Average Price: Modest
Area: Paddington
Address: 27-33 Oxford Street
Paddington New South Wales 2021
Phone: +61 2 9360 4662

#398
Rainford Street Social
Category: Lounge
Average Price: Expensive
Area: Surry Hills
Address: 500 Crown St Surry Hills
New South Wales 2010
Phone: +61 2 9357 2573

#399
Drink Better Wine
Category: Wine Bar, Tapas
Average Price: Modest
Area: North Sydney
Address: 189 Miller St North Sydney
New South Wales 2059
Phone: +61 2 8061 2511

#400
London Hotel & Restaurant
Category: Pub, Steakhouse
Area: Balmain
Address: 234 Darling St Balmain
New South Wales 2041
Phone: +61 2 9555 1377

#401
Paddington Bowling Club
Category: Dance Club, Social Club
Average Price: Modest
Area: Paddington
Address: 2 Quarry St Paddington
New South Wales 2021
Phone: +61 2 9363 1150

#402
The Record Crate
Category: Music, DVDs, Bar
Average Price: Modest
Area: Glebe
Address: 34 Glebe Point Rd Glebe
New South Wales 2037
Phone: +61 2 9660 1075

#403
Sagra
Category: Wine Bar, Italian
Average Price: Expensive
Area: Darlinghurst
Address: 62 Stanley St Darlinghurst
New South Wales 2010
Phone: +44 28 307 0430

#404
Fiore Cafe And Bar
Category: Italian, Bar
Average Price: Modest
Area: Darlinghurst
Address: 13B Burton St Darlinghurst
New South Wales 2010
Phone: +61 2 9332 1194

#405
The Balmain
Category: Gastropub,
Beer Gardens, Pub
Area: Balmain
Address: 74 Mullens St Balmain
New South Wales 2041
Phone: +61 2 9810 7500

#406
New Hampton
Category: Cocktail Bar,
Wine Bar, Winery
Average Price: Inexpensive
Area: Potts Point
Address: 15 Bayswater Rd Potts Point
New South Wales 2011
Phone: +61 2 9331 1188

#407
Iguana Bar & Restaurant
Category: European, Bar
Area: Potts Point
Address: 15 Kellett St Kings Cross
New South Wales 2011
Phone: +61 2 9357 2609

#408
Tonic Lounge
Category: Dance Club
Area: Potts Point
Address: 62 -64 Kellett Street Potts
Point New South Wales 2011
Phone: +61 2 8354 1544

#409
Lotus Bar
Category: Bar
Area: Pyrmont
Address: 80 Pyrmont Street Pyrmont
New South Wales 2009
Phone: 1800 700 700

#410
The Chippendale Hotel
Category: Pub, Irish
Average Price: Modest
Area: Chippendale
Address: 87-91 Abercrombie St
Chippendale New South Wales 2008
Phone: +61 2 9310 5133

#411
Nevermind
Category: Gay Bar
Area: Darlinghurst
Address: 163 Oxford St Darlinghurst
New South Wales 2010
Phone: +61 2 9358 2955

#412
The Lord Nelson Brewery Hotel
Category: Pub, Beer Bar, Australian
Average Price: Modest
Area: Millers Point
Address: 19 Kent St The Rocks
New South Wales
Phone: +61 2 9251 4044

#413
Orient Hotel
Category: Venues, Event Space, Pub
Average Price: Modest
Area: The Rocks
Address: 89 George St The Rocks
New South Wales
Phone: +61 2 9251 1255

#414
Gazebo Group Pty Ltd
Category: Bar
Average Price: Expensive
Area: Elizabeth Bay
Address: 2 Elizabeth Bay Rd Elizabeth
Bay New South Wales 2011
Phone: +61 2 9357 5333

#415
The Club
Category: Dance Club, Lounge
Average Price: Modest
Area: Potts Point
Address: 33 Bayswater Rd Potts Point
New South Wales 2011
Phone: +61 2 9331 0511

#416
The Cottage Bar & Kitchen
Category: Lounge, Wine Bar, Tapas
Average Price: Modest
Area: Balmain
Address: 342 Darling St Balmain
New South Wales 2041
Phone: +61 2 8084 8185

#417
Crest Hotel
Category: Sports Bar
Average Price: Inexpensive
Area: Potts Point
Address: 111 Darlinghurst Rd Kings
Cross New South Wales 2011
Phone: +61 2 9358 2755

#418
Key Largo Bar
Area: Rushcutters Bay
Address: 98 Bayswater Road
New South Wales 2011
Phone: +61 2 9331 2941

#419
Zigi's Wine & Cheese Bar
Category: Wine Bar, Australian
Average Price: Expensive
Area: Chippendale
Address: 86 Abercrombie St
Chippendale New South Wales 2008
Phone: +61 2 9699 4222

#420
Altitude Bar
Average Price: Modest
Area: The Rocks
Address: 176 Cumberland St The Rocks
New South Wales
Phone: +61 2 9250 6123

#421
Heavy Feather
Category: Bar
Area: Darlinghurst
Address: 137 Oxford St Darlinghurst
New South Wales 2010
Phone: +61 2 9331 1229

#422
Sydney Symphony Box Office
Category: Music Venues
Area: The Rocks
Address: Corner Harrington & Argyle
Streets The Rocks New South Wales
Phone: +61 2 8215 4600

#423
Kurrajong Hotel
Category: Hotel, Pub
Average Price: Inexpensive
Area: Erskineville
Address: 106 Swanson St Erskineville
New South Wales 2043
Phone: +61 2 9519 3609

#424
Abbotts Hotel
Category: Pub, Beer Bar
Area: Waterloo
Address: 45 Botany Rd Waterloo
New South Wales 2017
Phone: +61 2 9395 0000

#425
Pyrmont Point Hotel
Category: Bar
Average Price: Modest
Area: Pyrmont
Address: 59 Harris St Pyrmont
New South Wales 2009
Phone: +61 2 9660 1908

#426
Glasgow Arms Hotel
Category: Pub, Hotel
Area: Ultimo
Address: 527 Harris St Ultimo
New South Wales 2007
Phone: +61 2 9211 2354

#427
Michelle's
Category: Adult Entertainment
Area: Darlinghurst
Address: 135 Bayswater Rd
Rushcutters Bay
New South Wales 2011
Phone: +61 2 9357 6133

#428
Paragon Hotel
Category: Pub, Sports Bar, Music
Venues
Average Price: Modest
Area: Sydney
Address: Circular Quay
New South Wales
Phone: +61 2 9241 3522

#429
The Midnight Shift
Category: Gay Bar
Area: Darlinghurst
Address: 85 Oxford St Darlinghurst
New South Wales 2010
Phone: +61 2 9360 4463

#430
Longrain
Category: Wine Bar, Thai, Lounge
Average Price: Expensive
Area: Surry Hills
Address: 85 Commonwealth St Surry
Hills New South Wales 2010
Phone: +61 2 9280 2888

#431
Tipple Bar And Bistro
Category: Bar, Fast Food
Average Price: Modest
Area: Surry Hills
Address: 28 Chalmers St Surry Hills
New South Wales 2010
Phone: +61 2 9212 0006

#432
Mansions Hotel
Category: Bar
Area: Potts Point
Address: 18 Bayswater Road Potts
Point New South Wales 2011
Phone: +61 2 9358 6677

#433
Brighton Bar
Category: Bar
Average Price: Inexpensive
Area: Darlinghurst
Address: Oxford Street Darlinghurst
New South Wales 2010
Phone: +61 2 9331 5153

#434
21
Category: Dance Club, Lounge
Average Price: Modest
Area: Potts Point
Address: 12 Kellet Street Potts Point
New South Wales 2011
Phone: +61 2 9380 6060

#435
The Moose
Category: Jazz, Blues, Bar
Average Price: Expensive
Area: Newtown
Address: 530 King St Newtown
New South Wales 2042
Phone: +61 2 9557 0072

#436
Quarrymans Hotel
Category: Pub
Average Price: Modest
Area: Pyrmont
Address: 214- 216 Harris St Pyrmont
New South Wales 2009
Phone: +61 2 9660 4520

#437
La Tana Spritz Bar & Restaurant
Category: Wine Bar, Italian
Area: Redfern
Address: 648 Bourke St Redfern
New South Wales 2016
Phone: +61 2 9310 2311

#438
Buzzz Bar
Category: Coffee, Tea, Café, Wine Bar
Average Price: Modest
Area: Newtown
Address: 349 King Street Newtown
New South Wales 2042
Phone: +61 2 9557 9191

#439
L'aperitivo By L'incontro
Category: Cocktail Bar, Italian
Area: North Sydney
Address: 196 Miller St North Sydney
New South Wales 2060
Phone: +61 2 9957 2274

#440
Hampshire Hotel
Category: Pub, Bistros, Beer Gardens
Area: Camperdown
Address: 91 Parramatta Rd
Camperdown
New South Wales 2050
Phone: +61 2 8068 8418

#441
Maloney's Hotel
Category: Pub, Restaurant
Average Price: Modest
Area: Sydney
Address: 81 Goulburn Street Haymarket
New South Wales
Phone: +61 2 9211 2992

#442
Docks Hotel
Category: Dance Club,
Music Venues, Pub
Area: Sydney
Address: Shop 225, Harbourside Darling
Harbour New South Wales
Phone: +61 2 9280 2270

#443
Sam I Am Cafe Bar
Category: Café, Bar, Breakfast & Brunch
Average Price: Modest
Area: Glebe
Address: 99 Glebe Point Rd Glebe
New South Wales 2037
Phone: +61 2 8065 9156

#444
Railz On Regent
Category: Pub
Area: Redfern
Address: Cnr Regent & Redfern St
New South Wales 2016
Phone: +61 2 9699 2099

#445
Victoria Hotel Pub
Area: Annandale
Address: 176A Young St Annandale
New South Wales 2038
Phone: +61 2 9569 2383

#446
Candy's Apartment
Category: Dance Club
Area: Potts Point
Address: 22 Bayswater Road,
New South Wales 2011
Phone: +61 2 9357 4611

#447
Cauliflower Hotel
Category: Hotel, Pub, Sports Bar
Area: Waterloo
Address: 123 Botany Rd Waterloo
New South Wales 2017
Phone: +61 2 9698 3024

#448
Reggio Lounge
Category: Italian, Bar, Café
Average Price: Modest
Area: Darlinghurst
Address: 85A Stanley St Darlinghurst
New South Wales 2010
Phone: +61 2 9332 1140

#449
Sette Espresso Eatery Bar
Category: Café, European, Lounge
Area: Eveleigh
Address: 8 Central Ave Eveleigh
New South Wales 2020
Phone: +61 2 9698 7561

#450
Gotham
Category: Bar
Area: Surry Hills
Address: 35 Oxford St Darlinghurst
New South Wales
Phone: +61 2 9283 1891

#451
Q Bar
Category: Dance Club
Area: Surry Hills
Address: 44 Oxford St Darlinghurst
New South Wales 2010
Phone: +61 2 9360 1375

#452
Nevada Lounge
Category: Bar
Area: Surry Hills
Address: 34-44 Oxford St Darlinghurst
New South Wales 2010
Phone: +61 2 9331 2956

#453
Haymarket Hotel
Category: Cocktail Bar, Australian
Area: Haymarket
Address: 661 663 George St Haymarket
New South Wales
Phone: +61 2 8221 0226

#454
Stanley Street Station
Category: Bar, Café, European
Area: Darlinghurst
Address: 85A Stanley St Darlinghurst
New South Wales 2010
Phone: +61 2 9331 5375

#455
Evening Star Hotel
Category: Pub
Area: Surry Hills
Address: Cnr Elizabeth & Cooper Sts
Surry Hills New South Wales 2010
Phone: +61 2 9281 8177

#456
Bar Cleveland
Category: Venues, Event Space,
Sports Bar
Average Price: Modest
Area: Redfern
Address: 433 Cleveland St Surry Hills
New South Wales 2010
Phone: +61 2 9698 1908

#457
Spacekadets
Category: Dance Club
Area: Darlinghurst
Address: 134 Oxford St Darlinghurst
New South Wales 2010
Phone: +61 4 1309 8105

#458
Hermann's Bar
Category: Music Venues, Pub
Area: Darlington
Address: Corner City Road & Butlin
Avenue University of Sydney
New South Wales 2006
Phone: +61 2 9563 6000

#459
Tunnel Nightclub
Category: Dance Club
Area: Potts Point
Address: 1 Earl Place Potts Point
New South Wales 2011
Phone: +61 2 8065 8937

#460
Empire Hotel
Category: Dance Club, Pub
Area: Potts Point
Address: 32 Darlinghurst Road Potts
Point New South Wales 2011
Phone: +61 2 9360 7531

#461
Vice Wine Bar
Category: Bar
Area: Balmain
Address: 350 Darling St Balmain
New South Wales 2041
Phone: +61 2 8068 2441

#462
Absinthesalon
Category: Bar
Area: Surry Hills
Address: 87 Albion Street Surry Hills
New South Wales 2010
Phone: +61 2 9211 6632

#463
The Zoo Bar
Category: Bar
Area: Leichhardt
Address: 55 Norton St Leichhardt
New South Wales 2040
Phone: +61 2 9564 1777

#464
Phoenix Bar
Category: Dance Club
Area: Darlinghurst
Address: 34-44 Oxford Street,
Sydney Darlinghurst
New South Wales 2010
Phone: +61 2 9311 2956

#465
The Workers
Category: Pub
Area: Balmain
Address: 292 Darling St Balmain
New South Wales 2041
Phone: +61 2 9318 1547

#466
North Annandale Hotel
Category: Pub
Area: Annandale
Address: 105 Johnston St Annandale
New South Wales 2038
Phone: +61 2 9660 7452

#467
Alexandria Hotel
Category: Hotel, Pub
Average Price: Modest
Area: Eveleigh
Address: 35 Henerdson Rd Alexandria
New South Wales 2020
Phone: +61 2 9698 1933

#468
The Clare Hotel
Average Price: Inexpensive
Area: Chippendale
Address: 20 Broadway Broadway
New South Wales 2007
Phone: +61 2 9211 2839

#469
Soho Bar & Lounge
Category: Dance Club, Lounge
Average Price: Expensive
Area: Potts Point
Address: 171 Victoria St Potts Point
New South Wales 2011
Phone: +61 2 9358 6511

#470
DOME
Category: Dance Club, Australian,
Jazz, Blues
Average Price: Modest
Area: Surry Hills
Address: Cleveland St Surry Hills
New South Wales 2010
Phone: +61 2 9699 3460

#471
Enmore Theatre
Category: Music Venues
Average Price: Modest
Area: Newtown
Address: 130 Enmore Rd Newtown
New South Wales 2042
Phone: +61 2 9550 3666

#472
The Bearded Tit Bar
Category: Music Venues, Beer Bar,
Wine Bar
Average Price: Modest
Area: Redfern
Address: 183 Regent St Redfern
New South Wales 2016
Phone: +61 2 8283 4082

#473
Löwenbräu Keller
Category: Bar, German
Average Price: Modest
Area: The Rocks
Address: Corner of Playfair & Argyle St
The Rocks New South Wales
Phone: +61 2 9247 7785

#474
K1 Karaoke Lounge
Category: Karaoke, Lounge
Average Price: Inexpensive
Area: Haymarket
Address: Level 2, 31-37 Dixon St
Haymarket New South Wales
Phone: +61 2 9211 1776

#475
The Bear
Category: Cocktail Bar
Average Price: Modest
Area: Haymarket
Address: Thomas Lane Haymarket
New South Wales
Phone: +61 4 5102 9226

#476
Happy Endings Comedy Club
Category: Comedy Club,
Performing Arts
Average Price: Modest
Area: Potts Point
Address: 154 Brougham St Kings Cross
New South Wales 2011
Phone: +61 2 9300 9060

#477
Rock Lily
Category: Music Venues
Average Price: Modest
Area: Pyrmont
Address: 80 Pyrmont St Pyrmont
New South Wales 2009
Phone: 1800 700 700

#478
The Animal At Newtown Hotel
Category: Greek, Bar
Average Price: Expensive
Area: Newtown
Address: 174 King St Newtown
New South Wales 2042
Phone: +61 9 5576 399

#479
Newtown Social Club
Category: Music Venues, Bar
Average Price: Modest
Area: Newtown
Address: 387 King St Newtown
New South Wales 2042
Phone: +61 2 9550 3974

#480
Ester Restaurant And Bar
Category: Wine Bar
Average Price: Expensive
Area: Chippendale
Address: 46-52 Meagher St
Chippendale New South Wales 2008
Phone: +61 2 8068 8279

#481
Cat And Fiddle Hotel
Category: Irish Pub
Average Price: Modest
Area: Balmain
Address: 456 Darling St Balmain
New South Wales 2041
Phone: +61 2 9810 7931

#482
Royal Hotel Leichhardt
Category: Hotel, Karaoke
Average Price: Expensive
Area: Leichhardt
Address: 156 Norton St Leichhardt
New South Wales 2040
Phone: +61 2 9569 2638

#483
Wooloomooloo Bay Hotel
Category: Pub Food, Pub
Average Price: Expensive
Area: Woolloomooloo
Address: 2 Bourke St
New South Wales 2011
Phone: +61 2 9357 1177

#484
Pyrmont Bridge Hotel
Category: Pub
Average Price: Modest
Area: Pyrmont
Address: 96 Union St Pyrmont
New South Wales 2009
Phone: +61 2 9660 6996

#485
Mr Coopers
Category: Wine Bar, European
Average Price: Modest
Area: Paddington
Address: 438 Oxford St Paddington
New South Wales 2021
Phone: +61 2 8084 5465

#486
Dry Dock Hotel
Category: Pub
Average Price: Modest
Area: Balmain
Address: 22 Cameron St Balmain
New South Wales 2041
Phone: +61 2 9555 1306

#487
Wembley Snooker Center
Category: Pool Hall
Average Price: Modest
Area: Haymarket
Address: 841 George St Haymarket
New South Wales
Phone: +61 4 1327 7003

#488
Pocket Bar
Category: Wine Bar, Cocktail Bar
Average Price: Modest
Area: Darlinghurst
Address: 13 Burton St Darlinghurst
New South Wales 2010
Phone: +61 2 9380 7002

#489
Buzzz Bar
Category: Wine Bar, Café,
Breakfast & Brunch
Average Price: Modest
Area: Newtown
Address: 349 King Street Newtown
New South Wales 2042
Phone: +61 2 9557 9191

#490
Town Hall Hotel
Category: Pub, Pizza, Music Venues
Average Price: Modest
Area: Newtown
Address: 326 King St Newtown
New South Wales 2042
Phone: +61 2 9557 1206

#491
Cohibar
Category: Cocktail Bar
Average Price: Modest
Area: Sydney
Address: Shop 359 Darling Harbour
New South Wales
Phone: +61 2 9281 4440

#492
Hugo's Bar Pizza
Category: Pizza, Lounge, Gluten-Free
Average Price: Expensive
Area: Potts Point
Address: 33 Bayswater Road Potts
Point New South Wales 2011
Phone: +61 2 9332 1227

#493
Berkelouw Books
Category: Bookstore, Wine Bar, Café
Average Price: Modest
Area: Leichhardt
Address: 70 Norton St Leichhardt
New South Wales 2040
Phone: +61 2 9560 3200

#494
The Commons Local Eating House
Category: Breakfast & Brunch,
Mediterranean, Cocktail Bar
Average Price: Modest
Area: Darlinghurst
Address: 32 Burton St Darlinghurst
New South Wales 2010
Phone: +61 2 9358 1487

#495
Oscar's Hotel Restaurant
Category: Bar, Austrian
Average Price: Modest
Area: Pyrmont
Address: 84 Union St Pyrmont
New South Wales 2009
Phone: +61 2 9660 5933

#496
Longrain Bunker Bar
Category: Asian Fusion, Lounge,
Cocktail Bar
Average Price: Expensive
Area: Surry Hills
Address: 8-10 Hunt St Surry Hills
New South Wales 2010
Phone: +61 2 9280 2888

#497
Gleebooks
Category: Comedy Club, Bookstore
Average Price: Modest
Area: Glebe
Address: 49 Glebe Point Road Glebe
New South Wales 2037
Phone: +61 2 9660 2333

#498
Hartsyard Seed & Feed
Category: Bar, Australian, American
Average Price: Expensive
Area: Newtown
Address: 33 Enmore Rd Newtown
New South Wales 2042
Phone: +61 2 8068 1473

#499
Norfolk Hotel
Category: Pub, Gastropub
Average Price: Modest
Area: Redfern
Address: 305 Cleveland St Redfern
New South Wales 2016
Phone: +61 2 9699 3177

#500
Hugos Lounge
Category: Lounge
Average Price: Expensive
Area: Potts Point
Address: 33 Bayswater Road Potts
Point New South Wales 2011
Phone: +61 2 9332 1227

29967504R00099

Printed in Great
Britain
by Amazon